Word 97 Further Skills

Sue Coles

Department of Business and Management Studies
Crewe and Alsager Faculty
Manchester Metropolitan University

Jenny Rowley

School of Management and Social Sciences
Edge Hill University College

Letts

1998

Acknowledgments

This book would not have been completed without the support that the authors received, during its production, from many of their colleagues and family. They are particularly grateful to husbands Martyn and Peter, children Helen, Shula, Lynsey and Zeta, who had to make do with even less of their time than usual.

Windows 95™, Excel™ and Access™ © Microsoft Corporation, all rights reserved. Screen displays from Access 7, Excel 97 and Windows 95 reprinted with permission from Microsoft Corporation.

A CIP record for this book is available from the British Library.

ISBN 1 85805 222 X

Editorial and production services: Genesys Editorial Limited

Typeset by Kai, Nottingham

Printed in Great Britain by Martins the Printers, Berwick upon Tweed

Contents

About this book

Aims

This book is intended for users of Word 97 for Windows '95 who already have a working knowledge of the package and wish to progress further to improve both their productivity in document production and the quality of documents produced.

You can use it

- as part of a college course
- for independent study
- for reference.

Although the book uses a business orientated approach for the practical activities, this approach will be easily adaptable to other situations where documents for other purposes, such as assignments or projects, are being produced.

It is assumed that you are familiar with the following activities in Word 97:

- text formatting – fonts, margins, alignment, basic bullets and numbering
- navigating around a document; working with more than one document
- moving, copying, deleting, and finding and replacing text
- tabs and tables
- borders and shading
- basic chart and image creation.

If you need to brush up on your basic skills you may find it useful to refer to the companion book S Coles and J Rowley *Word 97 Basic Skills* Letts Educational 1997. That book assumes no prior knowledge of word processing. Following and completing the activities and Tasks will provide you with extensive word processing skills.

Word 97 Further Skills aims to develop your word processing skills further. The focus is on document control and enhancement, particularly in relation to more lengthy documents. The use of Word as part of the Office '95 suite of applications is explored as well as Word's Web authoring tools. *Word 97 Further Skills* introduces the 'power applications' of Word 97. The topics that are threaded through the text are:

- the creation and management of long and, where appropriate, multimedia documents
- corporate applications, including establishing templates and styles, and group working
- internet and networking with documents.

Word 97 is a very sophisticated package. This book threads its way through a range of power features and applications, with a focus on the business environment. The extensive skills that are developed through this book are a good basis for exploring other yet more advanced applications of Word 97.

Structure

The book explores advanced word processing techniques through clear explanatory text and a series of applications orientated Tasks focusing on a range of end products, such as a report or a Web page. Each unit includes a series of Tasks that familiarise the user with the features and functions relating to the unit topic. Each unit takes approximately one hour to complete. As each new function is introduced, the book explains both why the function is useful and how to use it. The Tasks are designed to meet a business user's needs and they are orientated towards the production of business documents in a corporate environment.

The Tasks follow a theme. They create a range of documents that might typically be used in an Estate Agency, Chelmer Estates. The scenario for the Estate Agency evolves as you work through the text. Chelmer Estates is an entirely fictional organisation, and while documents have been selected and created to demonstrate the range of documents required in such an organisation, these are in no sense model documents: they are used simply to introduce a range of word processing features. In order to reduce the amount of keying necessary to complete the Tasks the early ones create documents that are re-used later in the book.

The units can be grouped broadly into the following sections.

a) Those that deal with the creation of corporate documents. This includes topics such as: text quality, advanced printing, templates, group working, styles, bookmarking and master documents.

b) Those that deal with advanced use of special features in Word. This includes topics such as: images and graphics, Word Art, charting, tables and calculations, sections and columns, the creation of on-line forms and macros.

c) Those that deal with networking and the integration of applications. This includes topics such as: object linking and embedding, integration with Office applications and HTML documents.

The appendices provide useful reminders of toolbar buttons, keyboard shortcuts and HTML tags. Appendix 3 focuses on an issue that becomes ever more pressing for the power word processor: file and version management.

In Word there are often many ways of achieving the same operation. This book offers the quickest and most user-friendly means of achieving the desired outcomes. Although at times other methods may also be indicated, preference is given to operations based on the use of the mouse and menu options. This approach makes maximum use of the self-explanatory nature of the menu options and dialog boxes, and does not ask the user to remember key combinations.

The learning material requires little, if any, input by lecturers, and can therefore be used in programmes based on independent learning. Students learn by practising the commands and techniques to produce specific types of documents.

Conventions

The following conventions have been adopted to distinguish between the various objects on the screen.

■ Commands are shown as File-Page Setup, which means choose the File menu and then select the option Page Setup from that menu.

■ Buttons, tabs and icons are shown as Cancel

■ Menu items and Dialog box names are shown as Columns

■ Keys are shown as *Ctrl*

■ Filenames, names of fields, documents or anything else named by the user are shown as **Letter1**

■ Text which you are instructed to type yourself is set in Times typeface which looks like this.

 indicates a tip providing a helpful hint or short-cut method.

 indicates a cautionary note.

 indicates a cross reference.

Ten tips for better documents

1. Always Select, then Do. For example, when you want to change text, first select it and then choose a command or click on a button that will do what you want.

2. Save your document regularly, say every 15-20 minutes. The fastest way to save is to click on the Save button on the standard toolbar or use *Ctrl-s*.

3. If you do not like what you have just done, undo it using Edit-Undo or by clicking on the Undo button in the toolbar. Word will allow you to undo more than one operation.

4. Avoid using a blank line to separate your paragraphs, use paragraph spacing instead. This will make page control much easier.

5. If you are not a trained typist make use of the AutoCorrect spelling facility, and use AutoText to save typing frequently used words or phrases.

6. Be sober in your application of styles, borders and shading. Look at professional publications for guidance.

7. Create templates for your standard business documents.

8. Incorporate charts to give instant visual impact to your presentation of data.

9. Use the headings styles so that you can plan your documents and produce automatic tables of contents.

10. Manage large documents by dividing them into several smaller documents and use a master document to group them as one.

Reviewing basic document creation

What you will revise in this review

This book assumes that you are familiar with the basics of document creation. In addition to the creation, saving and printing of documents, it is essential that you are familiar with all the functions that are available through the use of buttons and list boxes on the Word document screen. *Word 97 Basic Skills* by S Coles and J Rowley and published by Letts in the same series as this book, introduces these and many other functions associated with basic word processing. This unit is intended as a reference and reminder of some of these basic functions. This is a reminder and an opportunity to practice your skills in relation to:

- setting type font and size
- setting type font to bold, italic or underline
- text alignment
- bullets and
- indents.

Setting type font and size

The Font list box in the toolbar can be opened by clicking on the down arrow to the right. The box expands to show a list of the different fonts that are available. Printer fonts have a small printer symbol next to them. Some fonts have two 'T's next to them. These are True Type fonts; these are the most versatile of the fonts because they can be varied in size in steps of one point.

The font size box can be opened by clicking down the down arrow to the right of the box. The box expands to show the different sizes that are available; these will vary with the type font used.

 To create interesting but professional documents a limited number of type fonts should be used in any one document, or group of documents. Normally, it is good practice to use just one font, and to vary size and formatting to give variety and emphasis.

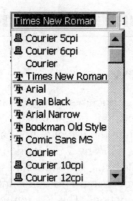 

Setting type font to bold, italic or underline

The following buttons on the toolbar can be used to set the type font to bold, italic, or underline, respectively, or some combination of these three:

Formatting can be applied in two different ways. Either:

■ click on the relevant type font button and then insert the text; as the text is created the formatting will be evident, or

■ type the text, possibly within an existing area of text, and then apply formatting after a significant quantity of text has been entered. Select the text to be formatted and click on the appropriate type font button.

Text alignment

Alignment is the position in which the text appears between the left and right margins. In Word there are four types of alignment: left, right, centre and full justification.

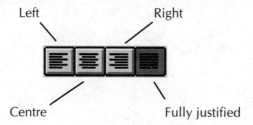

Left alignment causes the text to have a straight left margin and an uneven right margin.

Centre alignment causes each line to be positioned centrally between the left and right margins

Right alignment causes the text to have a straight right margin, and an uneven left margin

Fully justified is where both the left and right margins have straight edges. This is the type of alignment that is chosen for many documents

Alignment can be applied in two different ways. Either:

■ click on the relevant alignment button and then insert the text; as the text is created the formatting will be evident, or

■ type the text and then apply alignment after a significant quantity of text has been entered. Select the text to be formatted and click on the appropriate alignment button.

Using basic bullets

To distinguish a list of points from the rest of the text it is usual to highlight them using bullets or point numbers. There are two buttons on the toolbar which can be used to insert a numbered or bulleted list:

As with alignment, bullets can be inserted as the text is typed, or a block of text may be selected and the bullets or numbering applied after the text has been entered. Word automatically adds the next bullet or number when you hit *Return*.

Using indents

It is sometimes desirable to indent paragraphs, such as a quotation, or bulleted points so that they are indented from the left-hand margin. This can be achieved through the use of the **Increase indent** button. Indents can be removed, by applying the **Decrease indent** button.

Using borders

Clicking on the drop down list box next to the **Border** button shows the options for inserting borders. Simply click on the type of border that you would like to apply, and it will be inserted at the position of the insertion point.

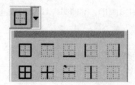

Task 1: Applying formatting

The purpose of this task is to encourage you to check whether you are sufficiently familiar with the basics of the creation of Word documents. The task can be completed using the buttons described earlier in this unit. If you find this task difficult then you are likely to need to spend some time familiarising yourself with more basic Word facilities, before proceeding with the tasks in this book.

1   Create the text below.

LIVING IN THE CITY

Preliminary Announcement

EXCITING NEW DEVELOPMENT

Show Flat Now Open

PARK LANE PROPERTIES

Presents

WHITWORTH HOUSE

53 WHITWORTH STREET, MANCHESTER

Elegant luxury apartments in the heart of Manchester City Centre, adjacent to UMIST

1 bedroom apartments from £56,000   2 bedroom apartments from £73,000

For further details contact:

Site office 0161-2361037   Open Thursday – Monday 10am-5pm

Or City Centre Specialist Office 0161-9053332

2   Format the text using a combination of:

■ type font sizes

■ text alignments

■ bold, italic and underline

3   Save the document as **Living**

Task 2: More text formatting

1   Create the document below.

FARM LANE
DISLEY

Offers around £300,000

* ❖ Substantial 4 bedroom residence
* ❖ 3 receptions, kitchen with breakfast area and utility
* ❖ Downstairs w.c., two en-suites plus family bathroom
* ❖ Double glazing, gas central heating.
* ❖ Double garage front and rear.

Contact:

Disley Branch for Further Details

01663-765253

---

2   In addition to the formatting that you have used in Task 1 you may like to try using borders, and formatting the bullets using Format-Bullets and Numbering

3   Save the document as **Disley**.

Text quality

What you will learn in this unit

This unit assumes that the user is familiar with basic text and page formatting and can create basic documents. The activities in this unit are concerned with proofing a document in order to achieve optimum accuracy and precision of expression. They cover:

- checking spelling and grammar
- using autocorrect
- using the thesaurus
- finding and replacing word forms.

There are various ways in which the word processor can help to improve the text in a document. Many word processor users are not trained typists and are prone to make errors while keying in their work. Word will check your work as you key it in for both spelling and grammatical errors. Mistakes are shown with a wiggly line underneath them, red for spelling errors and green for grammatical errors. You can instantly revise a mistake by clicking on the marked word or phrase with the *right* mouse button. This generates a shortcut menu through which you can choose a revision, or tell Word to ignore the word or phrase. Even so it is good practice to read your document to check for spelling and grammatical mistakes before printing the final copy. The word processor cannot proof-read a document, so after checking the spelling and grammar always proof-read your work. If the work would benefit from rewording make use of the thesaurus.

Checking spelling and grammar as you work

You will already have noticed Word's ability to check your work as you type. Word underlines spelling mistakes in red and grammatical errors in green. If you find this irritating, you may switch off either or both spelling and grammar checking as you work, using Tools-Options Spelling and Grammar and removing the tick from the 'as you type' check boxes.

Spelling mistakes are often the result of a typing error such as transposing letters in a word and these can easily be amended. However, there will be a number of occasions when Word will not recognise a word because it is not in its dictionary, as illustrated below.

Alsager

An example of a word not found in Word's dictionary

In this case point to the word and click the *right* mouse button. This displays a shortcut menu which will suggest alternatives, allow you to Ignore All occurrences of the word, add the word to the dictionary or to start the Spell Checker as described in the next section.

Grammatical errors may be due to misplaced apostrophes or commas that have been omitted or they may be due to the sentence structure. Word has a limited set of rules for grammar checking so if the revision suggested is not suitable, you can ignore the sentence and use your own judgement. The illustration below shows the shortcut menu (right mouse button) for a grammatical error.

Grammatical errors may be due to misplaced apostrophes or commas which have been omitted or they may be due to the sentence structure.

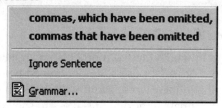

Grammar shortcut menu

Task 1: Correcting spelling as you work

In this task the following document will be created which will be saved as a template. A template is a document that contains standard text and it can be used to base other documents upon. The letter below is incomplete as it only contains text that would be found in all letters of this type, additional text would be added to customise the document. Templates are considered in more detail in Unit 3.

1   Start a new document and key in the standard letter shown on following page.

2   Experiment by keying in deliberately misspelt words and point to these words, click with the right mouse button to see the shortcut menu. Either choose one of the suggestions or Ignore All option, do not add any words to the dictionary or start the Spell Checker.

3   Save the document as a template by using File-Save As and choosing Document template from the Save as type list box. Give the document the name **Value and Saleability.**

Chelmer Estates

25 High Street

Chelmer

Cheshire

CH1 3QW

Our Ref:

Dear

Re:

We write as promised to confirm our comments with regard to value and saleability of the above mentioned property.

We found the property to comprise

We regard valuation

We enclose our terms and conditions in accordance with the Estate Agents Act 1979, Section 18 as amended with effect from 29th July 1991. If there are any aspects of these that you wish to discuss please do not hesitate to get in touch.

We trust you found our comments helpful and look forward to hearing from you.

Yours sincerely

H. D. Jones B.A., F.N.A.E.A

Director

Chelmer Estates

Task 2: Correcting grammar as you work

The following piece of text is deliberately incorrect. Key it into a new document exactly as shown below.

IMPORTANT QUESTIONS, HONEST ANSWERS TO HELP GET YOU MOVING

Buying or selling a property should be exciting and fun, but its certainly one of the most important decisions you'll ever make.

Its important that, before you make any decisions, you know the facts and seek out the soundest advice, so that you can turn what could be seen as hurdles, into easily managed steps.

Naturally, you'd expect Chelmer Estates to know all of the answers, and to offer you sound, honest and expect advice.

That's precisely why we've introduced an important service for anyone thinking of moving home.

It is called **Budgeting Advice** and the god news is that its absolutely free!

1   You should discover two instances of 'its' instead of 'it's', which are signalled with a wiggly green line.

2   Note that there are also two mistakes that neither the spell or grammar checker will find. These are 'expect advice' which should read 'expert advice' and 'god news' instead of 'good news'. Correct these.

3   Save the document as the document (not as a template) **Budgeting advice**.

Using the spelling and grammar checker

The spelling and grammar checker can be used to check a selection or the whole document. In large documents that are subject to repeated amendment, working on specific selections is more efficient than working through the full document.

If a selection is to be checked, select it first. Use Tools-Spelling and Grammar or click on the Spelling and Grammar button or use the shortcut key *F7* or choose Spelling or Grammar from the shortcut menu (right mouse button). If you have not made a selection Word will start the spelling and grammar check from the position of the insertion point.

The Spelling and Grammar dialog box appears as illustrated below. If you only want to check your document for spelling mistakes and not grammatical errors, then remove the tick from the Check Grammar check box.

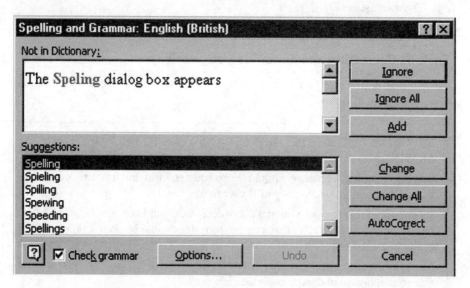

When the spelling and grammar checker comes across a misspelt word it shows it in red in the Not in Dictionary box. In the Suggestions: box the spell checker offers a list of correction options.

There are now a number of options available, shown by the buttons.

- If the correct spelling is highlighted in the Suggestions: box, click on the **Change** button.

- If the correct spelling is in the Suggestions: box, but is not highlighted, select it and click on the **Change** button.

- If you think that the mistake may be repeated throughout the document then use the **Change All** button instead of the **Change** button.

- If the word is correct but it is not in the spell checker's dictionary then choose **Ignore** or you may **Add** the word to the dictionary. Consult the Office Assistant for information about adding to or creating your own dictionary. Use **Ignore All** to ignore all occurrences of the word throughout the document.

- If the word is a mistake that you commonly make then you may add it to Word's list of AutoCorrect entries by clicking on the **Auto Correct** button. AutoCorrect is discussed later in this unit.

If a selection is not made, the spell checker will check the entire document, and when finished will return to the original place of the insertion point. If you are checking a selection, when that is finished you have the option to carry on and check the whole document.

If you are checking grammar as well as spelling, whenever the checker comes across a grammatical error, the error will be shown in the upper box that will have a title that states the type of error.

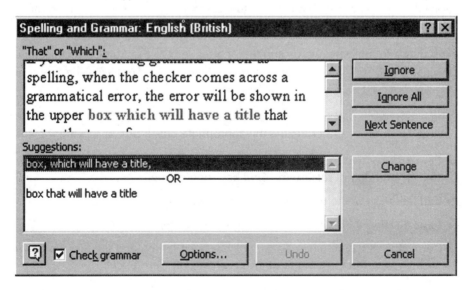

Words related to the suspected error are displayed in green type. The spelling and grammar checker displays suggested corrections in the Suggestions: box. The following choices of action are available.

- Make a suggested correction.

  Select one of the corrections from the Suggestions: box and click on the `Change` button.

- Make your own corrections in the document.

  Make the document window active by clicking on it. Edit the sentence and click on the `Resume` button in the dialog box to resume checking the document.

- Ignore the questioned word or sentence without making changes.

  Click on the `Ignore` button.

- Skip the entire sentence.

  Click on the `Next Sentence` button to start checking the next sentence.

- Customise the grammatical rules used for checking.

  Click on the `Options` button. Refer to the Office Assistant for the grammatical rules that are available.

AutoCorrect

You can tell Word about your common typing mistakes so that, as you type, Word will monitor your typing for these mistakes and automatically correct them. Word maintains a list of common 'mistypes' and their corrections and Word will correct you, if you mistype a word from this list. For example the word 'occurrance' would be corrected as 'occurrence'. If you do not wish Word to make automatic corrections then you can switch off this feature using Tools-AutoCorrect and remove the ✓ from the Replace Text As You Type check box.

You may add 'mistype' words and their corrections to the AutoCorrect list, either through using Tools-AutoCorrect or by clicking on the `Auto Correct` button in the Spelling and Grammar dialog box.

The Autocorrect dialog box also offers the following corrections which you may switch on or off by either ticking the appropriate check box or leaving it blank.

- Correction of two capitals at the beginning of a word (may happen if you type quickly and do not release the *Shift* key soon enough.

- Capitalisation of the first word of a sentence.

- Capitalisation of the names of the days of the week.

- Correction of typing when *Caps Lock* has been left on and the first word is lower case and the rest upper case (it also switches off *Caps Lock*).

Task 3: Making an AutoCorrect entry

1 Choose Tools-AutoCorrect and see that the Replace Text As You Type check box is checked.

2   In the Replace box type **usualy** (this is an example of a common mistake).

3   In the With box type **usually** (the correct spelling) and click on **Add** . Click on **OK** .

4   In a new document that you do not save experiment with misspelling this word. You may add other words that you commonly mistype.

Note if you click on the **Auto Correct** button in the Spelling and Grammar dialog box Word will add your mistake and the selected change to the list.

Using the Thesaurus

The Thesaurus can be used to add variety and interest to your work: it suggests synonyms and related words. The Thesaurus is used for one word at a time. Place the insertion point in the appropriate word and then choose Tools-Language Thesaurus (shortcut key *Shift+F7*). The Thesaurus dialog box is illustrated below.

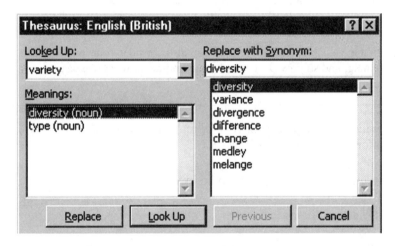

The word that was selected appears in the Looked Up box. Underneath this is the Meanings box that lists related words and indicates whether these words are nouns or verbs. Next to the Looked Up box is a Replace with Synonym box that contains a list of synonyms for the selected word. You can replace the selected word with any of the words listed by clicking on the word. It will then appear in the text box at the top of the list and clicking on the **Replace** button will put it into the document in place of the word selected.

If the list of synonyms is not extensive enough then the Thesaurus can be used to find synonyms for the word in the Looked Up box. To do this, click on the **Look Up** button. This procedure may be repeated until a suitable synonym is found.

The Thesaurus keeps a list of all the words you have looked up. To return to a previous word open the Looked Up list box, by clicking on the arrow at the end of the box. Words, which you have previously looked up, are displayed and the required word can be chosen from the list.

Task 4: Using the Thesaurus

Add the following text to the document **Budgeting advice** and save it.

Here's how Budgeting Advice works for you

Because buying a home is so important, it's equally important that you understand clearly your own financial position.

Our aim is simply to advise you so that you can be certain that the home of your dreams is realistic and affordable now, and in the years to come.

How to get Budgeting Advice working for you

Simply call into or telephone your nearest Chelmer Estates branch and arrange a mutually convenient date and time to meet one of our 'Budgeting Advice' team. You'll find them friendly, helpful and highly knowledgeable.

The initial formal chat will broadly cover your own requirements and analyse your financial situation. If a further meeting is necessary, then a more in-depth financial analysis will take place, to ensure that you can consider all of the mortgage options available.

In addition to this valuable, free service, we can also consider your long term financial planning, and so provide a sound programme that will keep pace with your prospects and your aspirations.

Using the Thesaurus investigate synonyms for the following words: **mutually**, **programme**, **affordable**, **aspiration**s.

1 Place the insertion point in the word to be investigated.

2 Use Tools-Language Thesaurus.

3 Consider whether a replacement should be selected from the list of synonyms.

4 Investigate the effect of 'looking up' a word. Remember that a list of words looked up can be viewed by opening the Looked Up list box.

Finding and replacing noun or adjective forms or verb tenses

No doubt you will be familiar with Word's ability to find and replace words. This facility can be used in a more sophisticated way to replace word forms. You can replace

■ singular and plural noun forms at the same time, for example, replacing "house" with 'property' and 'houses' with 'properties'

■ all adjective forms, for example, replacing 'worse' with 'better' at the same time as replacing 'worst' with 'best'

■ all tenses of a root verb, for example, replacing 'sell' with 'buy' at the same time as replacing 'sold' with 'bought'.

To find and replace word forms follow this procedure.

1 Choose Edit-Replace and in the Find What box, type the word to find, for example 'get', or click the down arrow to select one of the most recent four entries.

2 In the Replace With box, type the replacement word, for example '**obtain**', or click the down arrow to select one of the most recent four entries.

3 Click on More and tick the Find All Word Forms check box and click on Replace or Replace All .

Instead of choosing Replace All , choose Replace after Word finds each word form so that you can confirm that Word is replacing the correct forms of the words you've specified. You should always be careful with the Replace All option, even for an ordinary replace, for example, if you replace 'program' with 'programme' you could produce 'programmeme' where the original word was programme. One way to avoid this is to include a space at the end of both the 'find what' and 'replace with' words.

Task 5: Finding and replacing word forms

1 Key in the following text.

Our house advertising is planned in great detail, and designed to gain maximum coverage for your home. We have an excellent reputation for selling houses quickly, so why not come to see us first?

2 Using Edit-Replace replace all word forms of 'house' with 'property'. Click on More and tick the Find All Word Forms check box and click on Replace to make two replacements.

3 It is not necessary to save this document.

Printing

What you will learn in this unit

Having created and saved a document it is usual to print it. The activities in this unit are concerned with investigating the different print options available and also the printing of document statistics. Elements of document and file management are to be considered. (File management is further developed in Appendix 3). At the end of this unit you should be able to:

■ select a printer (if you have a choice of printers or fax), investigate printer properties and cancel a print job

■ control page margins and use the 'Shrink to Fit' option

■ print selected parts of a document, collate multiple copies and print 'double-sided' (i.e. on both sides of the paper)

■ print on different sizes of paper and envelopes.

Preparing to print

Selecting a printer

If you are using a stand-alone machine then it is likely that you will have a single dedicated printer connected to your computer and normally you will not need to think about selecting a printer. However, if you have a fax/modem installed on your computer you can print directly to this in the same way as you would print to a printer.

If you are using a network then you may have the choice of different printers for different applications. For example, you may use a laser printer for high quality, high volume, high speed printouts or a colour printer for smaller, low volume specialised jobs. You may also be able to 'print' to a fax/modem as mentioned above.

To select a printer proceed as follows.

1   Proof and save the document you intend to print or fax.

2   Choose File-Print and in the Printer section, open the Name drop down list. This will display the list of printers and fax systems that are available. If you are using a portable printer then check you have connected it to your machine and it is loaded and ready before trying to print to it.

3   Select the required printer or fax. Remember that changing printer can cause slight layout differences so preview the document before printing. Make any changes as necessary and use File-Print and click on   OK   or click on the   Print   button in the toolbar.

4   If you are faxing the document then your fax application will start and you should select the recipient from your address list or key in their details and then send the fax.

Investigating the printer's properties

Choose File-Print and click on the Properties button. The properties that you see will be dependent on the printer but you are likely to be able to control print quality, paper feed and orientation and collation of printed output.

Task 1: Preparing to Print

1   Open the document **Budgeting advice** and add the text below to the document and save it.

Make your next move with real peace of mind

On approval of your completed financial analysis, we will present you with your Personal Home Buying Certificate. This will give you the peace of mind that, when you are making an offer on a property, you'll know the level of mortgage you can afford.

It's nice to know that when you're ready to move, Budgeting Advice will have made it possible for you to move quickly. With all discussions out of the way, your mortgage application will be made easier, whether you buy from Chelmer Estates or not.

With Budgeting Advice, you need never take chances. Instead you'll enjoy the complete peace of mind that comes with friendly, expert and professional – Chelmer – advice.

Call in and see us soon

---

2   Choose File-Print and click on the Properties button. Investigate the printer properties. If you have a choice of printers then you may wish to select one of these from the Name drop down list and investigate its properties.

3   Print the document to a printer connected to your computer.

Background printing

You can print in background mode or not depending on the priority you wish to attach to printing. When background printing is on, you can continue to work in Word while you print. Background printing uses additional system memory, slowing the printing process. To speed up printing, switch off background printing (you will not be able to continue to work in Word until the print job has been sent). To turn background printing on or off:

1   choose Tools-Options, and then click the Print tab

2   under Printing options, tick the Background printing check box to switch on, remove tick to switch off.

Cancelling a print job

If background printing is turned off, click **Cancel** or press *Esc*. If background printing is turned on, double-click the printer icon on the status bar 🖨 . This will display the print job queue and you can select the print job and cancel it by pressing *Delete*.

If you're printing a short document and background printing is turned on, the printer icon may not appear on the status bar long enough for you to click it to cancel printing.

Page Setup

Page Setup, on the File menu, allows you to set a number of parameters that specify how the document will be displayed on the page. Four main options are available:

- Margins
- Paper Size
- Paper Source
- Layout.

Each of these has a separate dialog box which is displayed when the appropriate tab is clicked. Many of the options in these dialog boxes are self-explanatory and the preview helps to indicate the effect of modifications.

Controlling page margins

Under the **Margins** tab of Page Setup, there are two important characteristics:

- the part of the document to which the settings are to be applied
- whether facing pages need to be set with mirrored margins, as in a book, to allow for binding.

Margins can be adjusted in Page Layout View or Print Preview. Dragging the margin boundary on the ruler will change the margins in a section or an entire document.

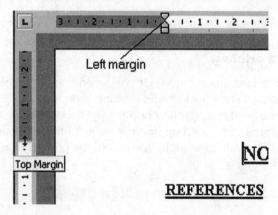

To display the measurements of the text area and the margins, hold down the *Alt* key as you drag the boundary.

If you plan to bind a document, defining a size for a gutter margin will add extra space to the inside margin. To create a gutter margin use File-Page Setup, choose the Margins tab and then set a width for your gutter margin.

You may wish to print a document on both sides of the paper, as in a book, and so you will have left and right-handed pages. To set margins on facing pages to mirror one another, i.e. so that inside and outside margins have the same width, use File-Page Setup, choose the Margins tab and check the Mirror margins check box. You may adjust the widths of the inside and outside margins as necessary.

Shrink to fit

When you preview a document you may find that a small amount of text appears on the last page. To prevent this you may be able to reduce the number of pages by clicking on the Shrink to Fit button in Print Preview. This feature works best with documents that contain only a few pages, such as letters and memos. In order to shrink the document, Word decreases the font size of each font used in the document.

If you do not like the result of the Shrink to Fit operation you can use Edit-Undo Tools Shrink to Fit on the menu. However, after you save the document and close it, there is no quick way to restore the original font size.

Printing selected parts of a document

It is not necessary to print a whole document, particularly if it is more than one page long. Through the Print dialog box a selected set of pages, the current page or a selection may be printed.

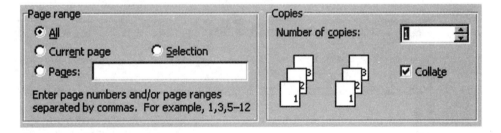

Collating multiple copies

If you are printing more than one copy of a document which is more than one page long, if you tick the Collate check box then the documents will be printed in proper binding order.

Printing in reverse order

Printing usually starts with the first page so that as the pages collect the first page is at the bottom and the last page at the top in the printer output tray. So that the document can be stapled straight away the order of printing should be reversed and to do this:

1   Choose **Tools-Options**, and select the **Print** tab.

2   Under **Printing Options**, tick the **Reverse print order** check box.

Word prints the document in reverse order, beginning with the last page. You should use this option when printing multiple collated copies that are to be bound. If you are printing an envelope don't select this option.

Printing on different sizes of paper and envelopes

In the UK the standard size of paper used for printing is A4. However, for some documents you may wish to use an alternative standard size or even non-standard size paper. Your printer will ultimately limit the width of paper that you can print on.

To change the paper size use **File-Page Setup** and select the **Paper Size** tab. Open the **Paper Size** drop down list and select the size of paper required. You may also change the orientation of the paper. If your paper is not a standard size then choose **Custom Size** and enter the size of the paper into the **Width** and **Height** boxes.

Printing an address on an envelope

If you only want to print an occasional envelope use the method described below. If you print many envelopes on a regular basis then you should use mail merge, which is dealt with later in this book.

To print on an envelope, proceed as follows.

1   Choose **Tools-Envelopes and Labels**, and select the **Envelopes** tab as illustrated.

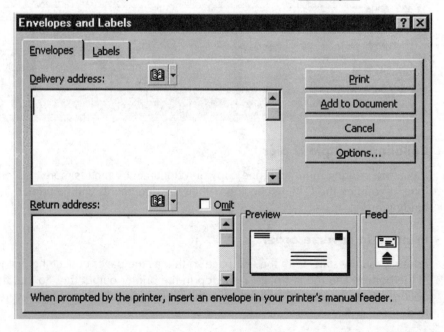

2   Enter the address information. To format the address, select the address text, click the right mouse button, and choose Font on the shortcut menu and apply the required formatting.

3   To select an envelope size, the type of paper feed and other options, click on the Options button.

4   To print the envelope, insert the envelope in the printer as shown in the Feed box, and click on the Print button.

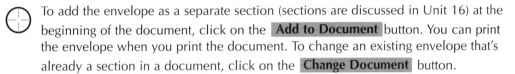

To add the envelope as a separate section (sections are discussed in Unit 16) at the beginning of the document, click on the Add to Document button. You can print the envelope when you print the document. To change an existing envelope that's already a section in a document, click on the Change Document button.

You can create a default return address that appears on all the envelopes you print, or you can include a logo or other graphic images with your return address.

Change the size of an envelope

1   Choose Tools-Envelopes and Labels, and select the Envelopes tab.

2   Click on the Options button, and choose the Envelope Options tab.

3   Open the drop down Envelope size box, and select the required envelope size. If the size you want is not listed, choose Custom size, and then enter the dimensions of your envelope.

Task 2: Adding an address to a document

In this task a simple letter is created and the address will be added so that both letter and envelope may be printed.

1   Create the following letter and save it as **Bailey P sale confirmation**.

Our ref: SJC/341/HDJ/CHELMER OFFICE

28 October 1997

Mr P. L. Bailey
55, Chestnut Drive
Meirton
Cheshire
CH7 6TD

Dear Mr Bailey

Re: 55, Chestnut Drive, Meirton, Cheshire.

We have pleasure in confirming the proposed sale of the above property to
Ms A McAllister for the agreed sum of £46,000 subject to contract.

We have passed the relevant information to your solicitor who will proceed with
the necessary contractual arrangements and keep us advised of developments.

If there is any further information that you require, please do not hesitate to
contact us.

Yours sincerely

H. D. Jones B.A., F.N.A.E.A.
Director
CHELMER ESTATES

---

2 Choose Tools-Envelopes and Labels, and select the `Envelopes` tab. The address
   used on the letter should already appear in the Delivery address box. Note that
   you could amend this address if so desired.

---

3 If you wish to specify the envelope size click on `Options` and choose the
   required size as described above. Click on `OK`.

---

4 Click on the `Add to Document`
   button and save.

The address is added to the document as
a separate section (see Unit 16 for more
detail on sections) and envelope and
letter can be printed later.

Templates and Auto Text

What you will learn in this unit

The activities described in this unit are aimed at reducing the amount of keying that might be performed in producing a document, by using templates and the AutoText facility. In business there are many occasions where standard documents, such as letters, memos, faxes, reports, invoices, delivery notes etc. are produced repeatedly. Often most features such as the firm's address, logo, text font and layout of boxes and lines are consistent across a set of documents. Using a template to hold such features is the best way to maintain consistency and to establish a corporate identity.

In Unit 1 Task 1 a very simple and plain standard letter template was created simply by typing the standard elements of a letter and saving them as a template. By basing other documents on this template only the more specific details need be added to complete the document.

AutoText allows you to assign a simple key combination to a long word or phrase. When the assigned key combination is used the word or phrase will appear in the document. AutoText is not limited to text entries; other objects such as graphics may also be made into AutoText entries.

The use of fields will be explored in this unit. Fields are used to add information to a document such as the date, the page number, the document file name, and the author. Fields are useful for document control and are often included in templates. By the end of the unit you will be able to:

- use a template

- create a template based on an existing template

- modify a template

- use fields and include them in a template

- create AutoText entries

- print AutoText entries.

Task 1: Using a template

1   Use File-New and select the **Value and Saleability** template, created in Task 1 Unit 1, from under the General tab.

2   Complete the letter as follows. Use Insert-Date and Time to add the date. Save the letter as **Pattison D. V&S** and print it.

Chelmer Estates
25 High Street
Chelmer
Cheshire
CH1 3QW

Our Ref: SJC/972/HDJ/CHELMER OFFICE

24 October 1997

Mrs D. Pattison
34 Cedar Close
Chelmer
Cheshire
CH5 7RY

Dear Mrs Pattison

Re: 34, Cedar Close, Chelmer

We write as promised to confirm our comments with regard to value and saleability of the above mentioned property.

We found the property to comprise a modern semi-detached dwelling.

We regard valuation as lying reasonably in the region of £75,000 and would suggest an initial asking price of £78,000 subject to contract, as a test of market reaction.

We enclose our terms and conditions in accordance with the Estate Agents Act 1979, Section 18 as amended with effect from 29th July 1991 If there are any aspects of these that you wish to discuss please do not hesitate to get in touch.

We trust you found our comments helpful and look forward to hearing from you.

Yours sincerely

H. D. Jones B.A., F.N.A.E.A
Director
Chelmer Estates

Creating templates

A template is a pre-defined format for a document. A template can be used to define not only standard text but also aspects such as the font, borders, page size and orientation. Once a template has been created it can be recalled and used to produce the required document.

Word comes with many pre-defined templates that you can use to create documents such as letters and memos. To create most documents the 'normal document' template, NORMAL.DOT is used. This is the template that you have been using to create your documents. If a document is started using File-New then a dialog box containing the names of the templates appears: these are grouped by type which you select by clicking on the appropriate tab. By choosing **General** you can select the normal template file. Template files have the extension .dot and are stored in the Template subdirectory.

Word provides other template files such as a standard letter and memo and it is possible to customise these.

You may base a new template on an existing template.

1 Choose File-New. Select a template that is similar to the one you want to create, click Template under Create New, and then click **OK** .

2 Choose File-Save As. From the Save as type list, choose Document Template (*.dot). This file type will already be selected if you are saving a file that you created as a template.

3 Word proposes the Templates folder in the Save in box. To save the template so that it will appear on a tab other than **General** , switch to the corresponding subfolder within the Templates folder.

4 In the File Name box, type a name for the new template, and then click on **Save** .

5 In the new template, add the text and graphics you want to appear in all new documents that you base on the template, and delete any items you do not want to appear.

6 Make the changes you want to the margin settings, page size and orientation, styles, and other formats.

7 Choose File-Save, and close the template document.

Task 2: Creating a memo template based on an existing template

This is the easiest way to create a template, particularly if your template is going to be very similar in layout to one of the ones that comes with Word.

1 Choose File-New and click on the **Memos** tab. Select the contemporary template, under Create New choose the Template option, and click on **OK** .

2 Choose File-Save As. From the Save as type list, choose Document Template. To save the template so that it will appear on the **Memos** tab, open the Memos subfolder within the Templates folder.

3 In the File-name box, type **Chelmer Estates Memo**, and then click on **Save** .

4   Customise the memo by making some formatting changes to the font of the text
    and by removing the instructions from the body of the memo. Save and close.

Task 3: Modifying a customised template

1   Choose File-Open and select Document Templates in the Files of Type box.

2   Open the Memos subfolder (in Templates, which is in Microsoft Office) and
    select **Chelmer Estates Memo**.

3   Make another formatting change and save and close the template document.

4   Use this template to create the following memo.

Chelmer
Estates

Memorandum

To: Jane Fellows

CC:

From: Peter Smith

Date: {an updateable date field is used by a memo template}

Re: Pattison, 34, Cedar Close, Chelmer

Our client has contacted me regarding the sale of her property and has asked us
to proceed with the sale, so please could you arrange for the property to be
photographed.

Using fields

In the previous task the date is added to the template using Insert-Date and Time,
selecting a suitable format and ticking the Update Automatically check box. There
are many types of fields that can be added to a document, those which are most
useful to standard letters and templates are the document file name, the author and
perhaps the template that was used to create the document. These fields would
usually be added to the document footer, often using a small type size, and provide
useful traceability for the document. In the following unit you will see how to add a
field to a document header or footer.

Creating AutoText entries

Word uses AutoText to save repeated keying of the same text. Some documents
contain text (and/or graphics) which is repeated several or many times. For example,
a company name, address or logo may appear several times in one document or

may be required in many documents. By defining the name, address or logo as an AutoText entry it may be recalled at any point in any document with a simple keying action. Take a simple example: the text *Yours sincerely* appears at the end of many business letters. If many letters are to be typed then defining this as an AutoText entry would help to save time keying.

Word maintains a list of AutoText entries that you can add to or delete from. An AutoText entry may be text, graphics or a mixture of text and graphics. You can save text or graphics that you use frequently as an AutoText entry. Then you can easily insert the text or graphics into a document with a simple keying action, rather than retyping or using copy and paste.

Making an AutoText entry

First type in the text (e.g. **Chelmer Estates**) that you intend to make into an AutoText entry. Check that spelling is correct and select the text. If you wish to store the paragraph formatting as part of the AutoText entry then include the paragraph mark in the selection. Choose Insert-AutoText AutoText, click on AutoText and the AutoCorrect dialog box appears:

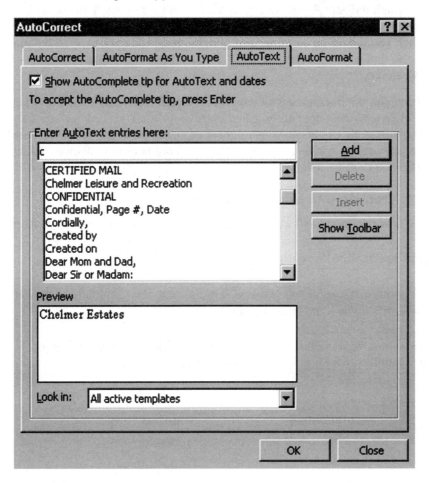

In the Enter AutoText entries here box type a name for the AutoText entry, in this example **c** for Chelmer Estates. Then click on the ▓ **Add** ▓ button. Alternatively use Insert-AutoText New, type in a name for the AutoText and click on ▓ **OK** ▓ .

Using an AutoText entry

The simplest method of using an AutoText entry is to type the AutoText name followed immediately by *F3* (function key 3). i.e. typing **c** and pressing *F3* would produce the text Chelmer Estates.

Alternatively, if you forget your AutoText names (for example, ys could be the glossary name for Yours sincerely) then use Insert-AutoText AutoText – in the dialog box will be a list of your previously defined AutoText entries. Type or select the AutoText name you wish to use and click on the ▓ **Insert** ▓ button.

AutoText prompts

You may have noticed that as you begin to type some words, for example, days of the week, Word prompts you with the completed word or phrase. This is another way in which the AutoText works. If, instead of using **c** as the AutoText name for Chelmer Estates, the full text was used as the name then, as you began to type '**Chelmer**' you would be prompted with the full text. You may have both names defined so that you can either use *c+F3* or expect to be prompted each time you type '**Chelmer**'.

Depending on the frequency with which you would use AutoText as a short cut you would choose to use either an AutoText entry or an AutoText prompt. For a shortcut that you frequently use an AutoText entry is probably preferable, and you would choose an AutoText name for the entry that you could easily remember (which could be one or more letters).

Task 4: Creating and using AutoText entries

Open a new document and try setting up and using the following AutoText entries.

1   Type out the AutoText entry in full, e.g. Yours faithfully

2   Select this text, use Insert-AutoText New, accept Yours faithfully as the name for the AutoText entry and click on ▓ **OK** ▓ .

3   Start typing **Yours faithfully** and you should be prompted when you reach the f of faithfully, press *Enter* to accept the prompt.

4   To create shortcut AutoText entries as follows:

AutoText name	AutoText entry
Ys	Yours sincerely
Yf	Yours faithfully
Ms	Microsoft Word

type out the AutoText entry in full, e.g. Yours sincerely.

5   Select this text. Use Insert-AutoText AutoText and in the Enter AutoText entries here box type the AutoText name, e.g. **ys**

6   Click on   **Add** . Move the insertion point to a place where the AutoText entry is to appear.

7   Type the AutoText name e.g. ys and press *F3*.

Experiment with creating other AutoText entries. Do not save this document.

Task 5: Assigning ClipArt to an AutoText entry

1   Start a new document. Add clipart to the document by using Insert-Picture Clipart. Choose the shape clipart that looks like a tick. Adjust the size of the clipart by dragging a corner sizing handle to make it smaller.

2   While it is selected choose Insert-AutoText New and in the Create AutoText box type the AutoText name e.g. tick. Click on   **OK** .

3   Move the insertion point to a place where the AutoText graphic is to appear.

4   Type the AutoText name **tick** and press *F3* . Do not save this document, however, the AutoText entry will be available to other documents. You may delete the AutoText entry following the steps below.

Deleting AutoText entries

To remove an AutoText entry

1   Choose Insert-AutoText AutoText. Scroll through the list of AutoText entries until you find the entry you wish to delete.

2   Highlight the entry click on   **Delete**   and   **OK** .

Printing AutoText entries

AutoText entries can be printed by selecting AutoText Entries from the Print What list box in the Print dialog box.

Page control

What you will learn in this unit

In this unit the activities concentrate on word processing features that are applicable to documents of more than one page. Features covered are:

- paragraph formatting
- controlling page breaks
- numbering pages
- adding headers and footers
- adding footnotes and endnotes.

For most long documents it is useful to know how to add headers, footers and page numbers and to be able to control page breaks.

You may be working on a document that will eventually be several or many pages long or you may wish to combine several documents, or parts of them, into one larger one.

Paragraph formatting

You will be very unlikely to find printed matter where the text is not divided into paragraphs, which are easily identifiable. Paragraphs are either denoted by an indent (first line set in slightly from the left margin), or by the use of space between them. The second method is more common, the first method is generally used where text is arranged in columns. Inexperienced users of word processors tend to separate paragraphs with a blank line. More professionally, instead of pressing _Enter_ to create a blank line between paragraphs Word allows you to define the amount of space before and after a paragraph.

Use Format-Paragraph to display the Paragraph dialog box and in the Spacing section the values in the Before and After boxes can be adjusted. Spacing is altered in increments of six points, which can be considered to be half a line. Note that if you have space after a paragraph and the following paragraph has space before it then the space between the paragraphs will be the sum of the before and after spacing.

Other paragraphs may require different spacing, for example headings or tables and these can be easily adjusted from the Paragraph dialog box.

Task 1: Controlling space between paragraphs

This task experiments with altering the spacing between paragraphs. Open the document **Budgeting advice**.

1   If you have blank lines in between paragraphs, remove them.
    To help you do this you can display the paragraph marks by clicking on
    the **Show/hide** icon.

2   Position the insertion point in the first paragraph. Choose Format-Paragraph and
    set the Spacing Before to 12 points (one line).

3   Position the insertion point in second paragraph. Choose Format-Paragraph and
    set the Spacing Before to 24 points (two lines).

4   Position the insertion point in third paragraph. Choose Format-Paragraph and set
    the Spacing After to 24 points (two lines).

5   Choose a suitable spacing, say six points before or after, and apply this to the
    entire document. **Save** .

Experiment with setting the line spacing before and after the paragraphs in this
document.

Page breaks

As the document being created gets larger, Word automatically inserts a page break
at the end of each page. Automatic page breaks are called *soft* breaks and are
shown in Normal View as a dotted line. As the document is edited and revised
Word repositions the page breaks accordingly. This is known as repagination.
Repagination occurs whenever you pause during keying. To alter the way in which
page breaks occur, then manual or *hard* breaks can be inserted.

Adding or removing page breaks

To add a page break

■ first position the insertion point at the place where the page break is to occur and

either

■ use Insert-Break and select Page Break from the Break dialog box.

or

■ the keyboard shortcut is to press *Ctrl+Enter* simultaneously.

In Normal View a dotted line appears at the point of the *hard* page break. In a *hard*
break the words Page Break appear in the middle of the line.

A *hard* page break may be selected in the same way as selecting a line of text, i.e.
by positioning the mouse pointer in the left edge of the screen, level with the page
break and clicking. Once selected the page break can be removed. It is not possible
to remove *soft* page breaks, these can be controlled either by inserting *hard* page
breaks or with paragraph formatting. If possible it is best to avoid *hard* page breaks
in a long document as they need to be revised manually whenever the document is
revised.

Controlling page breaks using paragraph formatting

This is controlled through the pagination section of the **Line and Page Breaks** tab in the Format-Paragraph dialog box. There are three types of formatting available.

```
┌─Pagination──────────────────────────────────────┐
│  ☑ Widow/Orphan Control      ☐ Keep with Next    │
│  ☑ Keep Lines Together       ☐ Page Break Before │
└──────────────────────────────────────────────────┘
```

1   Keep Lines Together: use this to prevent a page break within a paragraph. Word normally exercises Widow and Orphan control if the Widow/Orphan Control box is checked, that is to say that it will prevent Widows and Orphans from occurring. A Widow is a single line at the beginning of a paragraph left at the bottom of a page, and an Orphan is a single line at the end of a paragraph at the top of a page.

2   Keep with Next: use this to prevent a page break occurring between the paragraph and the following one. For example, to keep a sub-heading with its following paragraph or to keep the lines of a table together.

3   Page Break Before: if a paragraph such as a heading is formatted with Page Break Before then a page break will be inserted before the paragraph. If each chapter of your document is to appear on a new page, then format the chapter heading with Page Break Before by clicking in the appropriate check box. To remove this page break the formatting must be removed from the paragraph.

By making use of these formatting options the need for *hard* pages breaks to be inserted in a long document can be eliminated. When the document is altered the page breaks will follow the rules applied in the paragraph formatting and consequently should occur in sensible places.

Page numbering

There are two methods of inserting page numbers.

1   Page numbering using Insert-Page Numbers. Page numbers may be placed at the bottom of the page (footer) or at the top of the page (header). The alignment of the number can be chosen and whether or not all pages are to be numbered except the first. Remove the tick from the Show Number on First Page to omit the number from the first page, this is useful for documents that have a title page as the first page.

2   Page numbering as part of a header or footer. This is discussed in the next section.

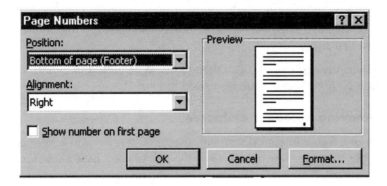

Task 2: Page numbering

Apply page numbering to the document **Budgeting advice**.

1 Use Insert-Page Numbers to add page numbers to the document.

2 Check that Position: Bottom of Page (Footer) and Alignment: Centre are selected.

3 Tick the Show Number on First Page check box. Click on ■ **OK** ■.

4 Choose View-Page Layout. In Page Layout View the page numbers should be visible at the bottom of each page.

5 Use File-Print Preview to see the effect. If the footer does not show properly, this may be due to the printer you have installed. Some printers are not able to print right to the bottom of the paper. Use File-Page Setup Margins and increase the size in the Footer box and preview again.

6 Save and close the document.

Headers and footers

A header is text or graphics that appears at the top of every page. A footer appears at the bottom of every page. They are useful in long documents as they can be used to indicate, for example, the chapter or section title. In business documents they may contain a reference number or company logo. If the work is a report, a header or footer could be used to put the author's name or the company name and logo on each page. Word prints headers in the top margin and footers in the bottom margin.

As well as being able to add headers and footers that are the same on every page, Word also offers choices of customising headers and footers.

■ If the document is to be printed on both sides of the paper then headers and footers can be set up so that *even numbered* pages have one header and *odd numbered* pages have a different one.

■ If the first page of the document is different from the rest of the document, for example, it is a title page, then headers and footers can be set so that they are *different on the first page*.

■ If the document is divided into sections then different headers and footers can be applied to *each section*. Sections are discussed in Unit 16.

Adding or removing a header or footer

To add a header or a footer to your document, use View-Header and Footer and the document switches to a page layout view with the text of each page shown in grey (or lighter than normal). A Header and Footer tool bar appears.

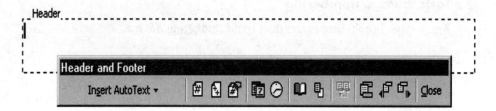

Headers and footers have pre-set tabs: there is a centre tab in the middle of the page and a right tab at the right edge of the page. By using the pre-set tabs, the headers or footers will be consistent through the document. Select a suitable font for your header or footer and tab across to the position required and type in the text. Using the buttons, as described below, enter text for headers and footers as required and when finished click on Close .

Icons and buttons in the Header/Footer Pane bar

The first button on the header and footer tool bar allows you to insert AutoText. The next set of three buttons are:

■ insert page number

■ insert number of pages

■ format page number.

The next set of two buttons are

■ insert date

■ insert time.

To put the date, the time, the page number, or the number of pages into a header or footer, position the insertion point and then click on the appropriate icon.

The next two buttons are Page Setup and Show/Hide Document Text .
Clicking on Page Setup will display the Page Setup dialog box. Clicking on
 Show/Hide Document Text will toggle between showing or hiding the document text.

The next button is the **Same as Previous** button. Click on the **Same as Previous** button if the header or footer is to be different from the header or footer in the previous section. Unit 16 discusses dividing the document up into sections.

The first button of the final group of three allows you to switch between the header and footer. The next two buttons allow forward and backward movement between different headers or footers. There will only be different headers and footers, if Different First Page, or Different Odd and Even Pages, in Page Setup have been selected or there are different sections in the document.

When the text for the header or footer has been typed in, click on the **Close** button to return to the document text body.

Before printing it is a good idea to preview the document; headers and footers can be positioned by choosing File-Page Setup and defining their required position in the From Edge section of the Page Setup-Margins dialog box.

Page numbering in headers or footers

By clicking on the **Page Number Format** button in the Header/Footer toolbar or, through using Insert-Page Numbers and clicking on the **Format** button, page numbering can be controlled. The Page Number Format dialog box shown below will be displayed.

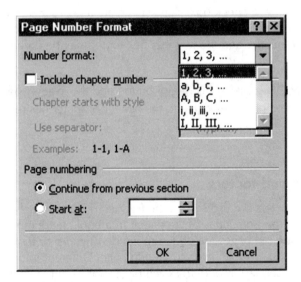

The format of page numbering may be chosen from the Page Number Format box, i.e. Arabic or Roman numerals or alphabetic sequencing. This can be done by opening the Page Number Format list box. It is also possible to alter the number at which page numbering starts. This can be useful if the document is long and is stored as separate files. The start page number of the second and subsequent files may be altered accordingly. This can be done by choosing Insert-Page Numbers, clicking on **Format**, then on **Start At** and typing in the start page number and clicking on **OK** and **Close**. Different formats of page numbering may be used in different sections of a document, for example, a preface may use Roman numerals and the following sections may use Arabic numerals.

Editing or removing existing headers and footers

To remove or edit an existing header or footer:

1   Use View-Header and Footer and display either the Header or Footer using the Switch Between Header and Footer button.

2   Edit the text in the header or footer in the normal fashion. Text may be pasted into the header or footer, or copied from it. To remove the header/footer simply delete all the text.

3   Click on Close .

Headers and footers that are different on the first page

It is useful to set headers and footers to be different on the first page to prevent a header appearing on the first page. As there is usually a title on the first page then a header does not look right. However, the same footer could be used by making the first footer identical to the footer, as follows.

1   Choose View-Header and Footer and click on the Page Setup button.

2   Click in the Different First Page check box. This will create a First Header and a First Footer as well as the normal Header and Footer. The text in a first header may be different from the header and the text in a first footer may be different from the footer.

3   Use the Switch Between Header and Footer button and the Show Next and the Show Previous buttons to navigate to the header or footer desired and key in the text.

4   Click on Close .

Odd and even headers and footers

Odd and even headers and footers are used when the finished document will be printed, like a book or leaflet, on both sides of the paper. In a book, left hand pages are even numbered and right hand pages are odd numbered. A header or footer can be defined so that it reads across from an even to an odd page. Different information about the document can appear on odd and even pages, for example chapter title on even pages and section title on odd pages. To achieve this:

1   Choose View-Header and Footer and click on the Page Setup button.

2   Click on the Different Odd and Even Pages check box. This will create an Even Header, an Odd Header, an Even Footer, and an Odd Footer. The text in the even header may be different from the odd header and the text in an even footer may be different from the odd footer.

3   Use the Switch Between Header and Footer button and the Show Next

and the Show Previous buttons to navigate to the header or footer desired and key in the text.

4 Click on Close .

Note that the odd and even headers/footers option may be used in conjunction with the different first page option.

Task 3: Exploring header and footer options

Before you start this task you will need to complete the document **Budgeting Advice** as given at the end of this unit.

1 Open the document **Budgeting Advice** and to simulate a long document we will edit it to start each headed section on a new page. To do this select each heading in turn and use Format-Paragraph, select the Line and Page Breaks tab and check the Page Break before check box. Aim to create about five pages. Save the document as **Headers and Footers**.

2 Using View-Header and Footer, add the text **Chelmer Estates** to the Header and position it on the right tab. To the footer on the centre tab add the text '**Page**' followed by a space, click on the Insert Page Number button, add a space, add the text '**of**' followed by a space and click on the Insert Number of Pages button. Add a top border to the footer using the drop-down border button on the formatting toolbar. Save and view the result in Page Layout view; it is also useful to Print Pre-View. If you don't see the footers in Print Preview this may be due to the type of printer you have installed. To remedy this use File-Page Setup and increase the measurement specified in the Footer part of the From Edge section.

3 As a header may look out of place on the first page, the headers and footers on the first page will be made different. Choose View-Header and Footer and click on the Page Setup button and tick the Different First Page check box under the Layout tab and click on OK .

4 Leave the first header blank. Switch to the footer and click on the Show Next button to display the footer text. Select and copy this, use Show Previous and paste into the first footer. Save and view the result.

5 Finally, assume that this document will be printed double sided. Choose View-Header and Footer and click on the Page Setup button and tick the Different Odd and Even check box under the Layout tab (leave the Different First Page check box ticked).

6 View the header and use Show Next to move to the Even header. Add the date using the Insert Date button at the left of the header. Try adding a bottom border to this header. Using Show Next move to the odd header which should still read **Chelmer Estates** and apply the same bordering as for the even header.

7   Move to the footer. Display the Odd Footer and move it to the right tab. Copy this and using ██ **Show Previous** ██ , paste this into the Even Footer (you may need to remove an extra paragraph mark). Delete the tabs so that the text is on the left.

8   View the result, you should see headers and footers on the left for even pages and on the right for odd pages. Save the document. If you wish you can experiment further with headers and footers. Shading as well as bordering can be used to good effect in headers and footers.

Using fields in headers and footers

If you add a page number, date or time to a header or footer you are adding a field. Fields are highlighted usually in grey to distinguish them from ordinary text. If you wish to delete a field you will notice that your first deletion action will select the field and the second deletion action will delete it.

Fields other than those available on the Header and Footer toolbar may be inserted into a header and footer, in exactly the same way as they could be inserted into the document text. Fields which may be useful to add to headers and footers include document filename, author and title.

To add a field:

■ display the header or footer into which the field is to go and position the insertion point there

■ choose **Insert-Field** and the **Field** dialog box appears

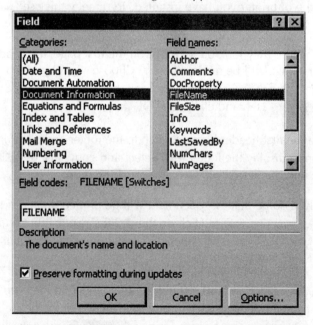

■ select the field category from the **Categories** box and the field from the **Field names** box and click on ██ **OK** ██ .

Task 4: Adding a field to a header

1   Open the template **Chelmer Estates Memo** by choosing File-New and clicking on the Memos tab.

2   Choose View-Header and Footer. Click on Page Setup and you will see Different first page ticked. Display the first page header.

3   Using Insert-Field as described above add the file name to the document header. Save the template.

4   Open the document **Headers and Footers** and display the first footer. Using Insert-Field , select Document Information and choose Author to add the writer's name to this footer. Save this document.

Footnotes and endnotes

Footnotes and endnotes are notes of reference, explanation, or comment. A word in the main text can be marked with a footnote or endnote reference mark [1]. Footnotes are found at the bottom of the page and endnotes are found at the end of the document. Word allows footnotes and endnotes of any length to be added to a document.

Text used in a footnote can be formatted just as any other text. To add a footnote or endnote:

1   In Normal View, first position the insertion point at the end of the word that the footnote or endnote is to refer to.

2   Use Insert-Footnote and the Footnote and Endnote dialog box appears:

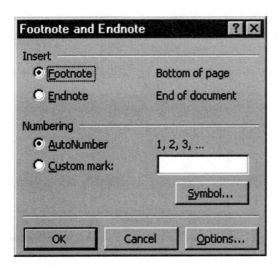

---
[1] *A number is commonly used for a reference mark.*

3 Click on **OK** and a footnote pane appears as shown below. A reference mark is positioned in the document at the position of the insertion point.

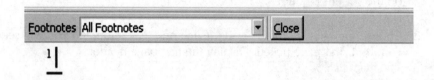

4 Key in the text. The insertion point is ready positioned following the reference mark.

5 Click on **Close** .

As footnotes or endnotes are added Word automatically numbers them. Word will automatically renumber footnote/endnote and reference marks whenever footnotes/endnotes are added, deleted, or moved. Footnotes are only visible in Page Layout.

BUDGETING ADVICE

Free advice if you're thinking of buying or selling a home

CHELMER ESTATES

In Short

Budgeting Advice provides you with information and guidance on all the financial matters of moving home, including the affordability of the move, the costs the actual move will incur, advice on insurance policies you may need, and a clear view of the on-going costs of running your new home.

What you can afford

Our fully trained staff will advise you on the mortgage options available, giving you the exact detail on what you can comfortably afford.

The Cost of the actual move

We will explain upfront costs incurred in the move, revealing any hidden costs that you may have overlooked.

Safeguarding the Transaction

We will also advise on insurance policies for your new home giving you peace of mind.

On-going Costs

We will help you consider your monthly on-going costs including regular bills such as council tax, water charges, insurance premiums, fuel, gas and electricity.

In Summary

Budgeting Advice is a flexible concept – based on giving you clear understandable comprehensive and vital information on the house moving process. If you have any queries or simply require further information, please contact your local Chelmer Estates branch.

IMPORTANT QUESTIONS, HONEST ANSWERS TO HELP GET YOU MOVING

Buying or selling a property should be exciting and fun, but it's certainly one of the most important decisions you'll ever make.

It's important that, before you make any decisions, you know the facts and seek out the soundest advice, so that you can turn what could be seen as hurdles into easily managed steps.

Naturally, you'd expect Chelmer Estates to know all the answers, and to offer you sound, honest and expert advice.

That's precisely why we've introduced an important service for anyone thinking of moving home.

It's called **Budgeting Advice** and the good news is that it's absolutely free!

Here's how Budgeting Advice works for you

Because buying a home is so important, it's equally important that you understand clearly your own financial position.

Our aim is simply to advise you so that you can be certain that the home of your dreams is realistic and affordable now and in the years to come.

How to get Budgeting Advice working for you

Simply call into or telephone your nearest Chelmer estate branch and arrange a mutually convenient date and time to meet one of our 'Budgeting Advice' team. You'll find them friendly, helpful and highly knowledgeable.

The initial formal chat will broadly cover your own requirements and analyse your financial situation. If a further meeting is necessary, then a more in-depth financial analysis will take place, to ensure that you can consider all the mortgage options available.

In addition to this valuable, free service, we can also consider your long term financial planning, and so provide a sound programme that will keep pace with your prospects and your aspirations.

Make your next move with real peace of mind

On approval of you completed financial analysis, we will present you with your Personal Home Buying Certificate. This will give you the peace of mind that, when you are making an offer on a property, you'll know the level of mortgage you can afford.

It's nice to know that when you're ready to move, Budgeting Advice will have made it possible for you to move quickly. With all discussions out of the way, your mortgage application will be made easier, whether you buy from Chelmer Estates or not.

With Budgeting Advice, you need never take chances. Instead you'll enjoy the complete peace of mind that comes with friendly, expert and professional – Chelmer – advice.

Call in and see us soon

Group working

What you will learn in this unit

In this era of network communication, and documents passing through a number of electronic versions, document creation is often a shared process. For example, in the creation of the manuscript for this book, the two authors passed drafts of the units between each other in electronic versions. Within organisations, a manager may key some basic text through the keyboard, and then e-mail that text as an attached document to a secretary who may undertake corrections and formatting, and then return the text for comment; the manager may suggest final corrections. Alternatively documents may be shared amongst a group; members of the group may have different levels of read and write access. In such environments, features such as 'Comments' can be valuable in allowing people to mark up documents with their comments. Version control and security are, however, particularly necessary. It is important to be able to identify the latest version of a document, and to be confident that only those people who should have access to a document do so.

At the end of this unit you will be able to:

■ use comments and alterations in exchanging documents between multiple authors

■ print document version information and statistics

■ be able to use e-mail to send documents to others

■ protect documents using passwords.

 This unit assumes that you are working in a networked environment. If this is not the case you will have difficulty in performing most of the tasks in this unit, and we suggest that you skip this unit.

Using comments

Electronic comments perform much the same function as comments on paper documents. The only additional feature supports multiple comments from several other authors; since it is no longer possibly to recognise their handwriting, it is necessary that they be identified through their user name. Accordingly each annotation has an associated user name. Once comments have been inserted into a document they may be saved with the document. When the document is returned to its original author the author can read the annotation by running the pointer over the text.

 The locations of comments are marked with yellow highlighting and, when the pointer is passed over the text, the comments themselves are shown in a box.

To insert a comment, position the pointer immediately after the relevant word (no space).

1   Choose either Insert-Comment, or display the Reviewing toolbar, using View-Toolbars-Reviewing, and click on the **Insert Comment** button (see Task 1).

2   In the Comments from box, check that your correct user name is identified. Type in your comment in the space in the lower half of the screen.

3   Click on **Close** and the annotation will be inserted in the text.

Instead of text comments, you can insert a sound file as an audio comment. After step 1 above, click on the **Insert Sound Object** button in the Comment window toolbar and then you can either record a message directly (provided you have a soundcard and microphone) or you can attach an existing file. Note that this could significantly increase the size of your document. See Unit 11 for more information about adding sound files to documents.

Task 1: Inserting comments into text

1   Open the letter created in Task 1 of Unit 3 (saved as Pattison D. V &S).

2   Display the Reviewing toolbar and click on the **Insert Comment** button on the Comment toolbar.

3   Choose the correct user name and type in a comment.

4   Moving between the comment window and the document, move the insertion point, click on the **Insert Comment** button, and type in further comments in the comment window.

5   Click on **Close** .

6   Check that your comments are as you planned by moving the insertion point over the text.

If you wish, send your document to a friend using e-mail (see below).

Sound or verbal comments can be embedded in a similar way, but in this case you need to click on the cassette icon in the comments entry window, and to be able to record your comment.

The Reviewing (Comment) toolbar

The Comment toolbar offers a range of buttons, the functions of most of which are clear. These fall into two categories.

Managing comments, including:

- **Insert Comment**

- **Edit Comment**

- **Previous Comment**

- **Next Comment** , and

- **Delete Comment** .

Managing alterations to the text, including

- **Track Changes** (when this button is clicked any changes are displayed in blue and can be identified as such)

- **Previous Change**

- **Next Change**

- **Accept Change** – this causes the selected change to be integrated into the text

- **Reject Change** – this deletes the change.

The toolbar also includes buttons to allow you to:

- change the highlight colour

- create a Microsoft Outlook task

- save versions, and

- send to mail recipient.

Task 2: Deleting comments

Open the document that you were using in Task 1 and, by selecting each comment in turn, delete the comments.

 Use the right click short-cut menu and select **Delete Comment** .

Task 3: Making alterations

1   Click on the **Track Changes** button and make six alterations to the text of the letter used in Task 2.

2   Reflect on your alterations, and accept or reject them. (Note: another author might often perform this process after the version had been e-mailed to them by the person proposing the alterations.

Task 4: Saving versions

Save the new version of your document, which incorporates the alterations. The Save Version dialog box will specify the date and time that the version is saved, who it has been saved by, and allow you to insert any comments on the revised version.

Printing document information and statistics

You may wish to print a draft of a document with comments, or just print the comments alone. In addition, when documents are subject to several drafts, possibly with the intervention of a number of authors, it is important to be able to identify which version of the document is currently being viewed or printed. Document information and statistics are designed to assist you to differentiate between different documents, and versions of a document. You can print document information, such as document properties, comments, field codes, hidden text or drawing objects, either with or without the text of the document.

To print only the document information:

1   Choose File-Print.

2   In the Print What: box, click on, for example, Document Properties, or Comments.

To print document information together with the document:

3   Choose Tools-Options-Print.

4   Select the option: Include with Document, and select the items to be included.

Once you have changed the Tools -Option-Print settings they stay changed for anything you print in future. So, until you change them back again, document information sheets will accompany every letter, memo or other document you print out.

Task 5: Printing comments

1   Open the letter, and insert six comments in the text of the document.

2   Print the comments with the text of the document.

3   Now print the comments alone.

Whether you choose to print the whole document or the comments alone depends on the length of the document and the extent of the alterations. With the short one page document that you have used above, it is easier to print the comments together with the document. In a long document with only a few comments, it is usually more effective and economical just to print the comments.

To complete this task, you may like to try to print document properties which will give information about the document, such as

■ Filename, Directory (folder), Template

■ Title, Subject, Author

■ Keywords, Comments

■ Creation Date, Change number

■ Last Saved On, Last Saved By, Last Printed On.

To edit properties such as Title, Subject, Author, Keywords use **File-Properties**.

E-Mailing documents as attached files

Word documents can be sent as files attached to an e-mail message, using a number of different e-mail systems. There are generally two different ways to do this, and depending upon the compatibility between your e-mail system and the system of the recipient of your messages, you may find it necessary to experiment with different approaches. The two main approaches are as follows.

1   In your e-mail package window, write a message, and then attach a file using the **Attach** option available in the e-mail package.

2   Using **File-Send To**, choose the option **Mail recipient** to send your document as an attached file to a friend. If he or she is sitting next to you, you will be able to see what is happening on both screens. If you are using Outlook, an e-mail dialog box will appear with an icon for the document in the message section. Complete and send the message as normal, adding your message text after the document icon.

If you have not used the e-mail system from within Word, this procedure may take you into the Set up Wizard. Just follow the steps in this wizard, to prepare for e-mailing.

The task below demonstrates how the **File-Send To** option can be used to send messages in Microsoft Outlook, the e-mail package within the Office suite.

While many of the recipients of your e-mail messages may work with Word, they will have a variety of different versions of Word, and others will work with other word processing packages. It will help your recipient if you save your document in a file format that they can import into their word processing package. If you cannot choose exactly the right format, rich text format (.rtf) files are often a good alternative.

Task 6: E-mailing attached documents

1   Open the letter that we have been using throughout this unit.

2   Using **File-Send To**, send your document as an attached file to a friend; if they are sitting next to you, you will be able to see what is happening on both screens.

3   Ask your friend to open the e-mail message.

4   In order to View the attached document, your friend will need to click on the icon for the attached document. This will open the document in a word processing package.

5   Sometimes such attached documents do not appear with full formatting. In order to display this, your friend will need to save the document as a word processed file, and then to open this new file.

6   Your friend should now be in a position to add comments or alterations to your document, and e-mail the modified document back to you.

Protecting documents

 If you assign password protection to a document and then forget the password, you can't open the document, remove protection from it, or recover data from it. It's a good idea to keep a list of your passwords and their corresponding document names in a safe place.

There are several ways in which you can restrict access to a document using a password. A password is case sensitive and can contain up to 15 characters. You can do any of the following.

■ Prevent unauthorised users from opening the document by assigning a password to open the document.

■ Prevent another user from modifying a document. Another user can read the document but they cannot save any changes without using a password. If the user opens the document without the password they can read the document and can only save the document by giving it a different file name.

■ Recommend that others open the document as a read-only file. If they agree to open the document as a read-only file and do change it, the document can only be saved by giving it a different file name. If they don't agree to open the document as a read-only file, the document opens as a normal read-write file and changes can be saved with the document's original file name.

■ Assign a password when you route a document for review, which prevents any changes, except by authorised users, for comments or tracked changes. This can be set using Tools-Protect Document.

To protect a document:

1   Open the document you wish to protect. Choose File-Save As and click on the
    Options button.

2   To password protect a document from being opened by an unauthorised user
    enter the password into the Password to Open box.

3   To password protect a document from being modified by an unauthorised user
    enter the password into the Password to Modify box.

4   To give the user the choice of opening the document as read only or not, check
    the Read Only Recommended box.

Styles and bullets

What you will learn in this unit

A style provides a means of recording formatting for future use. Every time you want a particular set of formatting you can apply a style that has that set of formatting rather than having to format manually. Word also allows you to copy a style from one document or template to another.

Often documents contain lists, numbered or bulleted, and this unit explores the ways in which such lists may be customised.

In this unit you will see how to

■ define and use a custom style

■ customise bullets and numbering

■ use multilevel bullets.

Using styles

A style is the name applied to the 'look' of the text in a document. The 'look' of the text depends upon the formatting instructions that have been applied to it. A heading is usually made to look different from the body of the text, i.e. it has a different style. In a document there may be different levels of headings, for example chapter or section headings and within these are sub-headings. Word has the facility for different styles to be created and stored under different names. Different styles can be used for different headings.

Various formats may be applied to create a style.

1   Character formatting such as typeface, size, bold, italics or underlining, special effects such, as shadow or outline.

2   Paragraph formatting such as alignment, spacing, margins, pagination.

3   Layout formatting such as tabs, bullets and numbering, borders and shading.

4   Language formatting. If text is written in a different language then Word will know to use the appropriate dictionary (if available) when spell checking.

Selecting a style

Word comes with some pre-defined styles and these can be listed by opening the style list box at the leftmost end of the formatting tool bar.

Select a style as follows.

1 Position the insertion point, either to key in some new text, or in an existing paragraph. If you wish to alter the style of a portion of the document that is more than one paragraph long, then select the required portion.

2 Open the Style list box and highlight the required style.

3 If you have positioned the insertion point in an existing paragraph or selected a portion of text several paragraphs long then the chosen paragraph or portion will be changed into the new style. If you are about to key in new text as you type, text will have the selected style applied to it.

To see a definition of a style, position the insertion point in some text that uses the style, say Normal, and choose Format-Style. In the Style dialog box, shown below, a description of the style is given.

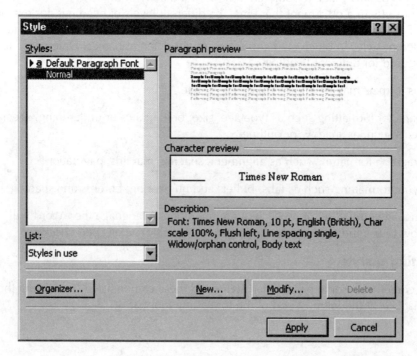

Styles may be used as the document is being keyed in or they can be applied after the text has been keyed in. The real advantage in using styles is in being able to define custom styles. Should an alteration in the style be desirable then by changing the definition of the style, all parts of the document that use that style will be altered accordingly. This makes it easier to produce consistent documents.

Defining a custom style

New styles can be defined, or existing ones modified using Format-Style. Consider defining the style for the main body of the text in the document.

1   Position the insertion point in a paragraph that is to take the main body style, or position it on a new line.

2   Use Format-Style to display the Style dialog box.

3   Click on the ▮ New ▮ button and in the Name box type in the name for the new style, e.g. **Text body**.

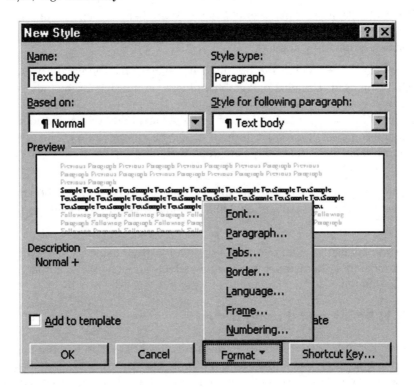

4   Select the appropriate formatting by clicking on the ▮ **Format** ▮ button and choosing from the list:

Font	–	produces Font dialog box.
Paragraph	–	produces Paragraph dialog box.
Tabs	–	produces Tabs dialog box.
Border	–	produces Paragraph Borders and Shading dialog box.

Language	–	produces Language dialog box.
Frame	–	produces Frame dialog box.
Numbering	–	produces Bullets and Numbering dialog box.

5   Make the required choices from these dialog boxes and click on **OK** .

6   Choose the Style For Following Paragraph from the list box. In this case it would be Text Body.

7   When the style is defined click on **Apply** . The defined style name will be available through the style list box.

At the top of the New Style dialog box there are two list boxes, a Based On box and a Style For Following Paragraph box.

■ The Based On list box allows you to choose a style on which to base your new style. By basing your custom styles on one particular style formatting changes can be made easier. If all the styles are based on a style that has a Times New Roman font and a decision is made to change to Arial, then altering the font upon which the others are all based will cause them to be altered too unless they have specific character formatting applied.

■ The Style For Following Paragraph list box defines the style that is to follow the one being used. The next paragraph will take on the style of the 'next style'. For the Text body style the next style should be Text body as the most likely paragraph to follow a paragraph written using the text body format is another paragraph using the same format. If the style is a heading style, e.g. Heading 1, then it is most likely that a text body paragraph will follow so for Heading 1 the next style should be Text body.

Note that heading styles (there are nine, Heading 1 to Heading 9) should only be used for headings. If a table of contents is required Word uses headings to generate it.

It is worth taking the extra effort to design various styles since it gives your work a professional look. Remember that the best effects are achieved with one or two fonts used in different sizes with a variety of typefonts, e.g bold or italic.

Task 1: Defining and using a style

1   From the disk, load in the file **Code of practice** or key it in without applying any formatting, as shown at the end of this unit. (As you work through these tasks, refer to the final version of this document, at the end of Unit 7, for guidance.) Position the insertion point in the first paragraph.

2   Use Format-Style, click on **New** and in the Name box type in the name **Point**.

3   Click on **OK** and then on the **Modify** button.

4   Click on **Format** and choose Paragraph. Set paragraph spacing to 3pt either before or after depending on your preference for using paragraph spacing. Click on **OK** .

5   Using **Format** again choose Numbering and customise the numbering as shown.

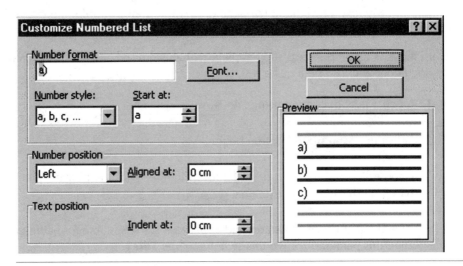

6   Click on **OK** , **OK** and **Apply** .

7   Apply this style to the following four paragraphs.

8   Save the document **Code of practice**.

Task 2: Modifying a style

You may change your mind about the styles that you have chosen and wish to make changes.

Using the document file **Code of practice** a change to the style Normal will be made.

1   Position insertion point in the paragraph '**You must do everything...**' following '**In Scotland**'. This text should have the default style Normal applied to it.

2   Choose Format-Style and click on **Modify** . Click on Format, choose Paragraph and set paragraph spacing to 3pt either before or after. Click on **OK** .

3   Click on **OK** in the Modify Style dialog box and click on **Apply** . All text throughout the document defined with this style will take on these new properties.

4   Save the document.

Task 3: Storing styles in templates

In Unit 3 the idea of using a template containing 'boilerplate' or standard text was introduced. The flexibility of templates can be further increased by defining a set of styles that can be stored with a template. In fact it is possible to have a template without any text. The default template of Normal is an example; it contains Word's standard styles.

In this task a compliments slip template with customised styles will be created. The document will also be a custom size.

1   Open a new document using File-New.

2   Select the **Template** option button.

3   Choose Blank Document from the list of templates as the new template is to be based on this template. Click on **OK**.

4   Type the text **Chelmer Estates** and apply to it some suitable formatting and right align this paragraph. Give this style the name **Title1.**

5   Type **Compliments slip** on the next line, applying suitable formatting and define this style as **Title2.**

6   Below this define a style Text body to be Times New Roman 12pt (or similar) with 6pt spacing either above or below the paragraph. You may wish to add a normal indent to this paragraph. If you type the words **text body** they can be left in the template.

7   Use File-Page Setup and adjust the height of the paper to 9.9cm. Also reduce the top and bottom margins and space for headers and footers. If you choose a dimension that is too small Word will automatically 'fix' this.

8   Add the date to the header.

9   Use File-Save and type **Chelmer Estates Compliments Slip** in the file name box. This file is saved as a .dot template file. Close the file using File-Close.

10 To use this template: start a new document using File-New and select **Chelmer Estates Compliments Slip** from the list of templates under the **General** tab. Replace the words **text body** (if you used them in the template) with the desired message, for example '**Please find enclosed the results of the recent survey on your property**'. If necessary, the completed slip can be saved in the usual manner but in this type of use it is more likely to be printed and discarded.

This document is not complete as it does not contain the business address and details of the agency. The neatest way to add these to the template is by using text boxes, this is covered in Unit 15.

Renaming and deleting styles

Both renaming and deleting are achieved through the Style dialog box (Format-Style). To delete a style, select the style in the Styles: box and click on the **Delete** button. To rename a style, select the style in the Styles: box, click on **Modify** and edit the name in the Name: box. Click on **OK** .

Adding styles to a template

As a document is created styles may be defined which it would be useful to store with the general document template. These may be added to the document template by clicking in the Add to Template check box in the bottom left hand corner of the Modify Style dialog box. When you save your document, Word will ask if you wish to save the changes to the template.

Task 4: Copying styles

If you wish to add new styles to the template file, or copy them from one document to another, then this can be done using the Organizer dialog box. In the list on the left of the dialog box the styles used in the active document or its template are shown. Styles used in the Normal document template are listed on the right.

If you wish to use styles that have been stored in a template or document that is different from the template currently being used, then the styles from that template can be copied into the current document. This can be achieved using the Organizer dialog box and is illustrated in the following task.

In this task a style saved in the template **Chelmer Estates Compliments Slip** is to be merged into a new document.

1   Start a new document.

2   Use Format-Style and click on Organizer.

3   Click on **Close File** on the right side of the dialog box. Next click on **Open File** and select the template **Chelmer Estates Compliments Slip**.

 You may select either a document or a template from which to copy styles. The Open dialog box allows you to change drive or directory or to list document or template files.

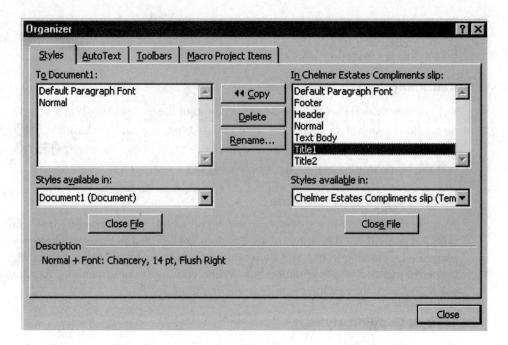

4   Select Title1 from the list of style names and click on **<< Copy** . Note that you could repeat this operation to copy other styles from the template.

5   Click on **Close** .

6   Open the Style list box (on the formatting toolbar) and you should be able to find the style that you have copied will be listed and can be applied in the new document.

7   Close the document without saving.

Bullets and numbering points

To distinguish a list of points from the rest of the text it is usual to highlight them using bullets or point numbers. A bullet is a symbol at the start of each point. Word offers two buttons on the formatting toolbar, which will help you to type a numbered or bulleted list.

Customising bullets and numbers

When you click on the **Numbering** or **Bullets** button, Word will apply the default numbering or bulleting to your document. You may customise this using Format-Bullets and Numbering. The Bullets and Numbering dialog box offers a choice of different styles of bullets under the **Bulleted** tab and different styles of numbering under the **Numbering** tab. The **Outline Numbered** tab allows multi-level bullets to be customised. Select the style you want and click on **OK** .

To alter the font of a point number, select the paragraph mark at the end of the point (click on ¶ to display them) and apply the formatting you require.

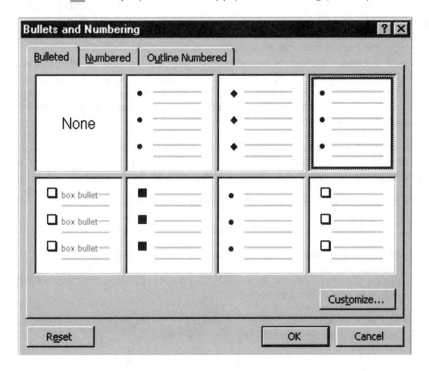

Task 5: Using a numbered heading style

The aim of this task is to use a numbered heading style in the **Code of Practice** document.

1 Open the document Code of Practice. Position the insertion point in the first heading 'General'.

2 Open the style list box and apply the Heading 2 style. Next use Format-Style and click on **Modify**. Use Format-Numbering to apply a numbered style to Heading 2 and apply this modification.

3 Apply the style Heading 2 to all the headings in the document (using the formatted version of this document, given at the end of Unit 7, as a guide) and note how the numbers increment.

4 Save the document **Code of Practice**.

Multi-level bullets

As well as creating straightforward bulleted and numbered lists, Word also allows you to create lists within lists, known as multi-level lists. The following task will illustrate the creation of multi-level lists.

Task 6: Multi-level lists

1   At the end of this unit is an extract from section 5 of **Code of Practice**. Open **Code of Practice** and select this portion of the text. In the style list box type '**Multi**'.

   a)   By law you must tell clients as soon as is reasonably possible about all offers that you receive at any time until contracts have been exchanged (in Scotland, missives have been concluded) unless the offer is an amount or type which the client has specifically instructed you, in writing, not to pass on. You must confirm such offers in writing at the earliest opportunity and keep a written or computerised record of all offers you receive.

   b)   You must not discriminate, or threaten to discriminate against a prospective purchaser of your client's property because that person refuses to agree that you will (directly or indirectly) provide services to them. Discrimination includes the following:

   ❖   Failing to tell the client of an offer to buy the property.

   ❖   Telling the client of an offer less quickly than other offers you have received.

   ❖   Misrepresenting the nature of the offer or that of rival offers.

   ❖   Giving details of properties for sale first to those who have indicated they are prepared to let you provide services to them.

   ❖   Making it a condition that the person wanting to buy the property must use any other service provided by you or anyone else.

   c)   You must take reasonable steps to find out from the prospective purchaser his source and availability of the funds for buying the property and pass this information to the client.

2   Choose Format-Bullets and Numbering.

3   Click on the   Outline Numbered   tab and select the multi-level bullets (top-left in the gallery). Click on   Customize .

4   Set up two levels of numbering as illustrated in the dialog box. Click on   OK   when finished.

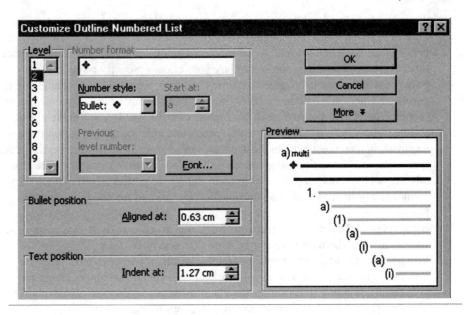

5 Position the insertion point in the third bullet point and click on the **Increase Indent** button on the formatting toolbar. Repeat for the other indented points.

The following text should be input as shown and saved as **Code of Practice**.

General

This Code applies to estate agency services (provided by a person or organisation who has agreed or is required to comply with it) in the United Kingdom for the selling and buying of residential property (see 10 a) below - all references hereafter in this Code to 'property' mean residential property as so defined) and related services. The Code aims to promote the highest standards of service. You must comply with all laws relating to residential estate agency (such as The Estate Agents Act 1979 and The Property Misdescriptions Act 1991, together with all relevant Orders and Regulations) and all other relevant legislation. You must offer equality of professional service to any person, regardless of their race, creed, sex or nationality. You must not be involved in any plan or arrangement to discrim- inate against a person or people because of their race, creed, sex, disability or nationality. You must always act both within the law and in the best interests of the client (see 10 b) below). You must offer suitable advice to meet the client's aims and needs. You must immediately (see 10 c) below) tell your client, in writing, about any circumstances which may give rise to a conflict of interest. However, this duty does not excuse you from considering fairly all those involved in the proposed sale or purchase. You must not release without your client's permission or misuse confidential information given by your client during the process of selling or buying a property.

You must make sure that you and all members of your staff keep to this Code and have a good working knowledge of the law of agency, the law of contract, and all relevant estate agency legislation.

Instructions

By law you must give your client written confirmation of his (see 10 below) instructions to act in the buying or selling of properties on his behalf You must give the client written details of your fees and expenses and of your business terms. You must give the client these details before he is committed or has any liability towards you. If appropriate, you must notify your client in writing if you or an 'associate' (see 8 a) below) or 'connected person' (see 10 d) below) wish to offer estate agency, surveying, investment, insurance or other services to people proposing to buy your client's property through you.

Except for any previously agreed expenses and fees, fees will only become due if a purchaser enters into a contract (in Scotland, concludes missives), through you, to buy the property, or as stated otherwise in your terms of business. If you use the phrase 'sole selling rights', 'sole agency' or 'ready, willing and able purchaser' within the terms of engagement, you must explain these phrases in writing, as set out in The Estate Agents (Provision of Information) Regulations 1991. Your client must be informed that, if any other agent introduces a purchaser to them during the period of your sole agency agreement this will be regarded as an introduction by you and the client will have to pay your fees.

If the client withdraws his instructions from you, you must advise him of any circumstances in which he may have to pay more than one fee.

You must try to get written confirmation if your client wishes to terminate your agency. You must give the client written confirmation that you are no longer acting for him and give details of any fees or charges the client owes you. You must also explain any continuing liability the client may have to pay you commission.

If you receive instructions from a client, you must give that client written notice that there may be a dual fee liability if:

-    that client has previously instructed another agent to sell the same property on a sole orjoint sole agency or a sole selling rights basis;

or

-    that client instructs another agent during or after the period of your sole agency or sole selling rights.

You must give up your rights to any commission if a purchaser first introduced by you goes on to buy the property through another agent, in circumstances where that purchaser was introduced by the other agent more than six months after the date your agency ended.

You must not instruct other agencies to assist you in selling a property without your client's permission. If the client gives permission, you must make sure any other agent appointed by you agrees to comply with this Code.

When you give advice to someone hoping to sell his property, any figure you advise either as a recommended asking price or as a possible selling price must be given in good faith reflecting current market conditions. You must never deliberately misrepresent the value of a property in order to gain an instruction.

You must not directly or indirectly harass (see 10 e) below) any person in order to gain instructions. Also, you must not repeatedly try to gain instructions in a way likely to cause offence.

You must not put any client's property on the market for sale without permission from that client or the client's properly appointed representative.

For Sale Boards

You can only erect a 'For Sale' board with the client's permission. When you put up a 'For Sale' board you must keep to the Town and Country Planning (Control of Advertisements) Regulations 1992 as amended; or in Scotland, the Town and Country Planning (Control of Advertisement) Regulations 1990. You must accept liability for any claim arising under these Regulations in connection with the board, unless the action arises as a result of a further board being put up by another person.

You must not erect an estate agency board at a property unless you have been instructed to sell that property.

If your 'For Sale' board relates to part of a building in multiple occupation it should, where desirable, indicate the part to which it relates.

You must not replace another agent's board with your own, or remove another agent's board from a property, without the client's permission. If you have the client's permission you must immediately tell the other agent, in writing, of the action you have taken.

Published Material

You must take all reasonable steps to make sure that all statements, whether oral or written, made about a property are accurate. Whenever possible, the written details of a property must be sent to the Seller for them to confirm that the details are accurate.

All advertisements must be fair, decent and honest.

Offers

By law you must tell clients as soon as is reasonably possible about all offers that you receive at any time until contracts have been exchanged (in Scotland, missives have been concluded) unless the offer is an amount or type which the client has specifically instructed you, in writing, not to pass on. You must confirm such offers in writing at the earliest opportunity and keep a written or computerised record of all offers you receive.

You must not discriminate, or threaten to discriminate against a prospective purchaser of your client's property because that person refuses to agree that you will (directly or indirectly) provide services to them. Discrimination includes the following:

Failing to tell the client of an offer to buy the property.

Telling the client of an offer less quickly than other offers you have received.

Misrepresenting the nature of the offer or that of rival offers.

Giving details of properties for sale first to those who have indicated they are prepared to let you provide services to them.

Making it a condition that the person wanting to buy the property must use any other service provided by you or anyone else.

You must take reasonable steps to find out from the prospective purchaser his source and availability of the funds for buying the property and pass this information to the client.

You must tell your client in writing as soon as reasonably possible after you find out that a prospective purchaser, who has made an offer, has applied to use your services or those of an associate or connected person in connection with that purchase.

When an offer has been accepted subject to contract, you must consult and take your client's instructions as to whether the property should be withdrawn from the market, or continue to be marketed. In the latter case, you must so advise the prospective purchaser in writing.

You remain under the legal obligation to pass on offers, as defined in 5 a) above.

In England, Wales and Northern Ireland

You must do everything you reasonably can to keep all prospective purchasers who have recently made offers through you, and which have not already been rejected, informed of the existence (but not the amount) of other offers submitted to the client. You must not misrepresent the existence of, or any details of, any other offer allegedly made, or the status of any other person who has made an offer. If you know that your client has instructed a solicitor to send a contract to an alternative purchaser, then you must tell your prospective purchaser in writing.

In Scotland

You must do everything you reasonably can to keep those who have told you that they intend to make an offer informed of the existence (but not the amount) of any other offers. All your negotiations must neither advantage nor disadvantage any of the prospective purchasers involved.

If you have received a note of interest (either orally or in writing) from someone intending to make an offer, you must do the following:

Immediately tell your client about the note of interest and confirm the details in writing, whenever this is practicable. (You must keep a written, or computerised, record of all notes of interest).

Do everything reasonably possible to tell the person intending to make an offer about any formal closing date for offers.

Access to Premises

Unless you and the client agree otherwise in writing, if you hold the keys to a property you must accompany anyone looking around that property. If you are arranging for someone to view an occupied property, you must agree the arrangements with the occupier beforehand, wherever possible.

You must make sure that all the keys you have are coded and kept secure. You must maintain records of when you issue keys and to whom, and when they are returned. These records must be kept secure and separate from the actual keys. You must only give keys to people providing you with satisfactory identification.

After exchange of contracts (in Scotland, conclusion of missives) you must not give the purchaser the keys to the property without specific permission from your client or their solicitor. (In Scotland, keys to the property must not be given to the purchaser without specific permission from the client's solicitor).

Clients' Money

In England, Wales and Northern Ireland

You must not hold a deposit or any other money belonging to a client, unless you are covered by adequate insurance.

All clients' money must be held in a separate client bank or building society account or accounts, as set out in the Estate Agents (Accounts) Regulations 1981. You must be able to account immediately for all money you are holding on behalf of a client.

You must refund immediately any deposit paid before exchange of contracts, together with any interest that may be due when you are asked, in writing, to do so. You should ask for a receipt for all the deposits you refund.

You must not deduct any cost or charges from any client's money you hold, unless your client has given you written authority to do so.

In Scotland, deposits should not be taken at any time.

Conflict of Interest

If your firm is instructed to sell a property and you, an employee or an associate (or an associate of the employee if you know about the relationship) is intending to buy it, you must, before negotiations begin, give all the relevant facts, in writing, to the client and his solicitor. If you or an employee is intending to buy a property which your firm is instructed to sell, that person must take no further direct part in marketing that property. (The term 'associate' includes a brother, sister, husband, wife, "partner" (ie co-habitee in an intimate relationship), aunt, uncle, nephew, niece, parents, grandparents, children and grandchildren. The definition also includes business associates).

If you are selling a property that is owned by you, an employee or an associate (or an associate of an employee); or you are selling a property in which you, an employee (or an associate of an employee) has an interest, you must, before negotiations begin, immediately give all the relevant facts, in writing, to the prospective purchaser.

You must make every attempt to avoid any conflict of interest which might not be in the best interest of the client.

Financial Services

You must keep to the rules of the recognised self-regulating organisation (as defined under the Financial Services Act 1986) which regulates the conduct of your investment business, or the life assurance company you represent, as the case may be.

Interpretation and Definitions

In this Code, references to the masculine include the feminine, the plural and organisations. The following interpretations and definitions also apply:

Residential property - property (land with buildings) used, last used, or to be used for residential purposes, to be sold or purchased with vacant possession.

Client - a person who has instructed you to sell or, for a fee, to buy a property on his or her behalf, in the United Kingdom - excluding the Channel Islands and the Isle of Man.

Immediately - as soon as is reasonably practicable in the circumstances.

Connected Person – "connected persons" include:

your employer or principal;

your employee or agent;

any associate including the term "business associate" as defined within Sections 31 and 32 of the Estate Agents Act 1979.

Harass - means act in a threatening or oppressive manner likely to cause alarm, annoyance and/or distress.

Outlining, contents and indexes

What you will learn in this unit

Outlining, contents pages and indexes are useful approaches to structuring long documents. If you are creating long corporate documents you should think about their structure at an early stage in their creation.

Outlining is a technique for viewing a document at various levels of its structure. By viewing major headings, without accompanying text (this is hidden), it is possible to check the structure and flow of topics in a document. An Outline View looks like a table of contents. Further, Word can create a table of contents using the document headings.

For long documents, indexes may be useful in allowing your reader to 'look-up' specific items in the document. An index refers them to the page (or pages) in the document where they will find the item discussed, exactly like the index you find at the end of a book.

By the end of this unit you will be able to:

■ apply heading styles so that you can use outlining

■ add a table of contents to a document, and

■ add an index to a document.

Outlining

If your document is more than a few paragraphs long then you should use headings. Word provides nine heading styles and these should be applied as styles to the headings in the document. Heading 1 is the most important and Heading 9 the least important. These levels of importance can also be given to any style, not just a heading style, by using the Outline level drop down list box in the Paragraph dialog box

Applying heading styles to headings is the basis for both using outlining as well as creating a table of contents. Outlining is a technique whereby a document is planned by noting the headings for the topics that are to be covered in the document. Topics can then be grouped under more major headings and their order in the document arranged. Before word processors this kind of planning took place on paper, and any restructuring could be a time consuming manual process, particularly if most of the document had been hand written or hand typed.

Word processors have automated this outlining technique and so a document structure can be re-worked at any stage of its production process. In Word, using Outline View, a document may be viewed in its entirety or at particular heading levels, with subordinate text being hidden. For example, if only heading level 1 is chosen, only the headings with the style Heading 1 will be displayed. It is easy to display whatever level of outlining is required and it is also easy to move sections of text from one part of the document to another.

Task 1: Applying heading styles

1   Create the document **Letting** (reproduced at the end of this unit)

2   Apply the heading styles as indicated by the numbers in brackets (don't type these in).

3   To use the style Heading 4, click in an appropriate heading, click in the style box and type **Heading 4**. Try altering the format of this style to be italic rather than bold. Save the document.

Outline view

To see the document in outline choose View-Outline and the document will take on a different appearance and the Outlining toolbar appears.

The buttons on this toolbar allow you to

■ promote or demote a heading level

■ demote a heading to normal 'body text', i.e. no heading level

■ move a heading (and its subordinate text) up or down within the document

■ expand or collapse a selected level so that you can choose whether or not to see subordinate levels and text

■ show the levels of headings, for example **3** will show all Heading 1, Heading 2 and Heading 3 levels of text; **All** will show all the text (with associated outlining symbols)

■ show the first line only; this allows you to see the opening line of subordinate text if that text is longer than one line

- show formatting; you can choose to see the formatting as used in the document or to ignore it; heading levels are indented in Outline View so you may prefer not to see the formatting; heading styles can be changed just as in other views

- switch to Master Document View. Master documents are the subject of units 9 and 10.

Outlining symbols

When a document is displayed in Outline View, the heading and text are shown indented, the larger the indent the higher the heading level. Each heading or text is prefixed by an outlining symbol as seen in the table below.

Symbol	Meaning
✿	The heading has associated subordinate text
▭	The heading does not have subordinate text
▫	Prefixes the first line of a paragraph of body text

Task 2: Viewing and manipulating a document in Outline view

1 Open the document **Letting** and choose View-Outline.

2 Click on the ▮ Show Heading 1 ▮ button to see just the one heading at this level. Try clicking on the other heading level buttons to display the document outline.

3 Display the four heading levels. Position the insertion point a level 4 heading and click on the ▮ Promote ▮ button. Try promoting this heading to level 1 and then use the ▮ Demote ▮ button to put it back to level 4

4 With the four levels of heading displayed in Outline View, position the insertion point in the heading **Expert advice** and click on the ▮ Expand ▮ button to display the text at this level. Click on the ▮ Collapse ▮ button to collapse the text. Expanding and collapsing of text can also be accomplished by double-clicking on the symbol prefixing the heading. Experiment with expanding and collapsing text and levels in this document.

If you expand or collapse a level that has subordinate levels, then expanding and collapsing works one level at a time and affects all subordinate levels.

5 Return the display to the four levels of heading. Position the insertion point in the **Preparing to let** heading and click on the ▮ Move Up ▮ button. This moves the heading and its collapsed subordinate text (and levels) with it. Use Undo to return the document to its original order.

Clicking and dragging the outline prefix symbol is another way in which the text can be re-ordered.

6 Toggle the **Formatting** button to switch between displaying heading formatting or not.

7 Click on **All** to display the whole document in Outline View. Toggle the **First Line Only** button and note its effect. Investigate collapsing and expanding levels with first line only switched on.

8 Return the document to its original formatting. The easiest way is to close it without saving.

Note that we have used outlining with an existing document in this task. You could create a new document using Outline View and key in headings and arrange their order and levels before adding text. It is easy to switch from one view to another (Normal to Outline) and back, to work either on text creation or document structure.

Creating a simple table of contents

Outline view resembles a table of contents, especially when only the major heading levels are displayed; all that is missing are the page numbers. Word uses the headings and notes their page numbers and thereby creates a table of contents. With a document open, create a table of contents as follows.

Choose Insert-Index and Tables and click on the **Tables of Contents** tab. You may select from a variety of formats and you can decide how many heading levels you want in your table of contents.

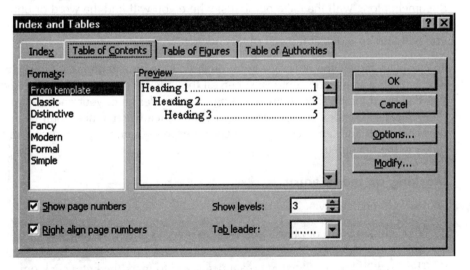

Task 3: Creating a table of contents

A simple table of contents is to be created for the document **Code of Practice**.

1 Open the document **Code of Practice**. Position the insertion point at the beginning of the document.

2 Choose Insert-Index and Tables. Set the Show levels value to 2.

3 Select the From Template format for the table of contents and click on   OK .
   The table of contents will be inserted at the beginning of the document.

Tables of contents may be put anywhere, so take care of where you position the
insertion point, usually they are placed at the beginning of a document and
sometimes in a separate section so as not to interfere with page numbering.

4 Save the document **Code of Practice**.

Updating and removing a table of contents

Should the document be revised the table of contents can be updated by positioning
the insertion point in the table of contents and pressing *F9*. You will be given the
choice of updating either just the page numbers or the whole table of contents.

A table of contents can be removed by simply highlighting the table and pressing
the *Delete* key. If you click in the left margin level with the first line of your table of
contents, the whole table should highlight.

You can use a table of contents to 'jump' to a specific heading in your document, by
double clicking on the page number of the heading to which you wish to go.

Creating an index

An index is an alphabetical list of important words or phrases that occur in your
document along with the page number(s) where you will find the word or phrase
used in the document. An index is usually found at the end of the document, just as
you will find an index at the end of this book.

To create an index, you must first go through your document and mark important
words or phrases as index entries. When all the index entries have been marked,
you can build the finished index selecting an index design of your choice. Word
then collects the index entries, sorts them alphabetically, references their page
numbers, finds and removes duplicate entries from the same page, and creates the
index in the document.

Marking an index entry

To mark an index entry

1 Highlight the word or phrase you wish to mark as an entry. Choose Insert-Index
   and Tables and select the   Index   tab and click on the   Mark Entry   button.
   The Mark Index Entry dialog box appears and to mark the entry click on
     Mark .

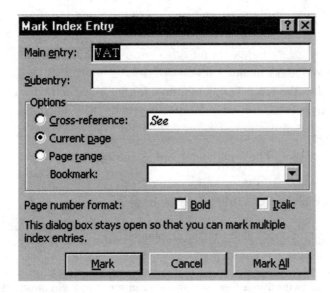

2   The **Mark Index Entry** box remains open so that you may scroll through the document and add all the index marks. Each time you add a mark highlight the relevant word and click in the **Main entry** box and then click on **Mark** . If the highlighted word appears several times throughout the document and you want to mark all the occurrences then click on the **Mark All** button.

3   When you have finished click on **Close** .

Adding the index

When you have marked all the index entries, move to the end of the document and choose **Insert-Index and Tables**, select the **Index** tab, select a format for the index and click on **OK** . The index will be inserted in a separate section. Sections are discussed in Unit 16

Updating and removing an index

Should the document be revised the index can be updated by positioning the insertion point in the index and pressing *F9*. In Normal view, if you click on the top section break marker, the whole index and section breaks should highlight. Press *Delete* to remove index and section breaks.

Task 4: Creating an index

1   Open the document **Letting**, highlight the word '**legislation**' and choose **Insert-Index and Tables**, select the **Index** tab, and click on the **Mark Entry** button. Click on **Mark** to mark this entry.

2   With the **Mark Index Entry** box open select the word '**rent**' and click in the **Main entry** box and then click on **Mark All** . Choose several other words which you think would be suitable in the index and either use **Mark** or

Mark All to add them to your index entries. When you have finished click on **Close** .

3   Move to the end of the document. Choose Insert-Index and Tables, select the **Index** tab, select the From Template format for the index and click on **OK** . The index will be inserted in a separate section. Save and close the document.

The shaded text below should be input and saved as **Letting**.

A Guide to Letting your Home (1)

Deciding whether to let or sell (2)

If you are currently undecided as to whether to let your property or sell it, then it's worth bearing in mind the increasing demand for good quality, rented accommodation.

Although home purchase is an attractive and very affordable option these days, an increasing number of people are choosing to rent – either as an alternative to buying, an intermediary step before embarking on the home ownership ladder, or simply because personal circumstances make renting the most practical solution.

It may be they are relocating to the area for work or retirement reasons, and need somewhere to live for a short term period or while looking for a property to buy. Similarly, there are companies seeking good quality residential accommodation for their employees or visitors, or there are people who divide their time between the UK and abroad, and require a home for time spent in this country.

So letting is an attractive option, as in our experience there is always a steady demand for good quality residential property let at sensible rents.

Professionals who care (3)

If you have a residential property to let then it makes economic and practical sense to put the letting in the hands of experts such as Chelmer Estates Property Services.

Our highly specialised Residential Letting and Management Services help safeguard your interests and protect your property during the letting period.

It's worth noting that although recent changes to legislation make the letting of a property an attractive proposition, it's still important to obtain professional advice on the rents you can charge and the different types of tenancies you may create.

Chelmer Estates Property Services Residential Letting and Management Services are designed to take the worry out of letting.

We provide invaluable advice on the complexities of letting and also information about current legislation on letting a property in England and Wales.

Advice on all types of furnished and unfurnished residential letting is readily available. We offer a complete letting and management package to ensure you receive the very best service.

However, we're flexible, so if you wish us to find a tenant for you without being involved in the subsequent management of your property, we'll be pleased to advise you about our letting-only service.

How much will it cost? (3)

Our letting and management fees are agreed at the start of any contract and are normally based on a percentage of rent. VAT is also payable. We'll also inform you if there are any additional charges, which arise while your property is let. These charges will be set out in our Terms of

Business, just ask our staff for details.

Full letting and management service for a trouble-free tenancy (3)

To ensure that the letting of your home is arranged with the minimum of fuss, and continues to run smoothly for the duration of the Tenancy agreement, we provide the following essential services:

Expert advice (4)

So you know exactly where you stand regarding current tax liabilities, rental levels, types of tenancy, and the effect on your existing mortgages and insurance policies.

Preparing to let (4)

We'll help you make all the necessary preparations, including arranging your household contents and legal expenses insurance, if required.

Completion of documentation (4)

We take care of all the paperwork, including completion of legal agreements and arrangements for the drawing up of an inventory of contents.

Finding a suitable tenant (4)

Our extensive network of Chelmer Estates Property Services offices attracts many people who are looking to rent. In addition, we often advertise your property to let in the local press.

Vetting applicants (4)

We make all reasonable enquiries and apply for references on all prospective tenants.

Collecting the rent (4)

We collect the rent and pay it into your bank or building society account at regular intervals.

Accounting (4)

Throughout the letting period, we provide detailed accounts for you.

Property visits (4)

We visit your property at quarterly intervals, or more frequently if required and, when considered necessary, submit written reports on the condition of the property and advise about the need for repairs.

Property maintenance (4)

We arrange any day to day repairs, in accordance with your instructions. We have a list of reliable contractors or, if you wish, we can use your own contacts.

Tenancy supervision (4)

During the tenancy we check that the tenant is complying with his or her obligations and also to organise the termination or extension of the Tenancy agreement.

Protecting your home during letting (4)

To give you peace of mind we can arrange to insure your property and contents, together with legal expenses cover. Please ask for details.

Should I inform my mortgage lender? (2)

It's essential that you obtain permission from your lender before you let your property. We'll be pleased to advise you how to go about this. Similarly, if your property is leasehold, you may need your head lessee's consent. We'll help you check your lease.

Do I have to pay tax on the rent I receive? (2)

This depends on your personal circumstances – mainly, whether you are resident in the UK for tax purposes or a non-resident living abroad. It's best to discuss your position with your tax adviser.

Tenancy (2)

What types of tenancy are available? (3)

Under current housing legislation, a choice of tenancies is available 'Assured Shorthold Tenancy' and 'Assured Tenancy'. Our letting specialist will be pleased to advise you which is the most appropriate to suit your needs

How long is the tenancy for? (3)

In our experience it isn't worth letting a property for less than six months, although 'Assured Tenancies' can be shorter.

Who prepares the tenancy agreement? (3)

We have our own tenancy agreement, which both you and your tenant sign. Alternatively, as your agent, we can sign the agreement on your behalf; this is particularly useful if you're living abroad.

How do you select tenants? (3)

This is one of the most important parts of letting a property. We make various enquiries, including taking up references on the prospective tenant. Where practicable we'll discuss the suitability of applicants with you - or you can simply rely on our professional judgement.

How long will it take to find a tenant? (3)

This depends very much on market conditions as demand for rented accommodation obviously varies from time to time and from area to area.

Rent and repairs (2)

What about a deposit and rent? (3)

We ask tenants for a deposit, which is usually equal to one or two months' rent. We only return it when the tenant has given vacant possession of the property and left it in a satisfactory condition, allowing for wear and tear, and complied with his or her responsibilities under the tenancy agreement.

Rent is usually payable at least one month in advance.

What happens if the tenant doesn't pay the rent? (3)

As part of our service, we endeavour to ensure that the rent is paid on time. Having carefully selected the tenant in the first place, there's unlikely to be a problem. However, people's circumstances do sometimes change during a tenancy and if the rent is not paid, we'll advise you on the appropriate course of action.

Who pays for the utilities and maintenance of appliances? (3)

It's usually the tenant's responsibility to pay Council Tax and all utility charges at your property, such as gas and electricity, during the tenancy agreement. The maintenance of appliances is your responsibility and you should ensure that the central heating is serviced and gas and electrical appliances are in good working order and comply with current regulations before the property is let.

Who's liable for repairs? (3)

Generally, you are expected to pay for most repairs to your property. We can arrange to have the work carried out for you, using our list of contractors we have found to be reliable, unless you instruct us otherwise.

What happens while my property is empty? (3)

Empty properties are always at risk, especially during the winter months. However, there are steps we can take to protect your property against damage by ice and frost etc., for an additional charge. If your property is to be left empty for more than 30 days, your buildings and contents insurer needs to be informed.

Does the tenant pay any insurance? (3)

Your tenant will be responsible for insuring any personal possessions brought into the property.

What about an inventory? (2)

This is essential and will be arranged by Chelmer Estates Property Services in consultation with you before the tenancy agreement is completed. We arrange a check of the inventory at the end of each tenancy, but you should expect some wear and tear to items you've left in the property. if the property should happen to be left in a poor condition at the end of the tenancy we'll arrange for professional cleaning at the tenant's expense.

What happens about the garden? (2)

The tenant is responsible for maintaining your garden, and you should leave the necessary tools available, especially a lawn mower.

Are pets allowed? (2)

They are specifically prohibited in our tenancy agreement, but we can make individual exceptions if you wish.

Need to know more? (2)

Chelmer Estates Property Services has many years' experience in the lettings market. So if you have any further queries about the ins and outs of becoming a landlord - or even buying a property with a view to letting - come and discuss your needs with our staff, who'll be happy to give you the very best advice, and provide you with our Landlord's Information Pack.

Decided to sell? (2)

If you decide to sell your property at some point in the future, Chelmer Estates Property Services can offer you a comprehensive range of services, designed to sell your home for the best possible price, in the shortest possible time. Ask staff for our brochure, Guide to Selling your Home, for more details.

Adapted and reproduced with the kind permission of the Halifax Building Society

The following text is the formatted version of **Code of Pactice**.

Contents

1. General

a) This Code applies to estate agency services (provided by a person or organisation who has agreed or is required to comply with it) in the United Kingdom for the selling and buying of residential property (see 10 a) below - all references hereafter in this Code to 'property' mean residential property as so defined) and related services. The Code aims to promote the highest standards of service. You must comply with all laws relating to residential estate agency (such as The Estate Agents Act 1979 and The Property Misdescriptions Act 1991, together with all relevant Orders and Regulations) and all other relevant legislation.

b) You must offer equality of professional service to any person, regardless of their race, creed, sex or nationality. You must not be involved in any plan or arrangement to discriminate against a person or people because of their race, creed, sex, disability or nationality.

c) You must always act both within the law and in the best interests of the client (see 10 b) below). You must offer suitable advice to meet the client's aims and needs. You must immediately (see 10 c) below) tell your client, in writing, about any circumstances which may give rise to a conflict of interest. However, this duty does not excuse you from considering fairly all those involved in the proposed sale or purchase. You must not release without your client's permission or misuse confidential information given by your client during the process of selling or buying a property.

d) You must make sure that you and all members of your staff keep to this Code and have a good working knowledge of the law of agency, the law of contract, and all relevant estate agency legislation.

2. Instructions

a) By law you must give your client written confirmation of his (see 10 below) instructions to act in the buying or selling of properties on his behalf You must give the client written details of your fees and expenses and of your business terms. You must give the client these details before he is committed or has any liability towards you. If appropriate, you must notify your client in writing if you or an 'associate' (see 8 a) below) or 'connected person' (see 10 d) below) wish to offer estate agency, surveying, investment, insurance or other services to people proposing to buy your client's property through you.

b) Except for any previously agreed expenses and fees, fees will only become due if a purchaser enters into a contract (in Scotland, concludes missives), through you, to buy the property, or as stated otherwise in your terms of business. If you use the phrase 'sole selling rights', 'sole agency' or 'ready, willing and able purchaser' within the terms of engagement, you must explain these phrases in writing, as set out in The Estate Agents (Provision of Information) Regulations 1991. Your client must be informed that, if any other agent introduces a purchaser to them during the period of your sole agency agreement this will be regarded as an introduction by you and the client will have to pay your fees.

c) If the client withdraws his instructions from you, you must advise him of any circumstances in which he may have to pay more than one fee.

d) You must try to get written confirmation if your client wishes to terminate your agency.

You must give the client written confirmation that you are no longer acting for him and give details of any fees or charges the client owes you. You must also explain any continuing liability the client may have to pay you commission.

e) If you receive instructions from a client, you must give that client written notice that there may be a dual fee liability if:

-    that client has previously instructed another agent to sell the same property on a sole orjoint sole agency or a sole selling rights basis;

or

-    that client instructs another agent during or after the period of your sole agency or sole selling rights.

f) You must give up your rights to any commission if a purchaser first introduced by you goes on to buy the property through another agent, in circumstances where that purchaser was introduced by the other agent more than six months after the date your agency ended.

g) You must not instruct other agencies to assist you in selling a property without your client's permission. If the client gives permission, you must make sure any other agent appointed by you agrees to comply with this Code.

h) When you give advice to someone hoping to sell his property, any figure you advise either as a recommended asking price or as a possible selling price must be given in good faith reflecting current market conditions. You must never deliberately misrepresent the value of a property in order to gain an instruction.

i) You must not directly or indirectly harass (see 10 e) below) any person in order to gain instructions. Also, you must not repeatedly try to gain instructions in a way likely to cause offence.

j) You must not put any client's property on the market for sale without permission from that client or the client's properly appointed representative.

3. For Sale Boards

a) You can only erect a 'For Sale' board with the client's permission. When you put up a 'For Sale' board you must keep to the Town and Country Planning (Control of Advertisements) Regulations 1992 as amended; or in Scotland, the Town and Country Planning (Control of Advertisement) Regulations 1990. You must accept liability for any claim arising under these Regulations in connection with the board, unless the action arises as a result of a further board being put up by another person.

b) You must not erect an estate agency board at a property unless you have been instructed to sell that property.

c) If your 'For Sale' board relates to part of a building in multiple occupation it should, where desirable, indicate the part to which it relates.

d) You must not replace another agent's board with your own, or remove another agent's board from a property, without the client's permission. If you have the client's permission you must immediately tell the other agent, in writing, of the action you have taken.

4. Published Material

a) You must take all reasonable steps to make sure that all statements, whether oral or written, made about a property are accurate. Whenever possible, the written details of a property must be sent to the Seller for them to confirm that the details are accurate.

b) All advertisements must be fair, decent and honest.

5. Offers

a)   By law you must tell clients as soon as is reasonably possible about all offers that you receive at any time until contracts have been exchanged (in Scotland, missives have been concluded) unless the offer is an amount or type which the client has specifically instructed you, in writing, not to pass on. You must confirm such offers in writing at the earliest opportunity and keep a written or computerised record of all offers you receive.

b)   You must not discriminate, or threaten to discriminate against a prospective purchaser of your client's property because that person refuses to agree that you will (directly or indirectly) provide services to them. Discrimination includes the following:

❖   Failing to tell the client of an offer to buy the property.

❖   Telling the client of an offer less quickly than other offers you have received.

❖   Misrepresenting the nature of the offer or that of rival offers.

❖   Giving details of properties for sale first to those who have indicated they are prepared to let you provide services to them.

❖   Making it a condition that the person wanting to buy the property must use any other service provided by you or anyone else.

c)   You must take reasonable steps to find out from the prospective purchaser his source and availability of the funds for buying the property and pass this information to the client.

d)   You must tell your client in writing as soon as reasonably possible after you find out that a prospective purchaser, who has made an otter, has applied to use your services or those of an associate or connected person in connection with that purchase.

e)   When an offer has been accepted subject to contract, you must consult and take your client's instructions as to whether the property should be withdrawn from the market, or continue to be marketed. In the latter case, you must so advise the prospective purchaser in writing.

You remain under the legal obligation to pass on offers, as defined in 5 a) above.

f)   In England, Wales and Northern Ireland

You must do everything you reasonably can to keep all prospective purchasers who have recently made offers through you, and which have not already been rejected, informed of the existence (but not the amount) of other offers submitted to the client. You must not misrepresent the existence of, or any details of, any other offer allegedly made, or the status of any other person who has made an offer. If you know that your client has instructed a solicitor to send a contract to an alternative purchaser, then you must tell your prospective purchaser in writing.

In Scotland

You must do everything you reasonably can to keep those who have told you that they intend to make an offer informed of the existence (but not the amount) of any other offers. All your negotiations must neither advantage nor disadvantage any of the prospective purchasers involved.

If you have received a note of interest (either orally or in writing) from someone intending to make an offer, you must do the following:

❖ Immediately tell your client about the note of interest and confirm the details in writing, whenever this is practicable. (You must keep a written, or computerised, record of all notes of interest).

❖ Do everything reasonably possible to tell the person intending to make an offer about any formal closing date for offers.

6 . Access to Premises

a) Unless you and the client agree otherwise in writing, if you hold the keys to a property you must accompany anyone looking around that property. If you are arranging for someone to view an occupied property, you must agree the arrangements with the occupier beforehand, wherever possible.

b) You must make sure that all the keys you have are coded and kept secure. You must maintain records of when you issue keys and to whom, and when they are returned. These records must be kept secure and separate from the actual keys. You must only give keys to people providing you with satisfactory identification.

c) After exchange of contracts (in Scotland, conclusion of missives) you must not give the purchaser the keys to the property without specific permission from your client or their solicitor. (In Scotland, keys to the property must not be given to the purchaser without specific permission from the client's solicitor).

7. Clients' Money

In England, Wales and Northern Ireland

a) You must not hold a deposit or any other money belonging to a client, unless you are covered by adequate insurance.

b) All clients' money must be held in a separate client bank or building society account or accounts, as set out in the Estate Agents (Accounts) Regulations 1981. You must be able to account immediately for all money you are holding on behalf of a client.

c) You must refund immediately any deposit paid before exchange of contracts, together with any interest that may be due when you are asked, in writing, to do so. You should ask for a receipt for all the deposits you refund.

d) You must not deduct any cost or charges from any client's money you hold, unless your client has given you written authority to do so.

In Scotland, deposits should not be taken at any time.

8. Conflict of Interest

a) If your firm is instructed to sell a property and you, an employee or an associate (or an associate of the employee if you know about the relationship) is intending to buy it, you must, before negotiations begin, give all the relevant facts, in writing, to the client and his solicitor. If you or an employee is intending to buy a property which your firm is instructed to sell, that person must take no further direct part in marketing that property. (The term 'associate' includes a brother, sister, husband, wife, "partner" (ie co-habitee in an intimate relationship), aunt, uncle, nephew, niece, parents, grandparents, children and grandchildren. The definition also includes business associates).

b) If you are selling a property that is owned by you, an employee or an associate (or an associate of an employee); or you are selling a property in which you, an employee (or an associate of an employee) has an interest, you must, before negotiations begin, immediately give all the relevant facts, in writing, to the prospective purchaser.

c) You must make every attempt to avoid any conflict of interest which might not be in the best interest of the client.

9. Financial Services

a) You must keep to the rules of the recognised self-regulating organisation (as defined under the Financial Services Act 1986) which regulates the conduct of your investment business, or the life assurance company you represent, as the case may be.

10. Interpretation and Definitions

In this Code, references to the masculine include the feminine, the plural and organisations. The following interpretations and definitions also apply:

a)   **Residential property** - property (land with buildings) used, last used, or to be used for residential purposes, to be sold or purchased with vacant possession.

b)   **Client** - a person who has instructed you to sell or, for a fee, to buy a property on his or her behalf, in the United Kingdom - excluding the Channel Islands and the Isle of Man.

c)   **Immediately** - as soon as is reasonably practicable in the circumstances.

d)   **Connected Person** – "connected persons" include:

   1)   your employer or principal;

   2)   your employee or agent;

   3)   any associate including the term "business associate" as defined within Sections 31 and 32 of the Estate Agents Act 1979.

e)   **Harass** - means act in a threatening or oppressive manner likely to cause alarm, annoyance and/or distress.

Bookmarks, captions and cross references

What you will learn in this unit

Bookmarks are the equivalent of strips of paper that you would put in a book so that you could find a particular page very quickly. If you wished to mark several places in a book you would make a brief note on the paper marker to remind you of the topic to be found on that page. You name electronic bookmarks in a similar manner so that you can easily find a particular point in a document.

A caption is the text that appears next to a table or figure, for example, 'Figure 1 Sales for South-West region'. By using a caption to number the tables and figures in a document, Word will automatically number them and will re-number them when you revise the document and either add, remove or rearrange your tables and figures.

If you wish to refer to a particular figure, table or other feature in a document then use a cross-reference. You may cross-reference across documents if the documents all belong to the same master document. Master documents are introduced in the next unit.

At the end of this unit you will be able to

- add, find and delete bookmarks in a document
- use a bookmark to create an index entry that contains a page range
- add and remove a caption
- use Auto Caption
- create a cross reference.

Bookmarks

Bookmarks are used to mark a location in a document so that you can

- 'jump' to that location
- refer to it in a cross-reference; this will be considered in the section on cross-references.
- use the location to generate a range of pages for an index entry.

Adding, jumping to, and deleting bookmarks

Bookmarks do not appear on-screen by default but they can be made visible as described in the next section. Insert a bookmark as follows.

1 Either select the text you wish to bookmark or position the insertion point next to it and choose **Insert-Bookmark**.

2 Key in a name for the bookmark and click on the ▎**Add**▎ button. Repeat this process to add all the bookmarks required in the document. Note that bookmark names can be up to 40 characters in length but that spaces in them are not allowed.

To move (jump) to a bookmark choose Edit-Go To and select Bookmark from the Go to What list, open the list of bookmark names, select the one to go to and click on ▎**Go To**▎ .

To delete a bookmark choose Insert-Bookmark and highlight the name of the bookmark you want to delete, and then click on the ▎**Delete**▎ button.

 To delete the bookmark and all the text associated with that bookmark, select all the text, and then press ▎**Delete**▎ .

Making bookmarks visible

You can show bookmarks that have been added to a document.

1 First change to normal view using View-Normal.

2 Choose Tools-Options and select the ▎**View**▎ tab. Tick the Bookmarks check box in the Show section and click on ▎**OK**▎ . Bookmarks will be shown enclosed by square brackets.

3 To make the bookmarks invisible again, remove the tick from the Bookmarks check box.

 You may add a bookmark at the insertion point without selecting any text; if you display this bookmark, it will appear as a large I as the brackets are on top of each other.

Task 1: Adding and jumping to bookmarks

1 Open the document **Letting**. Select the heading **Do I have to pay tax on the rent I receive** and choose Insert-Bookmark

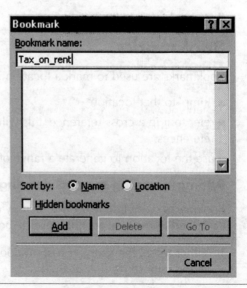

2   Accept the name **Tax_on_rent**, as suggested by Word, for the bookmark (or you could key in your own name) and click on **Add** . Don't use spaces in the name, use an underscore symbol instead.

3   Repeat this for several other headings in the document, choosing suitable bookmark names each time. Save the document.

4   Choose Edit-Go to, select Bookmark from the Go to What list, open the list of bookmark names, select **Tax_on_rent** and click on **Go To** .

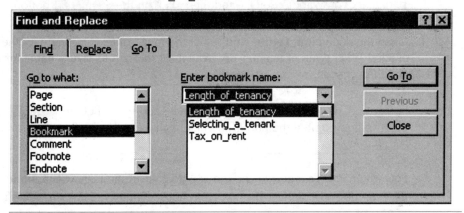

5   Make the bookmarks visible by first switching to normal view using View-Normal, choosing Tools-Options and checking the Bookmarks check box and clicking on **OK** . Review the document with the bookmarks visible, then make them invisible again by removing the tick from the Bookmarks checkbox.

6   Try deleting one of your bookmarks by choosing Insert-Bookmark, highlighting the name of the bookmark to be removed and clicking on the **Delete** button.

7   Save and close the document.

Using a bookmark to create an index entry that contains a page range

When you want an index entry to indicate a range of pages instead of a single page, you must mark that page range with a bookmark.

1   In the document, select the range of text you want the index entry to refer to, and then choose Insert-Bookmark.

2   In the Bookmark Name box, enter a name, and then click **Add** .

3   In the document, click the text that you marked with a bookmark.

4   Press *Alt+Shift+X.*

5   In the Main Entry box, enter the index entry for the marked text.

6 Select Page Range. In the Bookmark box, type or select the bookmark name for the range of pages from step 2

7 Click on [Mark]. When you use Insert-Index and Tables to add an index this page range index will be included.

The index entry can be removed in the same way as ordinary index entries, that is, by selecting the entry and pressing *Delete.*

Task 2: Using a bookmark to create an index entry that contains a page range

1 Open the document, **Letting** and select the range of text starting with the section entitled **What types of tenancy are available?** through to **Who's liable for repairs?** and then choose Insert-Bookmark.

2 In the Bookmark Name box, enter **Tenancy**, and then click on [Add]. Position the insertion point at the end of the first heading of the bookmarked range. Press *Alt-Shift-X*.

3 Enter the name **Tenancy** for the index entry. Select the Page Range option, open the drop down bookmark list box and choose **Tenancy**. Click on [Mark] and [Close].

4 Move to the end of the document and update the index by clicking in it and pressing *F9*.

Captions

Word can automatically add numbered captions when you insert pictures, tables, charts, and other items. For example, as you insert tables Word can add the captions 'Table 1', 'Table 2' and so on.

Insert a caption as follows.

1 Select the item that you want to add a caption to and choose Insert-Caption

2 Choose the label required from the drop-down Label list box. If the label you require is not in the list then click on the [New Label] button and key in the text of the label you require, for example, **Chart**. The new label will be added to the list ready for the next time you want to add a caption.

Note that you may remove any added labels from the list by choosing the label and clicking on the [Delete Label] button.

3 Select the position of the caption as either above or below the selected item.

4 If you wish, you may change the style of numbering using the [Numbering] button to display the Caption Numbering dialog box.

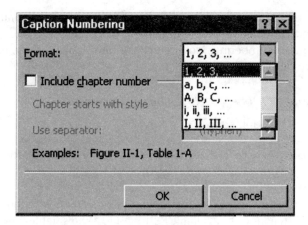

Different number formats include letters and Roman numerals as used in page numbering.

Task 3 Adding a caption

1 Create the document shown at the end of this task, which comprises three tables. The first table shows the number of new properties being offered for sale during the last quarter of the year, the second table the number of properties sold and the third table the average length of time properties remain on the books.

2 Click anywhere in the first table and choose Insert-Caption.

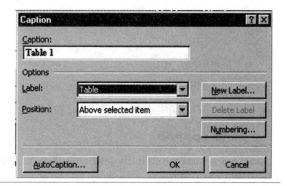

3 Choose Table as the option in the Label drop down list box.

4 Accept the position of the caption as above the selected item. If you wish, you may add some additional text in the Caption box after Table 1 by clicking at the end of the existing caption, for example, **New Additions**. Click on **OK**. Save the document as **Captions**.

5 Click in the second table and using Insert-Caption add a caption to this table. Notice that Word increments the table number. You could add the text **Properties sold** to this caption. Add a caption to the third table (**Average time on books**) and save.

6   Select the last table and its caption and cut and paste (or drag and drop) it between tables 1 and 2. Select the whole document (**Edit-Select All**) and press *F9* to update the caption numbering. Now return the new Table 2 to the end of the document and re-number the tables.

Price range £000's	October	November	December
0-50	6	8	3
50-100	4	7	2
100-150	2	0	1
150-200	0	1	1
200 and above	0	0	0

Price range £000's	October	November	December
0-50	8	6	5
50-100	6	7	3
100-150	0	3	2
150-200	1	0	1
200 and above	1	0	0

Price range £000's	Weeks
0-50	10
50-100	13
100-150	12
150-200	20
200 and above	25

Auto Caption

You may automatically add a caption to a table, figure, equation, or other item when inserting it.

1   Choose **Insert-Caption** and click on **Auto Caption**.

2   Select the items you want to be captioned automatically when you insert them in a document.

3   Select the options you want. Captions will now be inserted automatically when you add any of the types of item selected in the **AutoCaption** dialog box.

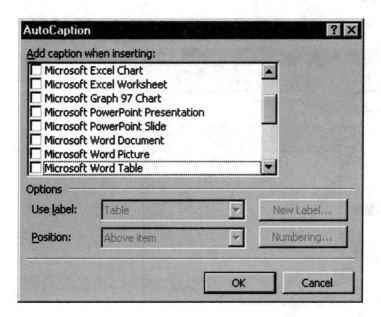

Updating caption numbering following document revision

If a table (or other captioned object) is added to a document which already contains captioned tables (or other captioned objects of the same type as the one being added) and the new table is added between existing tables, then when it is given a caption the following tables will have their caption numbers updated. However, if you delete a caption (by selecting and deleting) or if you rearrange the captioned objects in the document, then you will discover that the caption numbers are out of sequence. The caption numbers are fields and they are easily updated, simply select the whole document and press *F9*.

Cross-references

If you create a document that contains tables, charts, figures, numbered paragraphs etc. they are generally discussed in the text of the body of the document, for example, **'as illustrated in Figure 3'**. Instead of typing the words '**Figure 3**' you may insert a cross-reference to the figure. This is useful if you later modify the figure number as the document is revised, because when you update all the fields in the document the cross reference will update and therefore still refer to the correct figure.

Clicking on a cross-reference will 'jump' to the referenced item, provided the Insert as Hyperlink check box was ticked when the cross-reference was created, which may be useful for proof reading purposes.

Create a cross-reference as follows.

1   In the document, type the introductory text that begins the cross-reference. For example,'**as illustrated in**'

2   Choose **Insert-Cross-reference** and the **Cross-reference** dialog box appears.

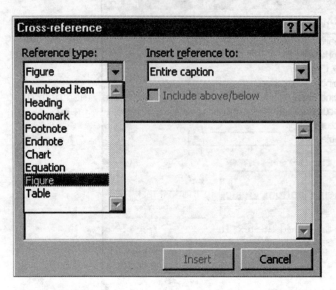

3   The drop down **Reference type** list box, as illustrated, allows you to select the type of item you want to refer to – for example, a figure or table. If you have created custom captioned items (e.g. charts) then these will be listed as well.

4   The drop down **Insert reference to** list box, allows you to choose the format of the cross-reference you want inserted in the document – for example, a chapter heading or just the caption name and number.

5   In the **For which caption** box, illustrated below, select the specific item you want to refer to. For example, if you chose **Chart** in the **Reference type** box and the document has three charts, select the chart you want to refer to.

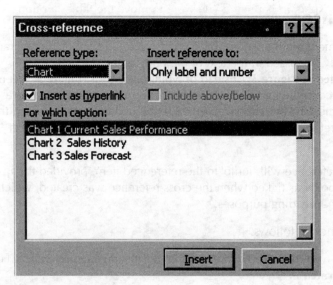

6 Click on the **Insert** button.

If you see an entry that looks something like {REF _Ref249586 * MERGEFORMAT} instead of text, Word is displaying field codes instead of field results. To see the field results, click the field code with the right mouse button, and then click Toggle Field Codes on the shortcut menu.

 If the item you want to refer to is located in another document, then both documents must be part of a master document. Master documents are the topic of the next two units.

Task 4 Adding a cross-reference

1 Open the document **Captions** created in the last task.

2 At the end of the table add the text **In**.

3 Choose Insert-Cross-reference and select Table from the drop down Reference type list box.

4 Choose Table 1 from the For which caption box and choose Only label and number from the Insert reference to box.

5 With Insert as Hyperlink checked click on **Insert** and **Close**. Continue the text of the sentence **the number of new properties appearing on our books is shown**.

6 Add two similar sentences with cross references to tables 2 and 3 respectively.

7 What would you expect to happen if you were to move the tables around as at the end of the last task? Try it to see the power of cross-referencing.

Creating a master document

What you will learn in this unit

Word offers many automatic features for document completion, such as tables of contents and indexes. When you are producing a long document, it becomes more cumbersome to work with as it gets longer and it makes sense to break it into two or more shorter documents.

In order to be able to create a table of contents or index for more than one document, which together comprise a publication, the documents can be grouped together using a master document. The master document allows you to work with the group of documents as a whole or individually.

Documents grouped using a master document are known as subdocuments. By using a master document, you can easily create cross-references, a table of contents, and an index across all of the subdocuments. You can also print several subdocuments without opening them individually.

At the end of this unit you should be able to

- create a new master document and subdocuments
- convert an existing document into a master document
- add existing documents as subdocuments to a master document
- add page numbering and headers and footers.

Before introducing master documents, which will require you to work in Master Document View it is worthwhile to review the different views offered by Word.

Different ways to view a Word document

When working with master documents, Master View is used, so a brief resumé of the different 'views' provided by Word are included here. The buttons to the left of the horizontal scroll are used to switch between the different views.

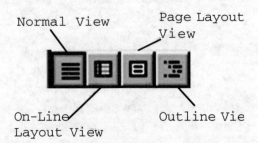

Normal View

Page Layout View

On-Line Layout View

Outline Vie

Normal View

In Word, Normal View is the usual view. It is the best all purpose view for typing, editing, and formatting text. Normal View shows text formatting but simplifies the layout of the page so that you can type and edit quickly.

Online Layout View

This view is designed for reading a document on-line. Text is displayed slightly larger and wraps to fit the window. If the document has heading styles, an outline of these can be displayed in a left hand window by clicking on the Document Map button. This provides a useful way of moving around the document.

Page Layout View

In Page Layout View, you can see how objects will be positioned on the printed page. This view is useful for editing headers and footers, for adjusting margins, and for working with columns, drawing objects, and frames.

Outline View

Outline View makes it easy to look at the structure of a document and to move, copy, and reorganise text. In Outline View, you can collapse a document to see only the main headings or you can expand it to see the entire document.

Master Document View

Master Document View is similar in some ways to Outline View but its major function is to group several Word documents so that you can work with them as if they were one document. You can then make changes to the long document – such as adding an index or table of contents, or creating cross references – without opening each of the individual documents.

By switching to Normal View from Master Document View, you can make specific changes to the subdocuments. In Normal View, each subdocument is displayed as a section of the master document.

Working with a master document

In Master Document View, the Master Document toolbar is displayed which enables you to organise the subdocuments comprising your long document.

The first two thirds of the tool bar should be familiar as the outlining tools, i.e. **Promote**, **Demote**, **Demote to Text Body**, **Move Up**, **Move Down**, **Expand**, **Contract**, **Display Level of Heading**, **Display First Line Only**, **Show Formatting** and **Master View**. There are also additional buttons which are to do with subdocument control which are:

| Collapse subdocument | , | Create Subdocument | , | Delete Subdocument | , |
| Insert Subdocument | , | Merge Subdocument | , | Split Subdocument | and |
| Lock Subdocument |

Creating a new master document with subdocuments

To create a new master document, type an outline in Master Document View, and then divide the headings into subdocuments. For example you may use Heading 1 for Chapter 1, Chapter 2, etc. and you wish each chapter to be a subdocument. Alternatively you may create your own style Chapter Title and apply a Level 1 heading priority to it.

1   Open a new document in Word and choose View-Master Document.

2   Type the outline for the master document. Use the built-in heading styles to create a heading for each subdocument. For example, you could use Heading 1 for the document title and Heading 2 for chapter titles. Alternatively create your own styles with the appropriate heading levels.

3   Select the headings and text you want to divide into subdocuments. Make sure that the first heading in the selection is the heading level you want to use at the beginning of each subdocument. For example, if your selection begins with Heading 3, Word creates a new subdocument at each Heading 3 in the selected text.

4   On the Master Document toolbar, click on the Create Subdocument button. Word displays a box around each subdocument.

5   To save the new master document and all its subdocuments, choose File-Save As. Enter a filename and location for the master document. Word assigns a file-name to each subdocument based on the first characters in the subdocument heading.

Task 1: Creating a new master document with subdocuments

This task and the following tasks relating to master documents will illustrate how a larger publication, such as a book, is produced. It is intended to take extracts from this book in these tasks to illustrate the features but without creating large amounts of text.

1   Open a new document in Word and choose View-Master Document. Key in the text as illustrated using Heading 1.

2   Click on each chapter heading in turn and click on the Create Subdocument button to divide the document into four subdocuments. Each heading is surrounded by a box which has a subdocument icon in the top left corner.

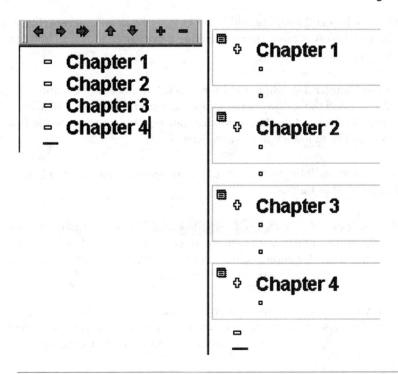

3 Choose **File-Save As**, enter the filename **Word 97 further skills** and select the location for the master document to be saved. Word assigns a filename to each subdocument based on the first characters in the subdocument heading.

4 Using **Explorer** you can verify that four files have been created **Word 97 further skills**, **Chapter 1**, **Chapter 2**, **Chapter 3**, and **Chapter 4**.

Working with subdocuments

You can open, edit, and print any subdocument from within its master document. To open a subdocument in Master Document View, double-click its subdocument icon. If you delete or rename a subdocument, make sure you do so within its master document.

Task 2: Working with subdocuments

1 Open the master document **Word 97 further skills** and click on the
`Expand Subdocument` button. When the subdocuments are collapsed you will see a link to the document. When the subdocuments are expanded the
`Create Subdocuments` button toggles to the `Collapse Subdocuments` button.

 2 Expand the subdocuments and under the heading **Chapter 1** add the heading **Checking spelling and grammar as you work** and the paragraph below it from Unit 1. Use a **Heading 2** style for the heading.

3   Under the **Chapter 2** heading add (from Unit 2) the heading **Preparing to print** (Heading 2), below it the heading **Selecting a printer** (Heading 3) and the following paragraph.

4   Under the **Chapter 3** heading add (from Unit 3) the heading **Creating templates** (Heading 2), and the following paragraph. Under the **Chapter 4** heading add (from Unit 4) the heading **Paragraph formatting** (Heading 2), and the first two sentences of the following paragraph. Save.

5   Investigate the outlining features available in Master View (refer to Unit 7 to remind yourself of these.

6   Double-click on the ▓ **Chapter 1 Subdocument** ▓ icon to display this document separately. You can then work with the document in Normal or Page Layout View as you wish. Try adding some additional text (the following paragraph), save and close. You will return to the master document.

7   With only the master document open try re-defining the style Heading 2. This will alter this style in all the subdocuments. If you use a master document then create and use styles to ensure consistency across all the documents.

Converting an existing document to a master document or sub-document

Any Word document can be a master document or a subdocument. An existing document can be converted to a master document and other existing documents can be added as subdocuments. To convert an existing document to a master document:

1   Open the document you wish to convert and choose View-Master Document.

2   Use the ▓ **Outlining** ▓ buttons to promote, demote, and arrange headings.

3   To prepare the document for division into subdocuments, use the built-in heading styles to create headings for each subdocument. For example, you could use Heading 1 for each subdocument title.

4   Select the headings and text you want to divide into subdocuments. Make sure that the first heading in the selection is the heading level you want to use at the beginning of each subdocument.

5   On the Master Document toolbar, click on the ▓ **Create Subdocument** ▓ button.

6   Choose File-Save As to save the new master document and all its subdocuments. Enter a filename and location for the master document. Word assigns a filename to each subdocument based on the first characters in the subdocument heading.

Insert an existing Word document into a master document as a subdocument as follows.

1 Open the master document to which you want to add an existing Word document.

2 In Master Document View, with the subdocuments in expanded view, position the insertion point at the place where you want to add the existing document.

3 On the Master Document toolbar, click on the `Insert Subdocument` button.

4 In the File Name box, enter the name of the document you want to add.

If the subdocument and the master document are based on different templates, or if they have different settings, the master document settings override the subdocument settings in the master document. If only the subdocument is opened, its settings are unchanged.

Task 3: Converting an existing document to a subdocument

1 Create a new document with the title Chapter 6 (Heading 1) and, from Unit 6, the heading Using Styles (Heading 2) and its associated paragraph. Save this document as Chapter 6 and close.

2 Open the master document **Word 97 further skills**. Click on the `Expand Subdocuments` button. With the insertion point at the beginning click on the `Insert Subdocument` button. Select the file **Chapter 6** and click on `Open`. This file has now become a subdocument. Save. This document has been deliberately put in the wrong place; Unit 10 deals with rearranging subdocuments.

Note that styles in the Master document are applied to the new document in Master Document View even though they may be different in the underlying document itself.

Page numbering and headers and footers in master documents

A master document treats all the component subdocuments as separate sections so that you can control page numbering and headers and footers separately in each section, or you can have sequential page numbering throughout the whole master document. Sequential page numbering is investigated in the following task.

Task 4: Page numbering and headers and footers

1 Open the master document **Word 97 further skills** and click on the `Expand Subdocuments` button. To make this task more realistic format the Heading 1 style to be Page Break Before.

2 Use **View-Page Layout** to see the document as it would be printed and you should see that page numbers have been added. Note that **Same as Previous** has been set so that numbering is continuous throughout the sections comprising the whole document. If you wish to format the page numbering then use **View-Header and Footer**.

3 Try adding a header that is different for each chapter, e.g. **Chp 1** etc. You will need to click on the **Same as Previous** button each time to make the headers independent. Save and close.

Working with master documents

What you will learn in this unit

Master documents allow you to use a number of word processor features across a collection of documents as mentioned in the previous unit. Before using these it is useful to be able to organise subdocuments and to protect them from accidental (or deliberate) revision. In this unit you will see how to

- use outlining to display and print the master document
- reorganise and rearrange subdocuments
- protect subdocuments
- create tables of contents, indexes, bookmarks and cross-references.

Using outlining to view a master document's organisation

If you formatted headings with the built-in heading styles, you can review the organisation of a document in Outline View by collapsing the subordinate text below the headings.

To collapse	Do this
Text below a specific heading level	On the Outlining toolbar, click the numbered button for the lowest level of heading you want to display. For example, click the button labelled **3** to display heading levels 1 – 3
	1 2 3 4 5 6 7
All subheadings and body text under a heading	Double-click the white cross ✪ next to the heading.
Text under a heading, one level at a time	Click the heading text, and then click the **Collapse** button **▬** on the Outlining toolbar.
All body text	On the Outlining toolbar, click on the **All** button **All** .

To display	Do this
All headings and body text	On the Outlining toolbar, click on the **All** button.
All collapsed subheadings and body text under a heading	Double-click the white cross ✿ next to the heading.
Only the first line of body text	On the Outlining toolbar, click on ☰ . An ellipsis (...) after the first line indicates that additional lines of text are collapsed
Collapsed text under a heading, one level at a time	Click the heading text, and then click the **Expand** button ✚ on the Outlining toolbar.

 If you select a heading that has collapsed subordinate text or select a heading by clicking its ✿ symbol, the subordinate text is also selected. Any editing, such as moving, copying, or deleting, also affects the subordinate text.

Printing a master document

1   To specify the amount of detail you want printed, display the master document in Master Document View.

2   Using the guidelines in the tables above, expand or collapse headings to display as much of the document as you want to print.

3   Choose **File-Print** and set your desired printing options.

To print the entire document, display the master document in Normal View, add page numbering or any other headers and footers and use **File-Print** as usual to print the entire document.

Task 1: Printing a master document

1   Open the master document Word 97 further skills. Display only the first heading level.

2   Choose **File-Print** and click on **OK** to print this Outline View. You may wish to try expanding one or two of the levels and then printing the document again.

3   Now view the document in Normal View or Page Layout View. Using **File-Print** will enable you to print the entire document as if it were one document.

Rearranging subdocuments within a master document

1   Display the master document in Master Document View.

2   Select the headings you want to move. To select an entire subdocument, click on its **Subdocument** icon ▤ .

3   Drag the selected headings to the new location. As you drag you will see a horizontal line with an arrow indicating the potential drop position. Remember that all subordinate text and headings will move with the selected heading. Headings and associated text may be dragged from one subdocument to another.

Renaming a subdocument

Display the master document in Master Document View. Select the subdocument you want to rename, by clicking on its icon. Choose File-Save As and enter a new filename for the subdocument.

Important Do not use any other means to rename a document that is a subdocument of a master document. If you use Windows 95 Explorer, Windows NT File Manager, or MS-DOS to rename or move such a document the master document will no longer be able to find or recognise the subdocument.

Removing a subdocument from a master document

Display the master document in Master Document View. Select the subdocument you want to remove, by clicking on its Subdocument icon and pressing *Delete*. Note that when you remove a subdocument from a master document, the subdocument file still exists in its original location.

Merging subdocuments

Display the master document in Master Document View. If necessary, rearrange the subdocuments so that they are next to one another in the master document. Click on the subdocument icon of the first subdocument you want to merge.

To select the next subdocument, hold down the *Shift* key and click on its Subdocument icon. If you wish to merge more than two subdocuments, repeat this process for each subdocument you want to merge.

On the Master Document toolbar, click on the Merge Subdocuments button. Note that when you save the master document, Word saves the merged subdocuments with the filename of the first subdocument.

Splitting a subdocument into two subdocuments

Display the master document in Master Document View. Using the built-in heading styles, create a heading for the new subdocument. Select the new heading. On the Master Document toolbar click on the Split Subdocument button.

Converting a subdocument into part of the master document

Display the master document in Master Document View and view the subdocuments in expanded View. If the subdocument to be converted is locked, unlock it by clicking on the Lock Document button. Locking and unlocking is discussed in more detail later in this unit.

Click on the Subdocument icon of the subdocument you want to make part of the master document. Click on the Remove Subdocument button on the Master

Document toolbar. When you convert a subdocument into part of a master document, the subdocument file still exists in its original location.

Task 2: Rearranging subdocuments

1   Open the master document Word 97 further skills. Expand the subdocuments and select the entire subdocument **Chapter 6** by clicking on its ▐ Subdocument ▌ icon.

2   Drag the selected subdocument to the end of the master document. Investigate the effect on the headers and footers. Save and close.

Locking or unlocking a master document or subdocument

Locking a document will prevent unintentional changes being made to the document. You can lock the entire master document or you can lock subdocuments individually. Locking the master document does not lock the subdocuments. To edit a locked document you need to unlock it first.

To lock or unlock a master document, display the master document in Master Document View and click anywhere in the master document but not any of the subdocuments. To lock or unlock a subdocument, click anywhere in the subdocument. To lock or unlock, click on the ▐ **Lock Document** ▌ button 🔒 on the Master Document toolbar.

When a master document is locked, it is marked as (Read-Only) in the title bar. When a subdocument is locked, the subdocument icon displays a padlock icon below it. 🔒 .

Limiting access for changing a master document or a subdocument

Just as for any other Word document you can password protect your documents if you are working in a shared environment. Use **File-Save As** and click on the ▐ **Options** ▌ button and set and retype a password for the document.

Task 3: Locking and unlocking

1   Using the master document Word 97 further skills, expand the subdocuments and first add some text to the master document, for example a title page at the beginning.

2   Investigate the effect of locking and unlocking the master and subdocuments.

Creating a table of contents of a master document

Display the master document in Master Document View. Expand the subdocuments. Position the insertion point at the place where you want to insert the table of contents. This may be in a separate section at the beginning of the master document.

Create the table of contents as for a normal document by choosing Insert-Index and Tables, and then selecting the Table of Contents tab.

Creating index entries and index

Display the master document in Master Document View. Expand the subdocuments. Add index entries to the subdocuments as you would for ordinary documents. If necessary refer back to Unit 7.

Create the index by positioning the insertion point at the place where you want to insert the finished index. This would usually be at the end of the master document. Choose Insert-Tables and Index , and then select the Index tab to choose the index format you require.

Using bookmarks, captions and cross-references in master documents

Open the master document and expand the subdocuments. Switch to Normal View. Create the bookmarks, captions and cross-references as described in Unit 8. Note that you can only create cross-references to other subdocuments within the same master document.

Task 4: Investigating tables of contents, index entries and indexes, bookmarks and cross-references in master documents

1   Open **Word 97 further skills** in Master Document View and expand the subdocuments. Position the insertion point at the start of the master document (after a title page if you've added one and check that the document is unlocked) and choose Insert-Tables and Index. Select the Table of Contents tab and heading levels 2, select a style and click on OK Change to Normal or Page Layout View to see the table of contents.

2   Switch back to Master Document View and move through the subdocuments (unlock them first) and select and mark various words to go in an index. Refer back to Unit 7 to see how to do this. Move to the end of the document and choose Insert-Tables and Index and select the Index tab and style of index and click on OK .

3   Add one of the tables from Unit 8 Task 3 to the subdocument **Chapter 4**. Using Insert-Caption add a caption to this table (as in Unit 8). In Master Document View add the text *The data in* to the subdocument **Chapter 2**. Using Insert-Cross reference select Table 1 from the list.

4   In Master Document View try adding bookmarks for all the chapter headings, refer to Unit 8 Task 1.

5   As the master document **Word 97 further skills** and its associated subdocuments will not be used elsewhere in this book you could now take the opportunity of experimenting further with these documents.

Images, graphics and multimedia

What you will learn in this unit

Word allows graphics from a variety of sources to be inserted into a document. Graphic images are integral parts of many documents and these may be embedded in the document if they were created outside Word or they can be created directly in the document using the drawing tools provided by Word. The drawing toolbar offers a means to construct such drawings.

In Word there are two types of image:

■ those that 'float' over the text

■ those that do not, known as in-line images.

Images that 'float' over text are not displayed in Normal View; they are only displayed in Page Layout View. In-line images can be seen in both Normal and Page Layout View. Floating images are usually the normal default type of image. Although they are more flexible with regard to the way in which they can be positioned on the page, they can be difficult to control.

Multimedia documents can be created by embedding sound and video files into a document. This can be achieved in a similar way to that used for images. As multi-media files tend to be large it may be preferable to link them to the multimedia file rather than embed them. This will save space in the document but puts more emphasis on file management as the document and media files remain separate.

In this unit various sources of image will be discussed with the emphasis on creating graphics using Word's drawing tools. At the end of this unit you will be able to:

■ create both floating and in-line images using Word's drawing tools

■ acquire an image by 'grabbing' a screen image and using Windows Paint

■ appreciate the creation and acquisition of images both by scanning and from other graphics applications

■ add sound and video to a document.

Creating basic shapes

In order to use the drawing tools, display the Drawing toolbar by clicking on the **Drawing** button in the standard tool bar. The brief resumé of basic shape creation given here is intended as a reminder of the basics of drawing shapes. It is, however, assumed that you have some familiarity with the drawing tools. For more detail on creating and controlling drawing shapes consult the companion book, *Word 97 Basic Skills*.

Drawing Lines

Click on the line drawing icon ⬉ , position the pointer at the start of the line, click and drag to the end of the line. Lines may be freely positioned or they may start and end on invisible grid points. The **Grid** option on the Drawing toolbar Draw menu can be used to turn this feature on or off and to set the spacing of the grid points. The grid is useful if you wish to 'line-up' parts of an image.

Drawing ellipses, circles, rectangles, and squares

The methods for drawing these shapes are summarised in the following table.

Ellipse/Circle	Rectangle/square	
To draw an ellipse from the corner of an imaginary bounding box	To draw a rectangle from one corner	Click on appropriate tool icon, position pointer at corner and drag to size required
To draw an ellipse from its centre	To draw a rectangle from its centre	Click on appropriate tool icon, hold down the *Ctrl* key, position pointer at centre and drag to size required
To draw a circle from the corner of an imaginary bounding box	To draw a square from one corner	Click on appropriate tool icon, hold down the *Shift* key, position pointer at centre and drag to size required
To draw a circle from its centre	To draw a square from its centre	Click on appropriate tool icon, hold down the *Ctrl* and *Shift* keys, position pointer at centre and drag to size required

Autoshapes

To draw shapes other than rectangles and ellipses, click on the **Autoshapes ▼** button in the Drawing toolbar. This displays a menu of different shapes from which you can choose. There are several categories of shape: lines, including arrows, curves and freeforms; basic shapes, including arcs, brackets and simple symbols; block arrows; flowchart symbols; and stars and banners.

A shadowed object can be constructed by clicking on the **Shadow** button ▣ in the Drawing toolbar and selecting the type of shadow required.

Creating a floating image

Working in Page Layout View you may draw directly on a document using the drawing tools. By setting the text wrap options you can control the way in which your image is displayed. If clip art is added as a floating image then it may be treated in the same way.

Text may be wrapped in a number of ways:

- tight – text follows closely the edge of the graphic
- square – text wraps in a rectangular fashion around the graphic
- through – text will show through open parts of the graphic
- none – text and graphic behave as layered objects
- top and bottom – text sits above and below the image.

A floating image may be converted into an in-line image by removing the tick from the Float over text check box. This is to found under the ▐ Position ▐ tab of the Format Picture (Object) dialog box. Conversely, an in-line image can be converted into a floating image by ticking this check box.

Creating an in-line image

A drawing may be created as a picture, and for diagrams in a document this is the best method as the picture is a separate entity. This is useful as the diagram can be positioned in the document as one image but can be edited as being composed of a collection of drawing elements. The picture can be left as a floating image or changed into an in-line image which is also visible in Normal View. To create a picture, choose Insert-Object and choose Microsoft Word Picture and a drawing workspace will be displayed as illustrated.

You can create your picture within the boundary shown. If your drawing element is outside the boundary click on the ▐ Reset Picture Boundary ▐ button to enclose all drawing elements within the picture boundary. When the picture is complete click on the ▐ Close Picture ▐ button to return to your document.

To edit a picture in a document simply double-click on it to display it in the drawing workspace.

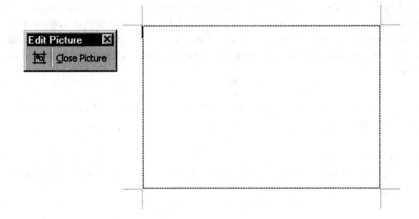

Task 1: Creating floating images

The text in the following example will be used in a later unit as part of a newsletter.

1 Key the following text into a new document, omitting the stars and the banner and save it as **Five star branch**.

Five Star Branch

The Oxley Branch has won the Chelmer Estates Five Star Award for sales achievements during April 96–April 97. This award is made for a notable success in sales during the year. The team at the Oxley Branch succeeded in increasing the number of sales processed by 10% over the total sales achieved during the previous year.

Running for Life

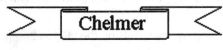

Four members of the staff from our Chelmer Branch, Joe, Jane, Louise and Peter, were successful in their bid to complete the Chelmer half marathon. They wish to convey their thanks to all staff and friends who supported them through sponsorship and to remind those of you who have yet to send in your sponsorship money that they will be collecting in person very soon! All proceeds go to support the Imperial Cancer Research Fund.

2 In Page Layout View add the stars by using Autoshapes-Stars and Banners, select the star shape and drag to size in your document. It does not matter where in the document you draw the star.

3 With the star selected set its text wrapping options to Top and Bottom and choose a fill colour for it.

4   Next copy and paste the star four times and position each copy so as to create a row of stars. Select all the stars either by clicking on each one in turn whilst holding down the *Shift* key or by using the arrow tool on the Drawing toolbar and drawing a box around all the stars to select them. Group the stars using **Draw-Group**.

5   Once the stars are grouped they can be moved as one to the correct position in the document. Save.

6   Create the banner using **Autoshapes-Stars and Banners**. Leave its text wrapping as Tight and position it in the top corner of the paragraph under the Running for Life heading.

7   Click on the **Text Box** button in the Drawing toolbar and draw a text box inside the banner. Add the text **Chelmer**. Choose a suitable font, centre the text and set 'no line' for the text box. Group these two objects so that if you wish to adjust their position in the document they will move together, as in step 4 above. Save the document.

Task 2: Creating in-line images

Exact instructions for the creation of the following in-line image are not given. It is composed of lines, arcs and text.

1   Start a new document and choose **Insert-Object** and select **Microsoft Word Picture**.

2   Using a combination of lines of varying thickness, arcs and text boxes either create the ground floor design below or attempt to produce a ground floor plan of your own home. It is useful to use the **Snap to Grid** feature. Set this using **Draw-Grid**; you might like to set the horizontal and vertical spacing to 0.1. The **Snap to Grid** feature makes it easier to 'line up' elements of the drawing.

3   If your plan exceeds the picture boundary reset it using the **Reset Boundary** button on the floating toolbar.

4   When the picture is complete click on the **Close Picture** button. The picture should be embedded as an in-line image and when selected it will have black sizing handles. If white sizing handles are seen then use **Format-Object**, select the **Position** tab and remove the check from the **Float over text** check box. Save this document as **Minerva** (the name of the design).

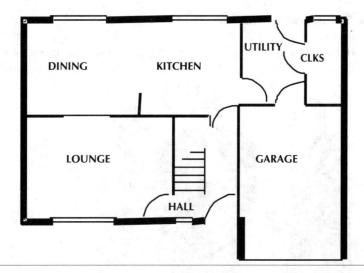

Picture formatting using the picture toolbar

When you add a picture to a document you may display the Picture toolbar so that you can edit the picture or insert other pictures. The Picture toolbar may appear as a floating toolbar when a picture is selected or you can display it using View-Toolbars Picture. The Picture toolbar is illustrated below.

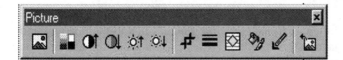

The buttons on this toolbar allow you to

- insert a picture
- change a colour image to greyscale
- adjust the contrast of the picture using the two contrast buttons
- adjust the brightness of the picture using the two brightness buttons
- crop a picture(i.e. cut it to size)
- choose a line style for the image border
- control text wrapping
- display the format picture dialog box
- set a transparent colour and
- reset the picture.

These controls will be explored in the following task.

Task 3: Picture formatting

1   Add the following text at the beginning of the **Five star branch** file and save.

Investors in People

As announced in the previous issue of the newsletter, Chelmer Estates will work towards the Investors in People Award. John Wall, Deputy Personnel Manager will act as champion for this project and will be preparing a regular report on progress for this newsletter. Watch this space!

2   In front of it add some clipart as a floating image. Click in the heading and choose the first image in the People at Work clipart. Make the clipart image smaller and position the image above the heading.

If you are positioning the clipart at the top of the page use Format-Picture, choose the   Position   tab and set the Horizontal and Vertical settings to zero. If at some point you might add text before the image then it is useful to have both the Move with text and the Lock anchor check boxes ticked.

3   If the Picture toolbar does not appear when you select the image then use View-Toolbars Picture to display it.

4   Select the clipart picture and experiment with the following.

Click on the   Image Control   button and investigate the effect of Greyscale and Black and White. You can return the image to normal using the   Automatic   setting.

- Increase and reduce the contrast and the brightness of the image.

- Add a border using the   Line Style   button. This can be removed by choosing   More Lines   and selecting No Line.

- Try cropping the picture using the crop tool, for example, to select out the head and shoulders of the centre figure.

- Investigate the text wrapping options available on the Picture toolbar and note that you can display the Format dialog box.

- Finally, to put the picture back to its original form try the `Reset Picture` button but be prepared for the image to return to the size it was when first inserted.

Wrapping text closely around the contours of an image

In the previous task you may have discovered the Edit Wrap points option available from the `Text Wrapping` button. Using this option you can have your text following the contours of the image as illustrated below.

Investors in People

As announced in the previous issue of the newsletter, Chelmer Estates will work towards the Investors in People Award. John Wall, Deputy Personnel Manager will act as champion for this project, and will be preparing a regular report on progress for this newsletter. Watch this space!

If you select the Edit Wrap points option you can alter the positions of the wrap points and add or remove wrap points. To alter the position of a wrap point simply drag it to a new location. To add additional wrap points, point to the dashed outline where there is no wrap point, press the *Ctrl* key and click. To remove a wrap point, point to it, press the *Ctrl* key (note that the pointer changes to a cross) and click. When you are happy with the positions of the points, click on the text to continue with the document.

Capturing a screen image

Both rectangular and irregular images can be captured or grabbed from the screen using the clipboard and Windows Paint, and inserted into a document.

1 Display on screen the image you wish to capture. Note that you can capture any part of the screen and discard the rest. Press the `Print Screen` button on the keyboard, this copies the image to the clipboard.

2 Click on the `Start` button in the Taskbar and choose Programs-Accessories-Paint to start Windows Paint.

3 Use Edit-Paste to paste in the image. Click on either the `Select` tool (for a rectangular image) or on the `Free Form Select` tool (for an irregular image) and choose Edit-Copy.

4 Click on the `Word` button in the Taskbar to re-display Word. Position the insertion point in the paragraph to which you wish to anchor the image and choose Edit-Paste. Save the document.

5 If you have chosen an irregular selection, it will be on a rectangular plain background. If you want the text to wrap to the irregularities of the image then the wrap points can be edited as described above.

Acquiring images from other sources

Images may be scanned or created from scratch using a graphics application or a computer aided design application. They may also be acquired using a digital camera and associated software. Provided that these are saved in a format that Word can import, they may be added to documents. Word can directly import Enhanced Metafile (.emf), Joint Photographic Experts Group (.jpg), Portable Network Graphics (.png), Windows Bitmap (.bmp, .rle, .dib), and Windows Metafile (.wmf) graphics. However, you do need a graphics filter installed to import other graphics file formats. Consult the Office Assistant to find out more about these. If Word has a filter available then you can install it using Setup.

If you are scanning images then you should check that you are not infringing copyright. This is also a consideration if you copy images from Web pages.

Multimedia

Both sound and video files can be inserted into a document in a similar way to inserting images. Usually your sound and video files are pre-recorded and inserting them is simply a matter of finding the right file.

Adding a sound file

1 Choose **Insert-Object** and click on the **Create from File** tab

2 Click on **Browse** and select the folder in which the sound or video file is stored, highlight the file and click on **OK** .

Alternatively, using Sound Recorder you can record, edit and play sound files. Sound Recorder is a Microsoft accessory and to use it you must have a sound card and speakers installed on your computer. If you want to record live sound, you also need a microphone. Record live sound while working on a document as follows.

1 With your Word document open use **Start-Programs Accessories Multimedia Sound Recorder** to start Sound Recorder.

2 Click on the **Record** button in Sound Recorder and speak your message into the microphone. You can play back your message and if you wish discard it and use **File-New** to start a new file to re-record the message. When you are happy with the message choose **Edit-Copy**.

3 Switch to Word, click where you want to insert the sound file and choose **Edit-Paste**. A sound file will appear as an icon (which looks like a speaker) in the document and to play the sound file, double-click its icon. Sound clips will increase the size of your document considerably so it is best only to embed short sound clips. For longer sound clips you can link to the sound clip stored as a

separate file; this will not increase the size of the document (see Unit 20 for more on Object Linking and Embedding). To insert the sound file as a linked object, choose Edit-Paste Special and click on Paste Link. In the As box, choose Wave Sound Object.

Task 4: Adding a sound file to a document

If you don't have multi-media sound capability then skip this task. The task assumes that you do not have the means to create a sound file so one of the Windows sound files will be added to a document in this task.

1 Start a new document. Choose Insert-Object, select the `Create from File` tab and click on the `Browse` button.

2 You will find Windows sound files in the Windows\Media folder. Select The Microsoft sound and click on `OK`. Click on `OK` again.

3 A speaker icon will appear in the document, double-click on this icon to play the sound. Close the document without saving.

Adding a video file

You can insert a video file into a Word document by using Media Player, a Microsoft Windows accessory that lets you play audio, video, or animation files. To use Media Player, you need to have a sound card installed on your computer.

1 Open both the Word document and Media Player. To open Media Player use Start-Programs-Accessories-Multimedia-Media Player.

2 Switch to Media Player, and select Device-Video for Windows.

3 Open the video file you want to insert. Video files usually have the extension .avi.

4 Choose Edit-Options to specify options such as the caption that will appear.

5 Choose Edit-Copy Object, switch to Word and click where you want to insert the video file.

6 To insert the video file as an embedded object, use Edit-Paste. The video will appear as an image (of the first frame) and can be played by double clicking on it.

To insert a video file as a linked object, choose Insert-Object, and then click the `Create from File` tab. Select the video file you want, and then select the Link to file check box. To play a video file, double-click on its icon.

Tables and calculations

What you will learn in this unit

Tables can be used to format text in parallel columns within a document. A more basic means of achieving the same effect is to use tab stops. However, formatting text in tables instead of using tab stops makes it much easier to apply text formatting to columns and rows, and borders can be used with tables to create quite complex documents such as forms and questionnaires. If columns have previously been created using tab stops it is relatively easy to convert the text into a table, should this be necessary.

At the end of this unit you will be able to:

- understand the difference between using tab stops and tables
- create and use a table to format text in columns
- do calculations in tables
- sort and re-arrange data in tables
- use borders in tables.

Reviewing tabs

It is assumed that as an experienced user of word processing packages, you are familiar with the concept of tabs, and are aware of the difference between left, centre, right and decimal tabs. This is a quick reminder of how to set and clear tab stops in Word, as a preliminary to the task below.

Tab stops can be simply set using the ruler and the mouse. Tab stops are set before creating text as follows.

1   Select the paragraphs to which you want to add tab stops, or position the insertion point where you want the formatting with tab stops to start before you type the document.

2   Click on the ▧ Tab ▧ button until it displays the tab type that you wish to use, i.e. left, right, centre or decimal.

3   Point to where you wish to place the tab on the ruler and click to place a tab stop at that point. The tab should appear on the ruler as a tiny version of the tab symbol on the button.

To clear custom tab stops with the ruler:

1   select the paragraph that contains the tab stops to be cleared

2   on the ruler, drag the marker for the tab stop that you want to remove down out of the ruler.

The above operations can also be achieved through the use of the command Format-Tabs, which will cause the Tabs dialog box to be displayed.

Task 1: Reviewing tabs

Start to create the first five lines of type in the handbill that is displayed below.

Bishop's Place

Development	Bishop's Place, Eyebrook Road, Bowdon
Sales Negotiator	Ann Dilorenzo
Telephone No	0161-926-9392
Sales Office opening Hours	Open 7 days 10 am – 5 pm

Plot No	House Type and Accommodation	Completion Date	Sales Price
3	5 bed detached with double garage	February 98	£322,500
4	5 bed detached with double garage	February 98	£327,500
5	5 bed detached with double garage	March 98	£325,000
6	5 bed detached with triple garage with games room over	March 98	£355,950

SHOW HOME: PLOT 2 – SOLD

RESERVATION DEPOSIT £300   TENURE: FREEHOLD

Completion Dates:	These are for guidance only, and our Sales Negotiator will keep you advised of any variations.
Sales Price:	These particulars are subject to contract and availability at the time of mailing. We would recommend you contact our Sales Office as soon as possible.

1 Insert and format the heading '**Bishop's Place**'. Select it and create a bottom border using Format-Borders and Shading. In the Borders sub-dialog box, choose a style for the border.

2 Set tab stops for the second column in the next section.

3 Using Format-Font, choose an Effect, such as Emboss or Engrave for the text in the first column.

4 Enter the text in both columns.

5 Save as **Pricelist**.

Notice that it is fiddly to work with text that is differently formatted in both columns and to use tab stops. This would be much easier with tables, since all the text could have been entered, then the text in the first column selected and formatted.

Converting existing text into a table

If you already have a table laid out using tab characters, or some columns of text separated by commas, this can be converted into a table by:

1 selecting the original text and

2 choosing Table-Convert Text to Table.

Word will examine the existing text and convert it to a table with suitable column widths. If Word cannot determine how to convert the text, it displays a dialog box listing different conversion options.

The reverse process, the conversion of a table into text, can be achieved by choosing Table-Convert Table to Text.

Task 2: Converting text into tables

1 Enter the text in the example below using tab stops.

2 Use Table-Convert Text to Table, to convert the text into a table.

3 With the insertion point showing as an arrow at the top of a column, select a column and then apply appropriate formatting.

3 Months	£85.00
6 Months	£150.00
Annual	£275.00

Creating and using tables

A table can be inserted in a document either through the use of the **Insert Table** button on the toolbar, or by choosing Table-Insert Table. Choose the number of columns that you want in the table. The number of rows can be expanded as you add text.

Text can be entered into a table, simply by placing the insertion point in the table and starting to type. The key operations that you are likely to use in entering text in a table are shown below.

Action	*Operation*
Move to next cell	Press Tab
Add another row of cells	Press Tab in the last cell in the table
Leave a table	Place the insertion point after the table, and start to type.
Move a row of cells	Select the row. Drag the selected rows to the new location. Position the mouse pointer at the beginning of the selected rows, then release the left mouse button.
Sort a table on the basis of the contents in a given column	Select the sort column. Choose Table-Sort. The Sort dialog box will be displayed. Select the appropriate column and then for Type choose Text. Select an ascending or a descending sort. Click on **OK**. Rows will be ordered alphabetically according to the text in the sorted column.
Inserting a row/column	Select the row where you want to insert a new row, and click the **Insert Rows** button on the toolbar, or choose Table-Insert Rows. Columns are inserted similarly using Table-Insert Columns.
Deleting a row/column	Select the row or column and choose Table-Delete Rows, or Table-Delete Columns, respectively.

 In addition to text, tab stops, charts, images, WordArt and any other objects can be inserted in the cells in a table.

Task 3: Creating and using tables

Continue with the document **Pricelist** that you started to create in Task 1.

1   Enter a table under the existing text.

2   Enter the text in the boxes of the table.

3 Select and format the first row to act as column headings.

4 Select the first column and apply centre alignment to centre the numbers with the box.

 5 Complete the handbill by entering the remaining text. Hint, use a table to format some of the text.

Doing calculations in tables

A basic range of calculations can be performed on the rows or columns in tables. If you wish to perform extensive calculations, it is generally easier to enter the data into an Excel spreadsheet and then to cut and paste appropriate summary data into a Word document. The facilities available in Word are intended to facilitate the occasional calculation of the type performed in Task 4 below.

To perform calculations on a row or column in a table:

1 With the insertion point in an appropriate cell in a table choose Table-Formula. This will display the Formula dialog box:

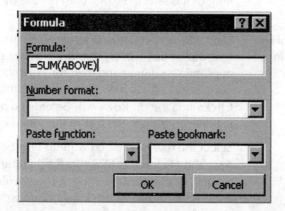

The Formula dialog box includes options for inserting formulae and for setting the number format. The functions available are shown in the Paste Function drop down list and include functions such as MAX, MIN, AVERAGE, COUNT, IF, FALSE, and SUM. Typically formula are entered in the format:

=FUNCTION(CELL RANGE)

For example:

=AVERAGE(ABOVE)

=MAX(A3:A20)

Such formulae will be familiar to spreadsheet users.

2 When you have entered an appropriate formula, click on ▆OK▆ .

Task 4: Calculations and sorting in tables

1 Enter the text and numbers below in a table.

	Vendor	Value	Completion Date
56 Bodmin Drive	Mrs J Kettin	56,000	4.12.97
187 Dairyground Road	Dr S Brown	100,000	16.12.97
16 Park Road	Mrs M Lingert	96,000	2.1.98
158 Moss Lane	Mr S Smart	81,000	15.1.98
15 Pownall Avenue	Mrs C Christie	189,000	17.1.98
3 Bude Close	Mr C Suttle	70,000	1.2.98
2 Woodford Close	Mr M Singh	150,000	3.2.98
16 The Close	Mr R Nettleton	39,000	14.2.98
	Total Sales Value	781,000	
	Average sales value	97,625	

2 Format the first row to create headings.

3 Select the bottom two rows and remove the borders, but leave the top border on, so that the row above still has a bottom border.

4 Calculate the Total Sales Value by placing the pointer in the box next to this text. Click on the **Auto Sum** button on the Tables and Borders toolbar. **Σ**

5 Calculate the Average Sales Value by placing the insertion point in the box next to this text, and then choosing Table-Formula. Choose Paste Function, and then the function Average. Delete the contents automatically shown then type the cell values in the brackets so that the formula reads **=AVERAGE(C2:C9)**.

6 Sort the rows on the **Completion Date** column, by selecting the rows in this column by which the table is to be sorted. Choose Table-Sort. In the Sort dialog box, accept the Type as Date and the Sort as Ascending.

7 Save the file as **Sales**.

Using borders in tables

Task 4 above asked you to experiment with removing borders from some cells in a table. Here we briefly introduce approaches to using borders and shading to format tables, and then apply these in Task 5 and 6. Borders and shading can be applied to paragraphs of text, graphics or the cells in a table. With a colour printer, you can print coloured borders and shading.

Quick borders and shading using Table AutoFormat.

A quick way to apply borders and shading to a table is to use Table-Table AutoFormat, which displays the Table AutoFormat dialog box. This dialog box lists a series of preset formats, and shows their format through a Preview box. These preset formats can be modified by changing: borders, shading, font, colour and AutoFit. It is also possible to apply special formats to heading rows, first column, last row and last column.

Task 5: Using Table AutoFormat

Open the file, **Sales**, that you used in Task 4.

With the pointer in the table, choose Table-Table AutoFormat, and from the Table AutoFormat dialog box choose a standard format.

Applying and formatting borders

To apply a border:

1   select the items to which a border is to be applied, and

2   choose Format-Borders and Shading. This displays the Borders and Shading dialog box.

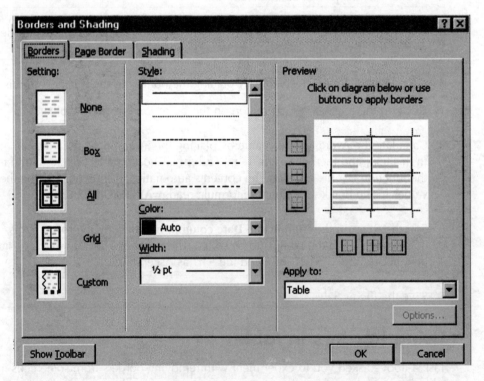

To **apply a box**, click on the box option under Setting:, and then click a line style under Style:. If you want to change the colour of the border, select a colour in the Color: box.

To **create a custom border** or to add lines within a box, click the Border Preview where you want to apply a border over one of the border buttons within the Preview, and then click a line style under Style: .

To **change the distance of the border** from the text, click on the ▐ Options ▌ button. Set the distance using the options in the Border and Shading Options dialog box.

To **change the width of a border**, click on the Width: box, and select and appropriate width from the options displayed.

To **remove all borders**, with the appropriate item selected and the Borders and Shading dialog box displayed click None under Setting.

To **remove selected borders**, click the border that you wish to remove on the border sample.

To exit the Borders and Shading dialog box, click on ▐ OK ▌.

As an alternative to using the Borders and Shading dialog box, you may click on the ▐ Border ▌ button on the toolbar to display the Borders list.

Task 6: Applying borders to tables

1   Type and format the text at the top of the example below.

   Sample – First Draft Showing Table Boundaries

   What to do next

   To help your company help you, simply complete and return this reply-paid coupon or call us on 01753-834257. Why not show this leaflet to the person in your company responsible for your relocation? **No stamp is required**.

Name		
Home Address		
Company Name		
Company Address		

2   Using Table-Insert Table, create a table with three columns and seven rows.

3   Drag the borders between the columns to make the columns appropriate sizes.

4   Drag the row boundaries to make the second and fourth rows much wider than the first and third rows.

5   Enter the text in the boxes in the first column.

(!)   6   Using **Format-Borders and Shading**, selectively remove and apply borders until your document appears like the one below.

This will probably need some experimentation and patience!.

7   Move column boundaries as appropriate.

Now complete the form so that it looks like the completed form below. You are asked to plan out for yourself where and how to use tables and borders.

Sample – Second Draft Showing Completed Exercise

What to do next

To help your company help you, simply complete and return this reply-paid coupon or call us on 01753-834257. Why not show this leaflet to the person in your company responsible for your relocation? No stamp is required.

Name

Home Address

Company Name

Company Address

Telephone   *Home*   *Company*

Please send me information on:

☐ *Home Sale Guarantee*   ☐ *Support Services*

☐ *Home Sale Assistance*   ☐ *Financial Services*

☐ *Group Move Programmes*   ☐ *Home Search*

Agency Address

Chelmer Estates

Meriton Branch

Meriton

Cheshire

MR1 3BV

Using WordArt

What you will learn in this unit

WordArt allows you to form interesting designs and graphics based on text, such as might be useful in signs, logos and other applications in which you wish to use text to draw attention an area of a document, or leave a graphical image in the memory of the user. Often WordArt is used alongside some other graphical image.

At the end of this unit you will be able to:

- select a WordArt style
- move, delete and edit WordArt
- format WordArt, using the WordArt toolbar.

Selecting a WordArt style

Creating a basic WordArt object is very straightforward. Once this object has been created, it is possible to either use it as it is, or to apply some of the more ambitious formatting that is available through the WordArt toolbar.

(!) Remember to work in Page Layout View throughout this unit.

Create a basic WordArt object as follows.

1   Click on **Insert-Picture-WordArt**. The WordArt Style dialog box will be displayed. (See following page). Choose a style from those that are displayed.

2   Click on **OK** . The WordArt Text dialog box will appear.

3   Type in your text. Set font size, and whether bold or italic formatting should be applied. Click on **OK** .

4   The WordArt will be inserted in your document.

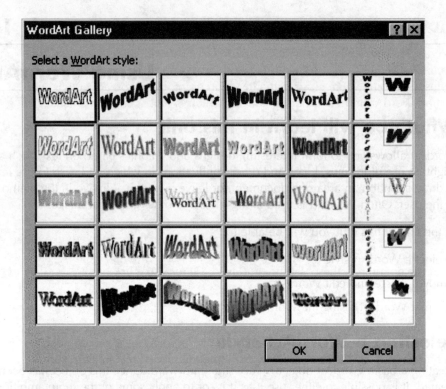

Task 1: Creating a Basic WordArt Object

Create a small document using the text below. Then insert WordArt as described.

1 Click on **Insert-Picture-WordArt**. The **WordArt Style** dialog box will be displayed. Choose the style from those that are displayed that seems to most closely match the WordArt shown above, for example, the style in the first row, fourth column.

2 Click on **OK**. The **WordArt Text** dialog box will appear.

3 Type in '**For Sale**'. Choose a font size, say 32 point. Click on **OK**.

4 The WordArt will be inserted in your document. Do not panic if the WordArt is not positioned in an appropriate place in your document.

Moving, deleting and editing WordArt

WordArt seems to have a mind of its own when selecting where to place itself in a document. If you are creating a new piece of WordArt from scratch, it will normally be inserted somewhere close to the insertion point, but if you are cutting and pasting WordArt from another document (which is quite common practice, since you will probably wish to re-use these images) then it seems that there is no knowing where the WordArt will position itself. It may take up a position in the middle of your text and trigger text wrapping. There are two solutions to this dilemma: move the WordArt, or, if you have not put too much effort into your design, delete it and start again.

To delete WordArt:

1   WordArt is selected when it has white boxes or handles displayed (like other floating objects that you will have encountered in Word). When initially inserted in the document, these will be displayed. Otherwise, click on the WordArt to select it and display these boxes.

2   Press the *Delete* key.

To move WordArt: simply move the mouse pointer over the WordArt until the pointer becomes a cross. Then click and drag the object to the desired position. Once selected, fine positioning of the Word Art image can be achieved using the arrow keys on the keyboard.

Alternatively, WordArt can be moved between documents and between pages within documents by using the normal cut and paste or copy and paste routines.

To edit WordArt a single click on the WordArt, will bring up the WordArt toolbar; we explore the functions of the buttons on this toolbar below.

A double click will recall the **Edit WordArt Text** dialog box, which allows you to change text and font size and choose whether bold or italic is applied.

Task 2: Editing WordArt

1   Click on the WordArt that you created in Task 1 to select it.

2   Choose **Edit-Copy**, move the insertion point down the page, and choose **Edit-Paste**

3   Double click on the copy of the WordArt, to display the **Edit WordArt Text** dialog box.

4   Edit the text to read: For Sale/To Let.

5   Click on **OK**, and insert the new WordArt in your document.

6   The WordArt will probably appear squashed. Using the selection handles stretch it until the text can be read more clearly.

For Sale/To Let

Task 3: Using the WordArt toolbar

Once you have created a piece of WordArt, the tools on the WordArt toolbar can be used to create a range of different effects. The table below shows some of the effects that can be created by clicking on the different buttons on the toolbar. Take a piece of WordArt that you have created and try to replicate the effects in this table. Note that we have not made use of colour since this book is printed in black and white, but you may also like to experiment with the use of colours. Logos and other applications of WordArt are often the main application for colours on standard documents.

Button	Function	Example
	Format WordArt	For Sale
	Choose a WordArt shape	For Sale
	Rotate WordArt	For Sale
	Adjust WordArt letter heights	For sale

 Swop from horizontal to
vertical text (and vice versa)

 Adjust alignment

 Adjust letter spacing

Task 4: Using WordArt in a poster

One common application for WordArt is in the context of posters and other
displays. Here we wish to demonstrate how WordArt can be used to effect on a
hand bill or small poster.

 Open the file **Pricelist**, that you created in Unit 12. We wish to insert WordArt at
the top and bottom of the page, so that the finished work looks like the example on
page 119.

1   Choose Insert-Picture-WordArt

2   Choose a shape from the WordArt Gallery.

3   Type in the text '**Bishop's Place**' and adjust its size to around 60 points (so that it
will fill the width of the page)

4   Choose a shape using the shape tool on the WordArt toolbar, for example, Can
Up.

5   Stretch the WordArt to fill the width of the page, and, if necessary move the
WordArt into position at the top of the page. You may wish to set text wrapping
to Top and Bottom.

6 Now to create the WordArt at the bottom of the page select the existing WordArt, choose Edit-Copy, and then Edit-Paste.

7 Move the new copy of WordArt to the bottom of the page.

8 Using the shape tool on the WordArt toolbar select an appropriate shape for this copy of the WordArt.

   Note that you now have similar, but differently shaped WordArt at the top and bottom of the page.

9 See if you can add the **Sold** tag using WordArt and a rectangle. Add the WordArt and draw a rectangle around it (you may need to 'send the rectangle to the back' to stop it obscuring the WordArt). Group the two objects and use the rotate tool to tilt the grouped object.

Creating WordArt as an in-line image

As you have seen in this unit, WordArt is by default a floating image. You cannot change it into an in-line image using the **Position** tab in the Format-Object dialog box as the Float over text check box is not available.

To create WordArt as an in-line image, first open a picture work space, using Insert-Object Microsoft Word Picture. Create the WordArt as described in this unit for normal WordArt, click on the **Reset Picture Boundary** in the Edit-Picture toolbar and **Close Picture** buttons to insert the picture into your document. This 'picture' of the WordArt can be formatted as an in-line image. Also, if you want to convert your document to HTML format (see Unit 22) then WordArt that has been created inside a picture object will be converted to a Web graphics file.

Bishop's Place

Development	**Bishop's Place, Eyebrook Road, Bowdon**
Sales Negotiator	**Ann Dilorenzo**
Telephone No	**0161-926-9392**

Sales Office opening Hours   Open 7 days   10 am – 5 pm

Plot No	House Type and Accommodation	Completion Date	Sales Price
3	5 bed detached with double garage	February 98	£322,500
4	5 bed detached with double garage	February 98	£327,500
5	5 bed detached with double garage	March 98	£325,000
6	5 bed detached with triple garage with games room over	March 98	£355,950

SHOW HOME: PLOT 2

RESERVATION DEPOSIT   **£300**   **TENURE: FREEHOLD**

Completion Dates:	These are for guidance only, and our Sales Negotiator will keep you advised of any variations.
Sales Price:	These particulars are subject to contract and availability at the time of mailing. We would recommend you contact our Sales Office as soon as possible.

Using Graph (advanced)

What you will learn in this unit

Graph can be used to create charts. After a summary review of the basics of entering data in order to create a chart through the Datasheet window, and the fundamentals of formatting charts, this unit explores some of the more advanced features in Graph and offers guidance on the use of different types of chart.

At the end of this unit you will be able to:

■ create basic charts

■ format charts

■ select appropriate charts for specific applications.

Choosing when to use Graph

Graphs can be created with the aid of a number of different types of package. How do you decide which package to use in the creation of graphs? In general the answer to this question depends upon the context in which you are seeking to create the graphs.

■ You should use a spreadsheet package, when you need to explore a range of different scenarios, or use financial functions such as internal rate of return or net present value, as when evaluating a range of different investment decisions. The chart created in a spreadsheet package may subsequently be cut and pasted to be included in a word processed document.

■ You should use a presentations package, when you are seeking to create a simple chart to summarise some data for inclusion in a presentation, either on screen or printed onto slides.

■ You should use a word processing package, when you are creating a document such as a report, and wish to summarise some data into a simple chart.

■ You should use a statistical package, when you wish to undertake some complex statistical analysis of a relatively large data set.

The Datasheet and Chart windows in Microsoft Graph

To enter Graph, with a Word document open, choose Insert-Object-Microsoft Graph 97 Chart or click the Insert Graph icon on the toolbar. If this icon is not shown on your toolbar then you may add it (see Customising toolbars in Appendix 1). The screen will display a linked data sheet and chart, which may show the default chart. Data entered on the data sheet will be displayed on the chart.

The Datasheet window

Document1 - Datasheet		A	B	C	D	E
		1st Qtr	2nd Qtr	3rd Qtr	4th Qtr	
1	East	20.4	27.4	90	20.4	
2	West	30.6	38.6	34.6	31.6	
3	North	45.9	46.9	45	43.9	
4						

The Datasheet window is like a simple spreadsheet worksheet. Labels for data are entered in the first row and column of the data sheet. Do not type data in these cells. This first row and column remain visible as you scroll the sheet. Various parts of the datasheet have names that we will use later. The important components of the datasheet are listed below.

The components of the Datasheet window

row and column headings	above the first row and to the left of the first column of the data sheet
cell	one rectangle of the data sheet
active cell	currently selected cell
data point	single cell value
data series	a row or column of data used to plot one set of bars, columns, one line, or one pie.
series names	names that identify each row and column of data
tick mark labels	when the data series are in rows, the tick mark labels are the column labels. When data series are in columns, the tick mark labels are the row labels.

The Chart

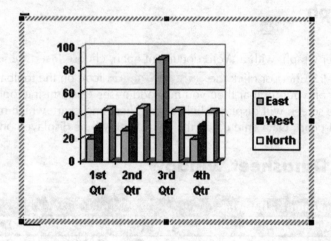

The data in the form of a chart appear in the document. Again, parts of the window have names that will be used later. The important components of the chart window are given below:

The components of the chart

chart	the entire area inside the Chart window
data marker	a bar, shape or dot that marks a single data point or value
data series	a group of related data points
axis	a line that serves as a reference for plotting data on a chart
tick mark	a small line that intersects the axis and marks off a category
plot area	the area in which Graph plots the data
gridlines	lines that extend from the tick marks across the chart
chart text	text that describes data or items in a chart
legend	the key

Managing the Datasheet and Chart windows

All the operations that can normally be performed on windows can be performed on the Datasheet window. It can be sized by moving its borders, or moved by dragging the title bar to a new position.

To work with the chart click on it and the icons on the toolbar will change to provide a range of charting tools. Once you have clicked on the chart the Datasheet window will become inactive. Simply click on the Datasheet window to re-activate it.

Task 1: Creating and formatting a chart

We wish to create the simple sales chart shown below.

1 Choose Insert-Picture-Chart to enter Graph. The datasheet should be displayed.

2 Leaving the first row blank, enter the following data in the first two columns of the datasheet (the data shows house sales for each of the years indicated).

1994	1221
1995	1178
1996	1360
1997	1555

3 Click on the Chart window to examine your chart. You should be able to see that the data is displayed as a chart, but that it will be necessary to apply some formatting to make the chart appear as the example below. At the moment, the chart should be a column chart that looks like this:

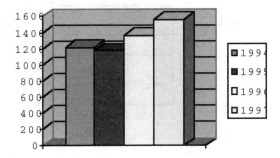

 Note that charts are embedded into the document as floating images. If you want to make them into in-line images that you may find easier to control, use Format-Object select the **Position** tab and remove the tick from Float over text.

The chart can be formatted as follows.

1 Double click on the chart to return to Graph.

2 Choose the chart type, either by clicking on the down arrow of the **Chart Type** button, or using Chart-Chart Type. Select a simple bar chart.

3 Change the display so that series are shown as rows, using Data-Series in Rows.

4 Click on the legend to delete it.

5 Choose Chart-Chart Options:

- in the Data labels box, click on Show values

- in the Gridlines box, choose not to show any gridlines

■ in the Axes box, take off the Value (y) axis labels

■ in the Titles box, add **Year** to the Category (X) axis and **Sales** to the Value (Y) axis.

■ click on **OK** .

6 Format the Axis titles thus:

■ click on the title to be formatted

■ click on Font, and choose a Font and size

■ if necessary use the Alignment box to adjust the orientation to make the label horizontal.

Your chart should now look like the chart below:

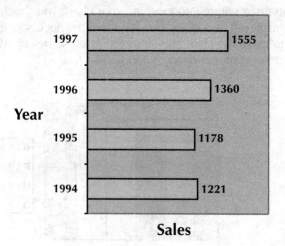

It is important to choose chart type first as any subsequent formatting applies to that specific chart type.

Selecting chart type

It is important to use the correct type of chart for displaying the data. This relates to what the chart is intended to show. The main types of graph and their purposes are as follows.

■ Scattergraph – shows the correlation between two continuous variables, or the distribution of points; this is useful for plotting series of readings.

■ Line graphs or curves – show how two continuous variables are related to each other, especially for changes in one variable over time. A third variable can be introduced by using a different line type. It is recommended that no more than four lines be charted on one graph.

■ Area, band or surface charts – these are difficult to use effectively. They are supposed to be used to show several line graphs or curves as portions of a whole. The shaded areas stacked on top of each other represent each category's contribution to the whole.

- Bar graphs, column charts – show values of a single continuous variable for multiple separate entities, or for one variable sampled at discrete intervals. Two variables (two data series) may be shown, so that the height of the charts can be compared.

- Composite bar charts – these are similar to bar charts, but each bar incorporates separate data series so that it is possible to see how the components contribute to the whole. Although superficially attractive these can be difficult for the reader to interpret.

- Pie charts – show the relative distribution of data among parts that make up a whole. A bar chart usually offers a more accurate interpretation. The number of segments should not exceed five or six. Segments can be moved out from the whole in order to draw attention to them.

Task 2: Choosing chart type

Here are some potential applications of charts. Consider which of the above chart types might be appropriate for these applications. Note that in some instances more than one chart type might be appropriate.

1   A chart designed to compare the sales performance during the last month of six different branches in the Chelmer group.

2   A chart designed to show the relative contributions of different branches to the success of the Chelmer group, as measured by the total value of property sold over the last year.

3   A chart designed to investigate whether there is any relationship between the month in which a sale takes place and the length of time that it takes to complete a sale.

4   A chart designed to compare the relative proportions of sales in the categories: house, flat and bungalow, across six branches.

5   A chart designed to show house price rises over the past five years.

6   A chart to investigate whether there is any relationship between the number of enquiries taken each month and the number of sales made each month. Data are available on a monthly basis, and there are data series for three branches.

Task 3: Creating a scattergraph

One branch manager is interested in the effect of the age of a property on the length of time that it takes to sell a property. He has collected the following data.

Age of Property (years)	Time Taken for Sale (days)
50	67
12	45
2	12
3	17
7	30
59	74
101	145
34	27
23	14
12	14
45	23
6	2
67	69
45	58
57	70
34	23

The manager would like to create a scattergraph of the data to embed in a report to management which makes a case for charging clients who are trying to sell older property at a higher rate. This task creates the following scattergraph

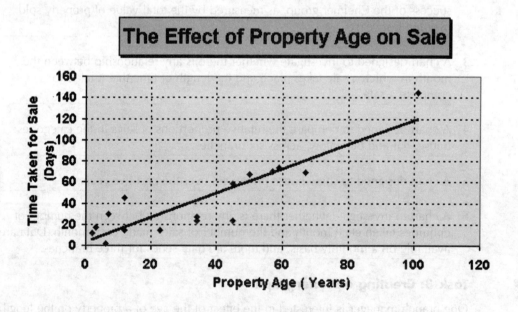

Task 4: Selecting data to appear in a chart

In this task we wish to demonstrate how you can re-use the same set of data to create different charts. In this chart we will use the sales data collected by the five branches over the last six months.

1   Start a new document and add the following data to the datasheet. You will notice that these data create a chart that looks 'busy' as it is displaying a lot of data. Instead of displaying all the data in one chart, several charts can be created from there data.

Branch	July	August	September	October	November	December
Chelmer	88	97	105	66	38	35
Meriton	54	54	39	44	27	22
Branford	30	55	56	37	58	60
Oxley	34	37	41	38	44	48
Easton	21	22	27	17	11	6

2   Display the data series in columns. Click at the left of the **Oxley** row, and choose Data-Exclude Row/Column. Repeat for the last two rows.

3   Click at the top of the **October** column, and choose Data-Exclude Row/Column. Repeat for the last two columns.

4   Note that the graph now shows only the third quarter sales for the three main branches.

5   Format the graph in a way that appeals to you, and makes sense for the data that you are seeking to display.

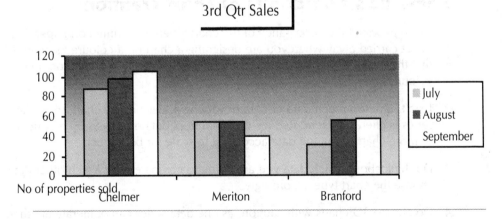

6   Embed the chart in the document and using Edit-Copy and Edit-Paste make a copy of it. Select the copy of the chart in the Word document. The following steps describe the changes you will make to this copy of the chart.

7   Click on the **By Row** button and include only the data for the Chelmer and Easton branches. Choose a two dimensional column chart, select the data series for Easton and choose a line graph format.

8   To create a secondary scale, choose **Format-Selected data series**, click on the **Axes** tab and select **Secondary axis**.

9   Again format the chart in a way that appeals to you, remembering to consider that the data are clearly displayed.

10 Experiment with chart types using the data and including and excluding data.

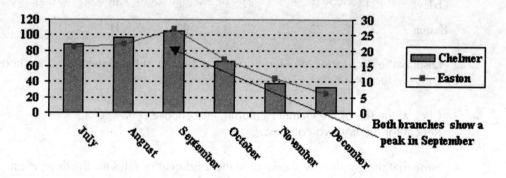

No properties sold by Chelmer and Easton branches

 Note that text boxes and arrows can be added from the Drawing toolbar.

Some do's and don'ts of chart creation

1   Do think about the appearance of the chart when it is printed on paper. It is easy to get carried away when you are designing a chart on a coloured screen. Check that the data series will be sufficiently differentiated when printed on a non-colour printer.

2   Don't have too much data or data of varying scales on one chart; three data series is often sufficient. Reduce the amount of data displayed by producing two or more charts grouping data according to scale for best effect.

3   Do think about which data you are trying to compare with which other data and choose the chart type accordingly.

4   Do choose 3D charts with caution, as one data series can obliterate another. Three-dimensional charts can have a good visual impact, but for a serious message, 2D charts are easier to interpret, and generally look better when printed.

5   Do use pie charts to display parts of a whole; it is inadvisable to explode more than one segment. The most helpful format shows data labels and percentages.

6   Do make full use of titles, axes labels, additional text and, if more than one data series is displayed, a legend or key.

7   Don't cover data markers with text, such as titles or legend.

8   Do examine the chart for legibility, and if necessary change the size of tick mark labels or turn them around.

9   Do make use of dual scale charts, using a secondary y-axis to compare data sets of different scales, which may be affected by a particular circumstance and are showing similar trends.

10 Do be careful when selecting a scale to avoid exaggerating the variation in the values of a variable.

11 Do develop a style across a set of charts, so that your documents have a consistent appearance.

Fun with colour and design

What you will learn in this unit

Unit 11 introduced the use of images and graphics, and in Unit 13 you have experimented with using WordArt. This unit builds specifically on Unit 11, and illustrates some of the ways in which shapes, borders, shadows and colours, can be used in conjunction with text boxes to create diagrams and other illustrations. At the end of this unit you will be able to:

■ use text boxes

■ apply colours, borders and shadows to objects

■ be able to create watermarks

■ be able to use combinations of these objects in order to be able to create diagrams and illustrations.

Most of these facilities can be accessed through the Drawing Toolbar, or through a range of other menu options. We shall focus on the use of the Toolbar. If the Drawing Toolbar is not displayed, before you start this unit display it by using View-Toolbars-Drawing.

Using text boxes

Text boxes are used for placing text in a document; the text can subsequently be moved or formatted as a unit. As initially created there is a border around the text to show the boundary of the text box, but this can be removed. You might wish to use a text box in a diagram as we do in this unit, or to create a banner, as we do in the newsletter in Unit 16. Alternatively text boxes may be embedded in text. They are like any other object or image in that text can be wrapped around a text box.

To create a text box:

1   click on the **Text Box** icon on the Toolbar

2   drag the pointer to open a box in an appropriate position on the document

3   the box should appear selected with white boxes embedded in its border

4   click inside the box and enter text as appropriate

5   to deselect the box, click outside the box.

To choose text wrapping around a text box:

1   Choose **Format-Text box-Wrapping**

2   Choose an appropriate style of wrapping and click on **OK** .

Task 1: Embedding a text box in text

1   Recall the document **Budgeting Advice** (the aim is to create the document below).

IMPORTANT QUESTIONS, HONEST ANSWERS TO HELP GET YOU MOVING

Buying or selling a property should be exciting and fun, but it's certainly one of the most important decisions you'll ever make.

It's important that before you make any decisions, you know the facts and seek out the soundest advice, so that you can turn what could be seen as hurdles, into easily managed steps.

Naturally, you'd expect Chelmer Estates to know all of the answers, and to offer you sound, honest and expert advice.

That's precisely why we've introduced an important service for anyone thinking of moving home.

It's called **Budgeting Advice** and the good news is that it's absolutely free!

Here's how Budgeting Advice works for you

Because buying a home is so important, it's equally important that you understand clearly your own financial position.

Our aim is simply to advise you so that you can be certain that the home of your dreams is realistic and affordable now, and in the years to come.

How to get Budgeting Advice working for you

Simply call into or telephone your nearest Chelmer estate branch and arrange a mut- ually convenient date and time to meet one of our 'Budgeting Advice' team. You'll find them friendly, helpful and highly knowledgeable.

Call in and see us soon

131

The initial formal chat will broadly cover your own requirements and analyse your financial situation. If a further meeting is necessary, then a more in-depth financial analysis will take place, to ensure that you can consider all of the mortgage options available.

In addition to this valuable, free service, we can also consider your long term financial planning, and so provide a sound programme that will keep pace with your prospects and your aspirations.

Make your next move with real peace of mind

On approval of your completed financial analysis, we will present you with your Personal Home Buying Certificate. This will give you the peace of mind such that, when you are making an offer on a property, you'll know the level of mortgage you can afford.

It's nice to know that when you're ready to move, Budgeting Advice will have made it possible for you to move quickly. With all discussions out of the way, your mortgage application will be made easier, whether you buy from Chelmer Estates or not.

With Budgeting Advice, you need never take chances. Instead you'll enjoy the complete peace of mind that comes with friendly, expert and professional – Chelmer – advice.

2   Click on the text box tool and create a text box in the middle of the text.

3   Click in the text box, and enter the following text: **Call in and see us soon**.

4   Using Format-Text box-Wrapping, format the text box wrapping to Tight.

Task 2: Using text boxes in a diagram

This task is designed to illustrate some of the features that can be applied to text boxes using the Drawing toolbar. We wish to create the diagram on page 134. First we create and format a text box and an arrow, then we copy these several times, move the copies into position, and insert text as required.

To create and format a text box:

1   open a new document

2   click on the Text Box button

3 type in the heading, and apply formatting

4 draw a text box in the middle of the page.

5 With the text box selected, use the options on the following buttons to format the text box:

- **Fill Colour**
- **Line Colour**
- **Line style** .

The text boxes and arrows on the next page are necessarily black and white. You should be able to create something much more imaginative through the use of colour and formatting.

To create an arrow:

1 click on the **Autoshapes** button, and display **Block Arrows**; choose an appropriate arrow style

2 the arrow should appear at the insertion point and should be selected; size and change the shape of the arrow until it resembles the arrow in this text

3 change the border style of the arrow, to give it a heavier border.

To copy text boxes and arrows:

1 use **Edit-Copy** and **Edit-Paste** to create a number of duplicate text boxes and arrows

2 drag these to an appropriate position.

To complete the diagram, enter the text shown in the diagram on the following page in the text boxes. Format the text and centre it within the box using the **Centre alignment** button.

Stages in HousePurchase

Mortgage Advice from Chelmer Estates

Review Property Options

View Properties

Select Property and Make an Offer

Sales Negotiation

Contract and Compliance

Moving House

Task 3: Using text boxes and objects in a diagram

You are asked to create the diagram on the following page concerned with Mortgage advice. In order to do this you will need to proceed as follows. The text and elipse on the following page are necessarily plain but you should be able to create something more imaginative with colour, shadows and formatting.

1   Create an ellipse for the centrepiece of the diagram. Format the ellipse using the **Line colour** button and the **Shadow** button.

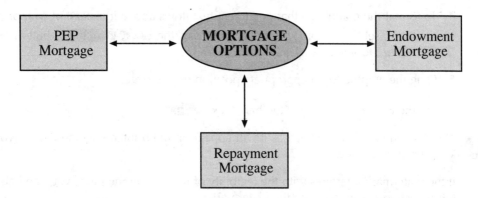

2   Add a text box to the centre of the ellipse and insert text in that box.

3   The text colour can be set using the **Font Colour** button. Centre, size and format the text.

4   Take the line off the text box by choosing the **No Line** option on the **Line Colour** button.

5   Create the arrows using the **Arrow Style** button.

6   Create and format another text box.

7   Make two copies of this text box and drag them into position around the central ellipse.

8   Enter the text into the text boxes in turn, and format it as necessary.

Creating watermarks

To print a watermark that will appear on every page, it must be inserted into a header or footer. The watermark is printed wherever you place it on the page, and will be printed on every page.

 If you only want to create a watermark on one page this can can be achieved in a similar manner to that outlined below, except that it is not necessary to insert the watermark in a header or footer.

1   In **Page Layout** view, choose **View-Header and Footer**.

2   Choose **Insert-Picture-ClipArt** (or some other object).

3   To format the graphic, select it, and then either use **Format-Picture**, or the Picture toolbar. If it is necessary to call up the Picture toolbar, use **View-Toolbars-Picture**. Choose the **Image Control** option. Click on **Watermark**.

4   To format the graphic so that document text flows above it instead of wrapping around it, set the wrapping to none, using say, the `Text Wrapping` button on the **Picture** toolbar.

5   Drag the graphic to an appropriate position on the page.

6   On the **Header and Footer** toolbar, click `Close`.

 The watermark can be viewed as it will appear on the printed page, in Page Layout View or print preview.

If the watermark interferes with the legibility of the text on the page, you can lighten the object you used to create the watermark.

Task 4: Creating a watermark

Insert an appropriate watermark into the document **Budgeting**.

1   In Page Layout View, Choose **View-Header and Footer**.

2   Choose **Insert-Picture-ClipArt**. Choose a piece of clipart that represents the subject of the document.

3   To format the graphic, select it, and then either use **Format-Picture**, or the Picture toolbar. If it is necessary to call up the Picture toolbar, use **View-Toolbars-Picture**. Choose the **Image Control** option. Click on **Watermark**.

4   To format the graphic so that document text flows above it instead of wrapping around it, set the wrapping to none, using say, the `Text Wrapping` button on the **Picture** toolbar.

5   Format the size and colour of the clipart.

6   Drag the graphic to an appropriately central position on the page.

7   On the **Header and Footer** toolbar, click `Close`.

8   Examine the watermark in **Print Preview** to confirm that it appears on each page.

136

Sections and columns

What you will learn in this unit

This unit draws together a number of the objects and documents that you have created in earlier units into an integrated document in the form of a newsletter. It demonstrates how relatively sophisticated documents can be created within Word. Specifically, by the end of this unit you will be able to:

■ create a document with columns

■ use section breaks so that different formatting can be applied to different parts of document

■ integrate text, tables, graphs and images to create an interesting document

■ control hyphenation.

The newsletter that is created in this unit uses too many different elements to be able to exhibit good design. If you are planning to create a 'real' newsletter you should be more conservative and selective concerning the features in Word that you use. The newsletter that we wish to create is printed at the end of the text for this unit. Note that it is designed to occupy two pages in this text, and is not exactly two A4 pages in length, since the book pages are shorter than A4.

Word is primarily suitable for the design of simply formatted newsletters. It offers a wide range of desktop publishing features and you will need to evaluate whether it is appropriate for any more significant applications that you might have, or whether to opt for a desktop publishing package.

Most of the skills that you will need to create this newsletter have already been introduced in earlier tasks. We will recap the steps about which we think that you might need reminding, but you do need to be reasonably confident with these earlier tasks, because it is not possible to cover everything that you might do wrong in this session.

You may find that in this unit, more than in earlier units, you have applied some formatting and are unable to retrieve the situation. Formatting the document into columns may require adjustment and patience. Do not forget to make use of **Edit-Undo**.

Working with Columns

Word allows you to produce two types of columns. Unit 12 dealt with columns in tables, or parallel columns. The second kind of column is the snaking column, in which text flows from the bottom of one column to the top of the next, as in newspaper columns.

When working with columns it is preferable to use Page Layout View, as it shows the columns side by side with objects such as graphics in the correct location. It is also useful for editing, manually inserting column breaks, and adjusting column width. The zoom in and out facility can also be useful.

To create a multiple column layout:

1   choose **View-Page Layout**

2   click in the section to be formatted

3   use **Format-Columns**

4   specify the number of columns, for example, 2

5   in the **Apply to:** box, select the portion of the document that you want to format

6   choose **OK**.

Alternatively:

1   Choose **View-Page Layout**

2   Click in the section to be formatted

3   Click on the **Columns** button on the toolbar

4   Drag to the right to select the number of columns that you want

5   When you release the mouse button, Word formats the section that contains the insertion point.

You can also use the Columns command to:

■ change the space between columns, through the **Width and Spacing** section

■ add a vertical line between columns, through the **Line Between** box

■ format the current section to start in a new column through the **Start New Column** box.

Working with sections

You can change the number of columns in all or part of a document. To change the number of columns on part of a document, make that part a separate section by inserting a section break. Within each section Word automatically adjusts the width of the columns. Word adjusts the space between columns to create equal amounts of space. You can customise this for unequal spacing throughout the Width and Spacing section.

To insert a section break:

1   choose Insert-Break, and in the Break dialog box choose a page or column break, and whether the break should be inserted in continuous text or whether it should cause the text after the break to start on a new page

2   click on OK .

Balancing column length for newspaper columns

1   If your text is not already formatted in columns, create the columns.

2   In Page Layout View, position the insertion point at the end of the columns you want to balance.

3   Choose Insert-Break and select the Continuous option.

Word inserts a continuous section break, which balances the text equally among the columns.

 If you want a new page to start after the balanced columns, click after the continuous section break, and either insert a manual page break or format the first line of text as Page Break Before.

Task 1: Setting up a multiple column document

The text below uses two columns. It is the two sides of a two-page leaflet.

1   Choose View-Page Layout so that you can see the columns.

2   Set the page set-up to landscape, using File-Page Setup. Display the Paper Size sub-dialog box, and select Landscape orientation.

3   Choose Format-Columns. In the Columns dialog box, choose two columns, with no line between, and click on OK .

4   Key in the text, formatting the headings as appropriate.

5   Size and format the text so that it fits into columns as shown here.

BUDGETING ADVICE

*Free advice if youíre thinking of
buying or selling a home*

Budgeting Advice provides you with information and guidance on all the financial matters of moving home,
including the affordability of the move, the costs the actual
move will incur, advice on insurance policies you may
need, and a clear view of the on-going costs of running
you new home.

What you can afford

Our fully trained staff will advise you on the mortgage
options available, giving you the exact detail on what you
can comfortably afford

The Cost of the actual move

We will explain upfront costs incurred in the move,
revealing any hidden costs that you may have overlooked

Safeguarding the Transaction

We will also advise on insurance policies for your new
home giving you peace of mind.

On-going Costs

We will help you consider your monthly on-going costs
including regular bills such as council tax, water charges,
insurance premiums, fuel, gas and electric.

CHELMER ESTATES

In Summary

Budgeting Advice is a flexible concept-based on giving
you clear understandable comprehensive and vital information on the house moving process. If you have any queries
or simply require further information, please contact you
local Chelmer Estates branch.

IMPORTANT QUESTIONS, HONEST
ANSWERS TO HELP GET YOU MOVING

Buying or selling a property should be exciting and fun,
but itís certainly one of the most important decisions you'll
ever make.

It's important that before you make any decisions, you
know the facts and seek out the soundest advice, so that
you can turn what could be seen as hurdles, into easily
managed steps.

Naturally, you'd expect Chelmer Estates to know all of the
answers, and to offer you sound, honest and expect advice.

That's precisely why we've introduced an important
service for anyone thinking of moving home.

It's called **Budgeting Advice** and the god news is that it's
absolutely free!

Here's how Budgeting Advice works for you

Because buying a home is so important, it's equally important that you understand clearly your own financial position.

Our aim is simply to advise you so that you can be certain
that the home of your dreams is realistic and affordable
now, and in the years to come.

How to get Budgeting Advice working for you

Simply call into or telephone your nearest Chelmer estate
branch and arrange a mutually convenient date and time to
meet one of our 'Budgeting Advice' team. You'll find them
friendly, helpful and highly knowledgeable.

The initial formal chat will broadly cover your own
requirements and analyse your financial situation. If a
further meeting is necessary, then a more in-depth financial
analysis will take place, to ensure that you can consider all
of the mortgage options available.

In addition to this valuable, free service, we can also
consider your long term financial planning, and so provide
a sound programme that will keep pace with your
prospects and your aspirations.

Make your next move with real peace of mind

On approval of you completed financial analysis, we will
present you with your Personal Home Buying Certificate.
This will give you the peace of mind that, when you are
making an offer on a property, you'll know the level of
mortgage you can afford.

It's nice to know that when you're ready to move,
Budgeting Advice will have made it possible for you to
move quickly. With all discussions out of the way, your
mortgage application will be made easier, whether you buy
from Chelmer Estates or not.

With Budgeting Advice, you need never take chances.
Instead you'll enjoy the complete peace of mind that
comes with friendly, expert and professional – Chelmer –
advice.

Call in and see us soon

Task 2: Setting up a newsletter

In this task we set up the basic format for the newsletter at the end of this unit. First we place a border around the page, and then we add the heading and the text box down the left hand side of the page. Then, after a section break we set the columns.

1   Open a new document, to be saved later, or at any stage where you wish to take a pause, as **News**.

2   Check that the correct printer is selected choosing **File-Print** and choose the correct page size using **File-Page Setup**. Choose **View-Page Layout**.

3   Apply a border to the page, using **Format-Borders and Shading**, selecting the **Page Border** tab and adding a single line page border.

4   Create a text box at the top of the page. Move and size the text box to place it just inside the border around the page. Choose a fill colour and a border colour and style. Type in the heading 'Chelmer Estates Staff Newsletter'.

5   Choose a Font size which almost fills the text box, choose a bold typeface, and apply **Centre** justification.

6   Create another text box on the left hand side of the page. Apply similar format- ting to that which has been used for the heading text box. Choose an appropriate orientation for the text, by using **Format-Text Direction-Orientation**. Click on **OK** .

7   Place the insertion point below the heading text box.

8   Choose **Format-Columns**, and select the number of columns at 2. Select **This point forward** in the **Apply To**: box. Check the **Line Between** check box. Click on **OK** . Word will automatically place a section break between the heading and the multiple columns.

 9   Save this as a template (see Unit 3) called **News**, which you can use again for subsequent issues of the newsletter.

Task 3: Entering text and objects into columns

This task illustrates the ease with which text, tables, images, graphics and other objects can be added to columns. The only problem is the adjustments that will be necessary to ensure that all the text fits on the two pages of the newsletter. This will certainly require patience, and may involve adjustments to type size, spacing, and the size of graphics. Effective design depends not only on technical competence, but also design sense!

1   Open the template **News**.

2 With the insertion point placed at the top of the first column, enter and format the heading for the first item in the newsletter.

3 You may continue typing all the text and go back to the insertion of images and graphs later. Some of the text in the newsletter was created in the document **Five Star Branch** (Unit 11) so you may wish to copy and paste it into your newsletter.

4 When you wish to add the graph, with the insertion point in the place where the graph should be added, select the graph in the document in which it was created (Unit 14), and Edit-Copy, Edit-Paste the graph into the document.

5 Next you may wish to add an image. The two images used here are selected from the clipart. To add a clipart image, choose Insert-Picture-Clipart, and select an appropriate item of clipart.

6 Continuing down the second column of the newsletter, you will see the use of bulleted points and a small table. These can be used in columns in just the same way that they are used in plain text.

7 On the second page the stars have been selected from the AutoShapes collection accessible, for instance through the Drawing toolbar. You have already created these stars in Unit 11, with the aid of AutoShapes. Remember that to add text inside the banner it was necessary to add a text box to the banner.

8 At the bottom of the page there is a paragraph of text to which borders and shading have been applied.

9 And finally, the For Sale WordArt has been added to the text, and wrapping has been set so that the text flows around the WordArt.

10 This final adjustment is likely to displace text and objects. Once all the text and objects that you wish to include in the newsletter have been added, spend some time adjusting the document so that it fits onto the page.

11 Examine the document in Print Review, and, if necessary, return to make any final adjustments.

If you have managed this task relatively easily, you may like to experiment with ways in which you might improve this document! Alternatively, you may wish to reflect on the design requirements for an on-line newsletter!

Hyphens and non-breaking spaces

Word wraps text at a convenient space between words. With normal documents that are in single column, irregularities due to long words in sentences rarely occur. However, in documents composed of more than one column this can become a problem, even when using a smaller point size for the text. If you look at professional newspapers and magazines you will see that hyphenation is often used to balance the length of lines in columns. Hyphenation can also eliminate gaps or "rivers of white" in justified text.

You can hyphenate text automatically or manually. If you hyphenate manually, Word searches the document for words to hyphenate and then asks you whether to include a hyphen and where to position it.

Hyphenate text automatically as follows.

1   Choose **Tools-Language**, and then select **Hyphenation**.

2   Check the **Automatically hyphenate** document check box.

3   In the **Hyphenation zone** box, enter the amount of space to leave between the end of the last word in a line and the right margin. To reduce the number of hyphens, make the hyphenation zone wider. To reduce the raggedness of the right margin, make the hyphenation zone narrower.

4   In the **Limit consecutive hyphens to** box, enter the number of consecutive lines that can be hyphenated.

 To prevent Word from automatically hyphenating part of the document, select the text, and then choose **Format-Paragraph**. Select the **Line and Page Breaks** tab, and then select the **Don't hyphenate** check box. Note that if you've marked text with the No Proofing format, Word won't hyphenate that text.

Hyphenate text manually as follows.

1   To hyphenate the entire document, make sure no text is selected, otherwise select the text you wish to hyphenate.

2   Choose **Tools-Language-Hyphenation** and click on the **Manual** button.

3   If Word identifies a word or phrase to hyphenate, and you want to insert a hyphen in the location Word proposes, click on the **Yes** button.

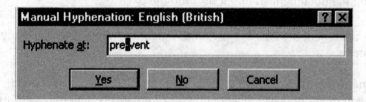

To insert the hyphen in another part of the word, use the arrow keys to move the insertion point to that location, and then click the **Yes** button.

Optional and non-breaking hyphens

For even more control over hyphenation, you can use optional hyphens and non-breaking hyphens. Use an optional hyphen to control where a word or phrase (such as "multimedia") breaks if it falls at the end of a line (for example, "multi-media"). If you amend the document so that this word falls at the end of a line then the hyphenation will come into effect, otherwise the word will look normal. Use a non-breaking hyphen to prevent a hyphenated word or phrase from breaking if it falls at the end of a line.

To add an optional hyphen position the insertion point where a hyphen should appear if the word was to fall at the end of the line. Hold down the *Ctrl* key while typing the dash (**hyphen**).

To add a non-breaking hyphen, hold down the *Ctrl* and *Shift* keys while typing the **hyphen**.

Non-breaking spaces

This works in exactly the same way as for non-breaking hyphens and prevents a line break between words, for example "Mr Jones". Remove the normal space and replace it with *Ctrl+Shift+Space*.

Task 4: Hyphenation

Make a copy of the newsletter you have just created and investigate some of the hyphenation techniques described above.

Chelmer Estates Staff Newsletter

Heatwave and New Government Lift Sales

The chart below shows the enormous boost to sales experienced by Chelmer estates over the past six months. Whilst these increases have been supported by exceptionally sunny weather in the early months of the year and the favourable economic climate associated with a new government, congratulations are nevertheless in order for all Branch teams who have contributed to this success.

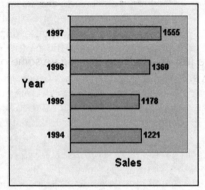

New Branch Opens in Meriton

Plans for the opening of a new branch in Meriton are well underway. The new branch will open on 1st December 1997. It will be managed by Neil Whiteley. Neil has spent over eight years running successful estate agency offices throughout Cheshire, and has gained a reputation for an efficient and dynamic approach to property sales. With a focus on residential lettings and sales, the Branch will seek to offer a customer service of the highest quality. Further staff appointments will be made over the

next few weeks, and information on contact numbers will be available soon.

New Computer Systems

This is the final reminder that from 1st October all networked computers will access the latest version of Microsoft Office, Office 97. Trainers will be visiting each of the branch offices to support you in this transition. If you have any further queries, please contact IT Support on Extension 4314.

Are Your Keeping Fit this Summer?

Six Tips from our sister company Chelmer Leisure:

1. Eat a low fat diet, including plenty of fresh fruit and vegetables.
2. Take aerobic exercise at least three times a week.
3. Take time to enjoy yourself and relax.
4. Apply sun cream 30 minutes before going out in the sun.
5. Make sure that all of the family keeps fit, and finally,
6. Remember that laughter is good for you!

Chelmer Leisure offers special membership rates to employees of companies in the Chelmer Group. The special rates for Gold Pass cards which include use of the Health Suite, Fitness Suite, Pool and Oasis are:

3 Months	£85.00
6 Months	£150.00
Annual	£275.00

New Appointments and Welcome

James Copeland, FVSA, Qualified Valuer and Surveyor, has been appointed as Manager of our Chelmer branch. Chelmer Estates longest standing branch manager, he started in Estates agency in 1978, and qualified as a Valuer and Surveyor in 1982. His last post was as Manager of Chelmer estates Residential Lettings Department. He also has experience with commercial and residential property,

sales in City Centres. For fun he plays golf, and has even been known to survive a game of squash!

Georgina Curry joins the Customer Service team at our Meriton branch. She brings experience as a member of the Customer services team at one of the larger building societies.

Pamela Young has been promoted from her previous post as secretarial assistant, to Personal Assistant to the Branch Manager of Branford Branch, John Wareing.

Investors in People
As announced in the previous issue of the newsletter, Chelmer Estates will work

towards the Investors in People Award. John Wall, Deputy Personnel Manager will act as champion for this project, and will be preparing a regular report on progress for this newsletter. Watch this space!

Five Star Branch
Oxley Branch has won the Chelmer Estates Five Star Award for sales achievements during April 96-April 97. This award is made for a notable success in sales during the year. The team at Oxley Branch succeeded in increasing the number of sales processed by 10% over the total sales achieved during the previous year.

Running for Life

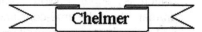

Four members of the staff from our Branch, Joe, Jane, Louise and Peter, were successful in their bid to complete the Chelmer half marathon. They wish to convey their thanks to all staff and friends who supported them through sponsorship and to remind those of you who have yet to send in your sponsorship money that they will be collecting in person very soon! All proceeds go to support the Imperial Cancer Research Fund.

New Free Appraisal Service
As from next month Chelmer Estates will be enhancing its free appraisal service. The appraisal will now cover the following points.

❖ An assessment of likely selling price together with recommended asking price.
❖ Recommendations, as necessary on improving the saleability of the property.
❖ Advice on marketing and presentation.
❖ Written confirmation of fees and expenses.
❖ Advice on the likely value of your next move.
❖ Advice on any other questions on any aspect of house sale or purchase.

> This Newsletter is edited by Catherine Newall, at Chelmer Estates Headquarters. The Newsletter is issued on a monthly basis. All contributions are welcome.

What you will learn in this unit

A macro is a series of Word commands and instructions grouped together as a single command to make time-consuming, repetitive tasks easier. You can assign a macro to a toolbar button, a menu item, or shortcut keys to make the macro as convenient to use as a built-in Word command.

Here are some typical uses for macros:

■ to speed up routine editing and formatting

■ to combine multiple commands

■ to make an option in a dialog box more accessible

■ to automate a complex series of tasks.

Word offers two methods for creating macros. The first is the macro recorder, which records a set of actions as a series of instructions in Visual Basic for Applications. The second is the Visual Basic Editor, which allows you to code instructions directly. The Visual Basic Editor can be used to open a recorded macro to modify the instructions. This way you can write very flexible and powerful macros that include Visual Basic instructions that you cannot record using the macro recorder.

After you have assigned a macro to a toolbar button, a menu item, or shortcut keys, running the macro is as simple as clicking the toolbar button or menu item or pressing the shortcut keys. You can also choose Tools-Macro to run a macro.

You use the Macros dialog box to create, delete, or rename a macro. By default, Word stores macros in the Normal template so that they are available for use with every Word document. However, if a macro stored in the Normal template is useful only for a particular type of document, you may want to copy the macro to the template for that type of document and then delete the macro from the Normal template. Macros can be copied using Format-Style Organizer under the Macro project items tab.

At the end of this unit you will be able to:

■ record and run a simple macro

■ delete a macro

■ assign a macro to a button, a shortcut key and a menu item

■ add a macro supplied with Word to the Normal template.

Recording and running a simple macro

Simple macros that automate a repetitive action are easy to record and use. The example that will be considered here is that of applying some specific formatting where certain words within a document will take on this formatting.

Task 1: A simple formatting macro

1   Choose Tools-Macro Record New Macro and in the Macro Name box type the name of the macro **RedShadow** and click on OK .

2   Choose Format-Font and select the shadow check box and change the colour to red. Click on OK . Click on the Stop Macro button.

3   To run the macro, select a word in a document, use Tools-Macro Macros, select Redshadow from the list and click on Run .

For such a small amount of formatting this macro is not really saving much time, but if your formatting involved more than this it would be advantageous. By assigning the macro **Redshadow** to a shortcut key the time saving becomes very evident.

Assigning a macro to a button, shortcut key or menu item

Once a macro has been created it can be run from the Macros dialog box. However, if the macro is to be used often then using Tools-Macro Macros can be time consuming. It is much quicker to run a macro by using a shortcut key or by clicking on a button in one of the toolbars. When recording a macro you can assign the macro to a shortcut key or a button using the Keyboard or Toolbars button.

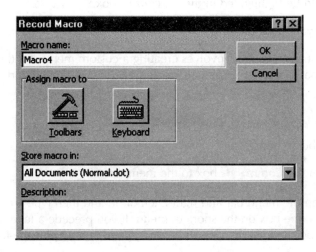

If you choose the **Keyboard** button the **Customize Keyboard** dialog box appears. You can try different keyboard combinations. The **Press new shortcut key** section will tell you whether the shortcut you have chosen has already been assigned to a command. Once you have decided on a shortcut key, click on the **Assign** button and continue to record the macro. When you have recorded it, the shortcut key chosen should run it in future.

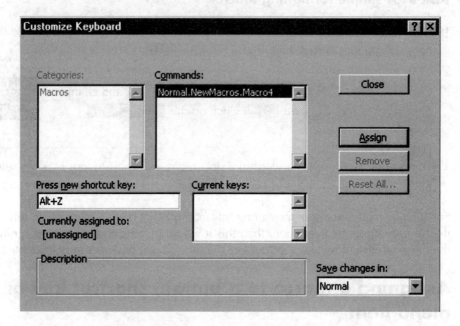

If you choose the **Toolbars** button, the **Customize** dialog box appears and, after selecting the **Toolbars** tab, you can add a button to a toolbar as follows.

1   Show the toolbar you want to add a button to and then click the **Commands** tab.

2   The **Macros** tab should be highlighted in the **Categories** box.

3   Drag the macro you want from the **Commands** box to the displayed toolbar.

To add a macro to a menu item usually involves creating a custom menu and then assigning the macro to that menu item. You can create new (custom) menu and add a macro to it.

1   Choose **Tools-Customize**, and select the **Commands** tab.

2   From the **Categories** box, choose **New Menu**.

3   Drag **New Menu** from the **Commands** box to the menu bar.

4   Point to **New Menu** on the menu bar and right-click on it, and then type a name (e.g. &Macro) in the **Name** box on the shortcut menu. If you precede a letter in the name with an ampersand (&) then it will be underlined and *alt* plus the letter

will open the menu, but choose a letter not already used by the existing menus. Press *Enter*.

5   To add a command to the Custom menu, click the custom menu name on the toolbar to display an empty box. Choose the Macro category in the Categories box, and then drag the macro from the Commands box to the empty box in the Custom menu.

Task 2: Assigning a macro to a shortcut key

In this task a macro will be recorded that produces the second of a pair of quotes. Word usually uses 'smart' quotes, i.e. handed apostrophes that generally occur in pairs. Sometimes, the right-hand apostrophe is needed on its own to indicate an abbreviation. This effect can be achieved by typing two apostrophes and deleting the first. This macro will be recorded and assigned to a shortcut key.

1   Choose Tools-Macro Record New Macro and in the Macro Name box type the name of the macro **RHapostrophe** and click on the assign macro to **Keyboard** button.

2   Choose the keyboard combination *Alt+'* and click on **Assign** .

3   You are now ready to record the macro. Use Insert-Symbol and choose ' (the right hand apostrophe) click on **Insert** and **Close** . Click on the **Macro Stop** button. This macro will run whenever you use the keyboard shortcut *Alt+'*.

Assigning a shortcut key to an existing macro

1   Choose Tools-Customize and choose the **Commands** tab. Click on the **Keyboard** button. Scroll down the list in the Categories and select Macros. In the Commands box select the macro you wish to assign to a shortcut key.

2   Choose a keyboard combination for the shortcut. Click on **Assign** and then **Close** . Test out the shortcut.

Deleting a macro

1   Choose Tools-Macro-Macros. In the Macro name box, highlight the name of the macro you want to delete by clicking on it.

2   Click on the **Delete** button, reply **Yes** to the message box and click on **Close** to close the dialog box.

If the macro doesn't appear in the Macro name box, select a different list of macros from the Macros in drop down list box. To delete more than one macro, hold down the *Ctrl* key whilst selecting the macros in the Macro name box you want to delete, and then click on the **Delete** button.

Task 3: Assigning a macro to a menu item

1 Choose Tools-Customize, and select the **Commands** tab. From the Categories box, choose New Menu and drag New Menu from the Commands box to the menu bar.

2 Point to New Menu on the menu bar and right-click on it, and type the name &Macro in the Name box on the shortcut menu. Press *Enter*.

3 Click on the Macro menu name on the toolbar to display an empty box. Choose the Macro category in the Categories box, select the macro Normal.NewMacros.RHapostrophe and then drag it from the Commands box to the empty box in the custom menu. If you right click on this new menu item its name can be edited to read say, Right-hand apostrophe. Press *Enter* and close the Customize dialog box. Test out the menu and macro.

An ampersand can be used in menu items to provide a shortcut to that item. Menu items and custom menus may be deleted through the Customize dialog box.

Using a macro supplied with Word

The macros supplied with Word are stored in templates installed in the Macros subfolder of the Microsoft Office\Office program folder. You will probably need to install this folder from the Office CD Rom. Using the CD Rom choose Add/Remove Office Components, choose the Word 97 options, select Wizards and Templates and tick the Macro Templates option. You can access the macros in these templates by making the templates global templates, by opening them in document windows, or by using the Organizer dialog box to copy the macros you want to use to the Normal template or to another template. There are two templates and a wizard supplied. The two templates are Macros8.dot and Support8.dot, the wizard is Convert8.wiz (file type conversion wizard). Only the Macros8 template will be considered as the others are beyond the scope of this book.

Macros8 template

This template contains macros you can use in your general work. The table below lists the macros in the template along with a brief description of their function.

Macro	Description
AnsiValue	Displays the ANSI value of any selected character.
AutoCorrectUtility	Creates a backup copy called "AutoCorrect Backup.doc" of the AutoCorrect entries in the active document. You can use this backup document to copy all AutoCorrect entries to another computer.
CopySpike	Works like the Spike command, in which several items are stored in the Clipboard at once, except that CopySpike copies to, rather than cuts to, the Spike.
FindSymbol	Adds functionality to the Find and Replace commands to help search for symbol characters in a document.

Macro	Description
InsertFootnote	Displays a wizard that helps you create footnotes using either the Modern Language Association (MLA) or The Chicago Manual of Style guidelines for various publication types.
NormalViewHeaderFooter	Displays header and footer panels in Normal View. In large documents, this may be a faster way to view headers and footers.
SuperDocStatistics	Provides information about formatting used in each document and section, such as fonts, styles, sections, hyperlinks and bookmarks.
TableCellHelper	Displays the table cell column and row in the status bar — for example, F17. This is useful for creating complex table formulas.

To use the macros:

1   choose **File-Open** and change to the **Microsoft Office\Office\Macros** folder

2   in the **Files of type** box, select **All Files**. Double-click **Macros8**.

Note that a **Warning** dialog box will appear which allows you to abandon the macro copying operation, as macros can contain viruses. A Word macro virus that can do damage, for example, by deleting all your files, could be part of an otherwise apparently innocent-looking useful macro. If you do acquire macros from other sources be aware of this. However, in this task, as the macros are supplied by Microsoft you may continue.

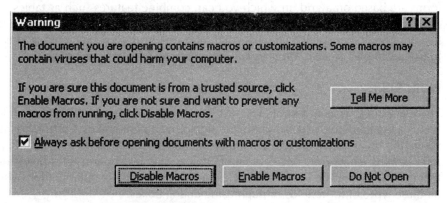

3   Click on the **Enable Macros** button. A document appears and using its **Sample Macros** toolbar buttons you can try out all or any of the macros.

4   To copy all or any of the macros to the **Normal.dot** template, follow the instructions in the document. When you have finished close the document.

5   Now whenever you choose **Tools-Macro** you will see the additional macros listed and you can run them if you wish.

Creating on-line forms

What you will learn in this unit

A form is a document that has demarcated empty areas that are to be filled in to collect and organise information. An online form can have text boxes to fill in, check boxes to select and clear, and drop-down boxes that contain a list of items from which to select answers. An on-line form needs to be created as a template so that it can be distributed to its target audience.

You can also create a form that is printed and then filled in on paper. The best way to create a form is by using tables. Tables enable layout, bordering and shading to be easily designed to give the form a professional appearance.

At the end of this unit you will be able to

- understand form fields
- design and create an on-line form.

Designing a form

Many forms, such as contracts, consist solely of text, with form fields inserted throughout the document so that users can provide specific information. Other forms are based on a grid, in which you can combine features such as tables to align text, borders to designate text areas to be filled in, and shading to emphasise headings and other special elements that make the form more attractive and easier to use. Examples of such forms would be invoices and purchase orders.

Form fields

There are three types of form fields: text boxes, check boxes and list boxes. A text box is a field where the person filling in the form can enter text. A check box is where the box may be 'ticked' to indicate a choice. Check boxes may be grouped to form options where only one of a set of choices may be chosen. A list box is one that may be opened to reveal a list of choices. You will be familiar with the use of all these types of form fields through using dialog boxes.

Forms toolbar

When creating a form, you will need to display the forms toolbar.

To do this, choose View-Toolbars and tick the Forms toolbar box and click on OK

You may wish to drag the toolbar to a convenient location on the screen, possibly at the end of another toolbar such as the Borders toolbar. When you have finished your form, the **Forms** toolbar may simply be closed.

Creating a form

You can create forms that are filled in online or printed and then filled in on paper. On-line forms can be distributed and collected via electronic mail or other kinds of networks. You can add Help messages to online forms to assist users.

Creating an online form

You *must* create and save an on-line form as a new *template* so that macros and AutoText entries are available to users who fill in the form. First sketch out a design for your form or base it on an existing form or template.

1 Either create a new template based on an existing document:

■ choose **File-Open**, and then open the document you want

or base a new template on an existing template:

■ choose **File-New**. Select a template that is similar to what you want or choose **Blank Document** (Normal template), choose the **Template** option, and then click on **OK** .

2 Choose **File-Save As**. In the **File Name** box, type a name for the new template.

3 In the **Save In** box, the **Templates** folder should be open. To add the template to a specific category of templates, e.g. memos, open the corresponding subfolder of the **Templates** folder.

4 In the **Save As Type** box, select **Document Template**, and then click on **Save** .

5 Add any text and graphics that you want to appear in the forms that will be based on the template, and delete any items you don't want to appear.

6 Make any changes you want to the margin settings, page size and orientation, styles, and other formats. Save.

7 Add the form fields. For each form field you want to add, position the insertion point in the document at the point where you want users to insert information, and then click on the appropriate button in the form toolbar.

8 To set options for the form field, double-click the form field.

9 When you finish designing the form, click on the **Protect Form** button on the **Forms** toolbar, so that users can enter information only in the form fields.

10 Save and close the template.

If you create or modify AutoText entries and macros, make the items available only to documents based on the new template, not to all documents. Save changes to menu settings, shortcut keys, and toolbars in the new template, not the **Normal** template.

Form fields are shaded for easy identification. You can turn form field shading off or on by clicking on the **Form Field shading** button on the Forms toolbar.

Text form fields

A text form field is a fill-in field where users can enter text. You can specify a default entry so that the user does not have to type an entry except to change the response.

Options in a text form field

Options in a text form field can be specified in the Text Form Field Options dialog box which can be displayed by double-clicking on the form field or by clicking on the **Form Field Options** button in the Forms toolbar. The Type list in the Text Form Field Options dialog box contains six field types you can use to achieve different results in a text form field. These are detailed in the following table.

Option	Characteristics
Regular Text	Accepts text, numbers, symbols, or spaces.
Number	Requires a number.
Date	Requires a valid date.
Current Date/Current Time	Displays current date or time. Users cannot fill in or change this field.
Calculation	Uses an =(Formula) field to calculate numbers, such as the VAT on a subtotal. Users cannot fill in or change this field.

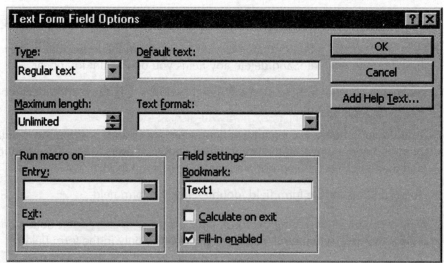

Through the Default text and Maximum length boxes additional specifications can be given to the expected text response. Text may be formatted to be upper case, lower case, or first letter upper case using the settings in the Text format box. Macros can be attached to a text box to run either on the text box being activated

(Entry) or on the text box being deactivated as another part of the form is selected (Exit). This will be illustrated in Task 2.

Pressing the **Add Help Text** button will display the Form Field Help Text dialog box into which help messages which appear in the status bar, or that appear when *F1* is pressed, when the field is selected, can be typed.

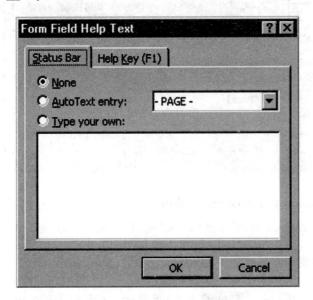

Check box form fields

A check box form field is where users can express a yes/no response in terms of a tick or a blank. Usually the tick indicates a 'yes' and the blank a 'no'. A check box is put next to an independent option that you select or clear. If you use more than one check box in a form note that they are independent so that the associated options you give in the form should also be independent.

Options in a check box form field

Double-clicking on a check box field will display the Check Box Form Field Options dialog box (see following page). Through this dialog box you can alter the size of the check box, set its default value to not checked or checked, attach macros and add help text.

List box form fields

A list box form when activated gives the user a drop-down list of choices which he or she can scroll through to select their response. The user is restricted to the choices that you supply in the drop-down list.

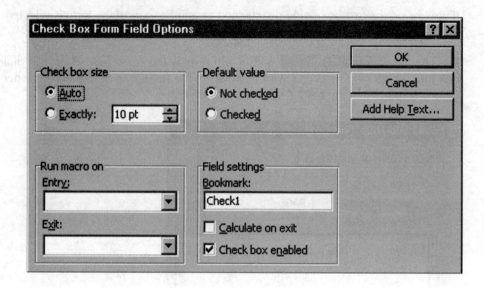

Options in a drop down list box form field

Through the Options dialog box, displayed by double-clicking on the field, the items in the drop down list are created. Type the first item into the Drop-down item: box and click on the **Add>>** button. Repeat this to add all the items to the list. To change the order of items in the list, since it is best to put those most likely to be chosen nearer the top, use the two **Move** buttons. If you wish to delete an item, select it in the Items in drop-down list and click on **Remove**.

In common with the other field types macros can be attached and help text added.

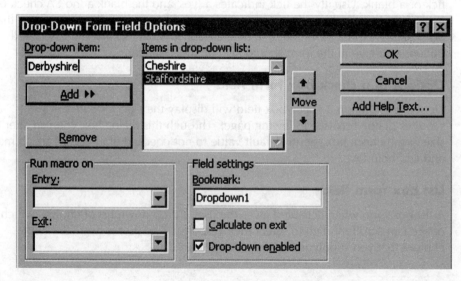

Retrieving the data

Data that is entered into an on-line form may either be printed or saved for exporting to a spreadsheet or database. To print the data from an on-line form

1 open the document saved from the form template and choose **Tools-Options**, and select the **Print** tab;

2 tick the **Print data only for forms** check box, click on **OK** and print the data. Word prints only the data entered in an online form, and no other part of the form.

If you based the design of the on-line form on a preprinted form such as a company invoice or record sheet, and provided that the form fields appear in the same locations, you can insert the blank preprinted forms in a printer and use this procedure to fill out the preprinted forms.

Save the data from an on-line form for use in a spreadsheet or database as follows.

1 Open the document that was filled in as an on-line form. Choose **Tools-Options**, and select the **Save** tab.

2 Check the **Save data only for forms** check box and click on **OK** . Choose **File-Save Copy As**, type a file name in the **File name** box.

3 In the **Save as type** box, select **Text Only**. Word saves the form field data in a comma-delimited text file, which can be imported into a spreadsheet or database for analysis.

Task 1: A simple customer details on-line form

In this task a form template which invites a prospective house purchaser to give their details is created. Text form fields are used to request name and address details, check box form fields are used to request customer preferences, and a drop-down list box is used to find out why they have chosen to place their custom with Chelmer Estates. An illustration of how the completed form might look is shown on the following page.

Exact instructions are not given, as you should be familiar with formatting and creating tables. Create the form template as follows.

1 Choose **File-New**, click to select the **Template** option and with **Blank Document** highlighted click on **OK** .

2 Choose **File-Save** and save in the **Templates** folder as **Customer details form**. Click on **Save** .

3 Add the Chelmer Estates logo to the form. Make it a floating image with square text wrapping. Add the instructions at the top of the form.

If you would like us to add your
details to our mailing list so that we
can send you up-to-date details of
our comprehensive list of
properties, please take five minutes to complete this form.

Your name:

Title: Mr ⬦   Initials: Lastname: 15/01/98

Your address:

| Street: | | Town: | |
| County: | | Postcode: | |

Check this box if you are a first time buyer ☐

Type of property you are interested in:

Leasehold	☐	Freehold	☐		
Detached	☐	Semi-detached	☐	Bungalow	☐
Terrace	☐	Flat/apartment	☐		

Please indicate your preferred price range:

| £30,000-£50,000 | ☐ | £50,000-£70,000 | ☐ | £70,000-£100,000 | ☐ |
| £100,000-£150,000 | ☐ | £150,000-£250,000 | ☐ | £250,000 and above | ☐ |

Thank you for your co-operation, please save the form by double-clicking here

4 Add tables and form fields as illustrated. To add a form field, position the insertion point and then click on the appropriate button in the Forms toolbar. Set
  appropriate text formatting for the text box fields, e.g. First capital for names and
  upper case for initials and post code. Use a text field to record the current date.

5 You may wish to experiment with adding help text, for example, to the freehold
  and leasehold check boxes to explain the meanings of these terms.

6 As a finishing touch you could add a Macrobutton field which when double-
  clicked would run the **File Save** command. Use **Insert-Field** and choose the
  Document Automation category and select **Macrobutton**. Click on **Options**
  and choose **FileSave**, click on **OK** and add the word 'here' to act as the display
  text.

7 To remove the need to worry about file names, include a reference in small type
  as the first line of the document so that this is used as the file name. Word will
  automatically number the names of subsequent documents when they are saved.

8 Remember to click on the **Protect Form** button before saving the completed
  template. Test the template by using **File-New** and selecting it to give a blank
  form to fill in. Fill-in the form and save as a normal document.

9   You may wish to open this completed form and save it as a comma-delimited text file by following the instructions above.

Task 2: An on-line purchase order

In this task an on-line purchase order as shown below will be created. The purchase order template will use form fields for the entries and a macro to calculate the sub-totals and totals.

1   Choose **File-New**, click to select the Template option and with Blank Document highlighted click on OK.

2   Choose **File-Save** and save in the Templates folder as Chelmer Estates purchase order. Click on Save.

3   Use a two column table for the heading section of the invoice as illustrated below. The borders are shown for clarity.

Chelmer Estates 23 Main Street Chelmer Cheshire CH4 4RT Tel: 01234 567899 Fax 01234 567988	*Chelmer* **Estates**
The following number must appear on all related correspondence, delivery notes, and invoices:	
P.O. NUMBER:	

4   To work with form fields display the Forms toolbar using **View-Toolbars**. After P.O. NUMBER add a text form field with the properties: Regular Text, maximum length 25, and give it the bookmark name **PO_number**.

5   Next create an area for the entry of the supplier's address. You could use four or five form text fields. Alter the bookmark names to read To_1 (for the first address line) through to To_5 (for the last).

6   Next create a three column table as illustrated below. Below P.O. DATE add a text field of type date, format dd/mm/yy and the bookmark name Date. Below REQUISITIONER add a text field with a default of your name (as branch manager you would be in control of purchases) and the bookmark name **Requisitioner**. Below TERMS use a drop down list form field with the options N/A, C.O.D., 30 days, 60 days, Special. Give this field the bookmark name **Terms**.

P.O. DATE	REQUISITIONER	TERMS

7 Next add a four column table as illustrated below. For quantity (QTY), set type as number, format as #,##0 and use the bookmark name **Quantity_1**. For DESCRIPTION use a regular text field with the bookmark name **Description_1**. For UNIT PRICE use a number type text field, format £#,##0.00;(£#,##0.00) and use the bookmark name **Price_1**. For TOTAL use a calculation type text field and for the expression type =PRODUCT(A2,C2), this will multiply together the values specified in the QTY and UNIT PRICE cells. Use the £#,##0.00;(£#,##0.00) format and use the bookmark name **Amount_1**.

QTY	DESCRIPTION	UNIT PRICE	TOTAL

8 Add a further six rows to the table and repeat the previous step except that your bookmark names should end in an underscore and the item row number, e.g. the last amount will have the bookmark name **Amount_7**. Also the expression for the amount should refer to the correct table row, i.e. last one is =PRODUCT(A8,C8).

9 The final part of the purchase order will be for totalling and adding VAT and delivery charges. Continue with the four columns (so that later table calculations will work), bordering as illustrated.

SUBTOTAL	
VAT	
DELIVERY	
TOTAL	

1. Please send two copies of your invoice.
2. Enter this order in accordance with the prices, terms, delivery method and specifications listed above.
3. Please notify us immediately if you are unable to supply as specified.
4. Send all correspondence to address above.

Authorised by .... Date ....

10 In the column to the right of SUBTOTAL add a text field of type calculation with expression =SUM(ABOVE) the currency format as for the other fields and the bookmark name **Subtotal**. To the right of VAT add a text field of type calculation with the expression =D9*0.175 a currency format and the bookmark name **ValueAddedTax**. The DELIVERY field is a text field of type number, format currency and bookmark **Delivery**. The TOTAL field is a text field of type calculation with expression =SUM(D9,D10,D11) i.e. adding the **Subtotal**, **VAT** and **Delivery**. It has a currency format and the bookmark name **Total**.

11 The order total is calculated whenever any of the **Quantity**, **Unit Price**, or **Delivery** form fields are exited. This is done by attaching a macro called Update to the **Run Macro on Exit** form field option of these fields. First the macro needs to be created.

12 To create the macro use Tools-Macro Macros, type the name of the macro Update in the Macro name box and select **Chelmer Estates Purchase Order.dot** in the Macros in drop down list. This is so that this macro is only available to this template. Click on Create and type in the following macro. Close the macro window.

```
Sub update
'*************************************************************
' This macro updates the fields that change as a result of leaving a
' cell in the Quantity or Unit Price columns or from leaving the
' Delivery cell.
'*************************************************************
Dim curType
Dim fieldName$
Dim split
Dim rownum$
     '*** First, get the name of the selected field:
     Dim dlg As Object: Set dlg=WordBasic.DialogRecordFormFieldOptions(False)
     WordBasic.CurValues.FormFieldOptions dlg
     curType = dlg.Type
     fieldName$ =  dlg.Name
     '*** Now check if we've changed Delivery
     If fieldName$ = "Delivery" Then Goto LastLine

     ' Each relevant field name is of the form heading_rownum.  So the
     ' second row under the Unit Price heading has the field name
     ' Price_2.  The following lines extract the rownum component.
     ' InStr returns the character position of the underscore, so for
     ' Price_2 this would be 6.
     ' Mid returns the portion of 'fieldName$' starting at 6+1 i.e. 7
     ' so for Price_2 this is 2.
     split = InStr(fieldName$, "_")
     rownum$ = Mid(fieldName$, split + 1)
     ' Update Amount for the current row, then update Subtotal
     ' and Total and ValueAddedTax fields:
     Wordbasic.SetFormResult  "Amount_" + rownum$
     Wordbasic.SetFormResult "Subtotal"
     Wordbasic.SetFormResult "ValueAddedTax"
LastLine:
     Wordbasic.SetFormResult "Total"
End Sub
```

13 Revisit the field properties of all the **Quantity**, **Amount** and **Delivery** fields and open the **Run** macro on exit box and choose the macro **Update**.

14 Lock the form and save the template. Using **File-New** and selecting the **Chelmer Estates Purchase Order** template, try creating a purchase order and save and print it. You should find that the row amounts, subtotal and total are calculated automatically.

Equation Editor and Organisation Chart

What you will learn in this unit

We have already met a number of 'objects' that might be embedded in a Word document such as a Word picture or a Word chart. Both these objects have an associated application which allow you to create and edit the object. Equation editor and Organisation Chart are two further examples of objects which can be created and embedded in a Word document and later edited.

Equation Editor is designed to support the creation of mathematical equations and formulae. Organisation Chart is a special graphics tool which supports the creation of organisational charts.

They are also available to the other applications within Office. By the end of this unit you will be able to:

■ use the Equation Editor to create formulae

■ use Organisation Chart to create structure charts.

The Equation Editor

One of the most difficult tasks in word processing is to write an equation, particularly if the equation has a complicated structure. Lining up numerator and denominator, positioning brackets, using subscripts and superscripts, to name but a few, are typical of the problems encountered when constructing an equation. Word provides a means to overcome this in the form of an equation editor. Only the basics of the Equation Editor will be covered here.

The Equation Editor works by providing a workspace in which to create the equation and the equation is constructed using Equation Editor toolbars and is then embedded into the document by clicking outside the equation. Later the equation may be edited by double-clicking on it to return to the Editor program.

Starting the Equation Editor

The Equation Editor is available through the Insert-Object command. An Object dialog box appears and under the Create New tab select Microsoft Equation 3.0 and click on OK .

The Equation Editor floating toolbars should appear and an equation editing work space. Note that only the menu bar remains at the top of the screen.

The Editor toolbars

The Equation Editor toolbars are composed of two palettes, the symbol palette and the template palette. The insertion point looks different; it is flashing vertical and horizontal lines inside a dashed rectangle, in the equation editing work space. The dashed rectangle, known as a slot, indicates a part of a template.

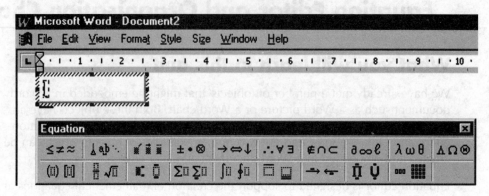

Building an equation

It is best to write down the equation to be created so that its method of construction can be considered. The basic rule for creating an equation is to set up a template first and then to fill the slots in the template with symbols. If the wrong template is inserted by mistake use **Edit-Undo** to remove it.

Templates are chosen from the lower palette bar. The icons in this bar represent the categories of template. By clicking and holding the mouse button on one of these icons a sub-menu appears showing all the templates available in that category. Still holding the mouse button down, move to the one required and release the button. Symbols can be inserted into the template to complete the equation.

The following table details the types of templates that are available:

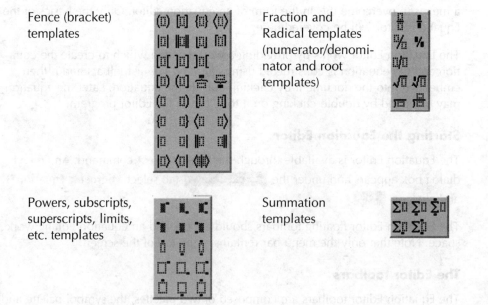

Fence (bracket) templates

Fraction and Radical templates (numerator/denominator and root templates)

Powers, subscripts, superscripts, limits, etc. templates

Summation templates

Integration templates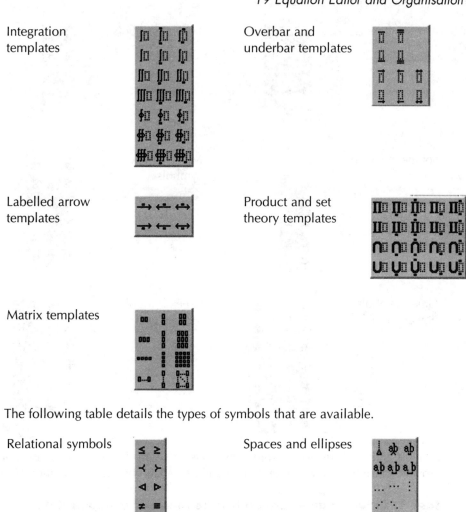

Overbar and underbar templates

Labelled arrow templates

Product and set theory templates

Matrix templates

The following table details the types of symbols that are available.

Relational symbols

Spaces and ellipses

Embellishments (symbol circum-flexes)

Operator symbols

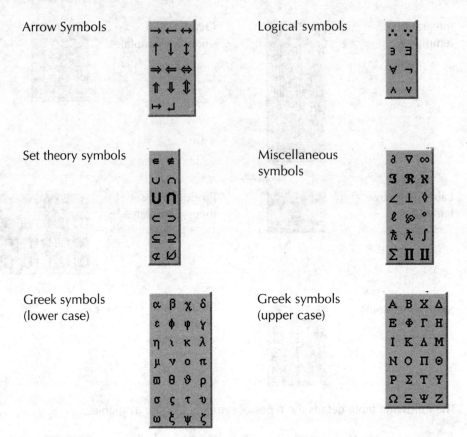

Arrow Symbols

Logical symbols

Set theory symbols

Miscellaneous symbols

Greek symbols (lower case)

Greek symbols (upper case)

By illustrating the creation of some basic business statistical equations, it is hoped to provide a firm base from which to explore the capabilities of the Equation Editor.

Task 1: Creating an equation for the mean of grouped data

The equation to be produced is that for calculating the mean value of a set of grouped data.

$$\bar{x} = \frac{\sum f x_{mid}}{\sum f}$$

Start a new document.

1   Position the insertion point at the place where the equation is to be and use **Insert-Object Microsoft Equation 3.0.**

2   Type x. Click on the third icon on the symbols bar and choose the bar symbol (fourth row, first column) ▓ . Type =

Note that you cannot type a space into an equation, the editor sorts out the spacing.

3   Choose a numerator/denominator template; the first one of the options is suitable, as illustrated. For the numerator, select a summation template (again choose the first one of the options). Type fx

4   Choose a subscript template (third icon on the template bar, second box in the first row). Type mid

5   Click on the denominator part of the equation. Using a template insert a Σ as for the numerator. Type f then click outside the working area to embed the equation in the document, which returns you to Word. Save as **Stats**.

Task 2: Creating an equation for standard deviation

Continuing work with the document just created, on a new line create the following equation for the standard deviation of ungrouped data:

$$\sigma = \sqrt{\frac{\Sigma\left(x - \bar{x}\right)^2}{n}}$$

1   Position the insertion point at the place where the equation is to be and use **Insert-Object Microsoft Equation 3.0.**

2   Enter a σ by selecting it from the ninth icon on the symbols bar. Click on the letter that is first on the sixth row . Type =.

3   Add a square root template (second icon on the template bar).

4   Add a numerator/denominator template and add a summation template to the numerator.

5   Add a round bracket template (first icon on the template bar). Type x-x.

6   Click on the third icon on the symbols bar and choose the bar symbol.

7   Press ⇒ to move to the insertion point to the end of the brackets. Choose a power template (third icon on the template). Type 2.

8   Click on the denominator slot. Make sure the insertion point is flashing in this slot.

9   Type n. Click outside the working area to embed the equation in the document and save.

Task 3: Creating the equation for the gradient of a line of best fit

Finally add the equation to find the gradient of a line of best fit.

$$m = \frac{\sum xy - \dfrac{\sum x \sum y}{n}}{\sum x^2 - \dfrac{(\sum x)^2}{n}}$$

1   Position the insertion point at the place where the equation is to be and use **Insert-Object Microsoft Equation 3.0.**

2   Type m=. Add a **numerator/denominator** template. In the numerator, add a summation template $\Sigma\Box$. Type xy-

3   Add a **numerator/denominator** template. In the numerator add a summation template. Type x.

4   Add another **summation** template and type y, click in the denominator slot of this part and type n.

5   Click in the main denominator slot to move the insertion point into it.

6   Add a **summation** template $\Sigma\Box$. Type x.

7   Add a **raise to a power** template. Type 2. Press ⬇ and type - ▊

8   Add a **numerator/denominator** template. Next add a round bracket template.

9   Add a **summation** template $\Sigma\Box$. Type x and press ➜ twice to move the insertion point to the end of the brackets.

10 Add a **raise to a power** template ▊ . Type 2. Click in the denominator slot. Type n. Embed the equation in the document. Save.

Adjusting settings in the Equation Editor

To make adjustments to the font and size of an equation use either **Style-Define** or **Size-Define**. **Style-Define** will allow different type fonts to be applied and **Size-Define** will allow the size of the individual parts that make up an equation to be altered.

Organisational charts

An organisational chart is one that is used to show the structure of an organisation. These structures are hierarchical with, say, a managing director at the top level and at each succeeding level representing a lower level of management. As there are generally more managers at the lower levels, this chart takes on a 'root-like' (upside-down tree) structure. An example of a simple structure is shown below.

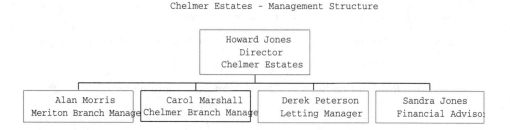

Starting Microsoft Organisation Chart

To enable you to add professional organisational charts to your documents, Microsoft Office supplies an application called MS Organization Chart 2.0. This application is used to create a chart, which is embedded into a document when complete. An embedded organisational chart may be revisited later if editing is required.

To start Microsoft Organisation Chart, choose Insert-Object and select MS Organization Chart 2.0.

The Organisation Chart application starts with a default chart displayed. Use the View menu to alter the size of the default chart to suit.

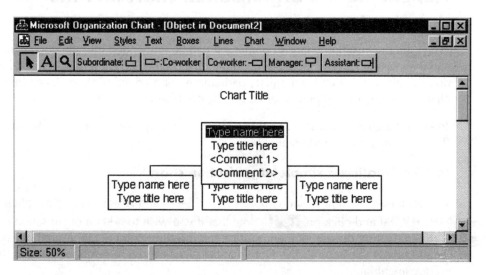

When working with the chart window it is useful to click on its ▌Maximize▐ button to prevent accidental clicking on the document window behind.

Selecting and entering information into chart boxes

Before any editing or reformatting of chart boxes can be performed, the box or boxes must be selected. When the default chart loads, the top level box is selected and appears highlighted.

To	Do this
Select one box	Click on the box
Select a set of boxes	Drag a selection rectangle around the boxes
Select the whole chart	Choose **Edit-Select All**
Select one level or one branch of the chart	Choose **Edit-Select** and either **All Managers**, **Branch**, or **Lowest Level**.

With a chart box selected, text may be entered. When the box is clicked a larger text box appears with the following placeholders:

Type name here

Type title here

<Comment 1>

<Comment 2>

To alter the placeholder text, highlight it by clicking and dragging and then type in the required text. The comment lines are optional; if no text is added to them they do not appear on the chart. When the text is added click on a blank part of the screen to add the box into the chart.

Embedding the organisation chart into the document

When the organisation chart is complete it can be embedded into the document and then saved. As you need to embed the chart before saving it may be useful to do this before the chart is complete, particularly for a complex chart. An embedded chart can easily be re-opened for editing by double-clicking on it.

To embed a chart into a document use **File-Exit and Return to** *filename*. Answer Yes to the update object in file dialog box.

Task 4: Creating a simple organisation chart

1   Start a new document and choose **Insert-Object** and select **MS Organization Chart 2.0** and click on **OK**. Note that if you wish to add an organisation chart to an existing document then position the insertion point at the desired place and follow the steps above. Note that the chart can be re-positioned within the document later.

2   Click on the **Maximize** button of the **Organization Chart** window.

3   To note the appearance of a selected box, click one of the four boxes in the default chart to select it. Click on another box to select that. Finally select the top level box.

4   Double-click on the selected top level box to display the text box. Select the first three text placeholders in turn and replace them with

Howard Jones

Director

Chelmer Estates

5   Now click on a blank part of the screen.

6   Repeat the process for the other lower level boxes adding the following people to the chart: Alan Morris, Meriton Branch Manager; Carol Marshall, Chelmer Branch Manager; and Derek Peterson, Letting. Sandra Jones will be added in the next task.

7   In the same way edit the **Chart Title** (select then type) to read: Chelmer Estates – Management Structure.

8   Choose **File-Exit and Return to** *document* and click on **Yes** to update the chart in the document. Save the document as **Chelmer Estates Management Structure**.

Adding and deleting chart boxes

The default organisational chart is unlikely to be the structure that you require and you will wish to modify it by adding and removing boxes and levels. In this activity we shall concentrate on simple structure charts and use the buttons on the Organisation toolbar to create such charts. These buttons are summarised in the following table.

Button	*Function*
Subordinate: ⎿⌐	Click on this button and then click on the chart box for which you wish to create a lower level.
⌐⊢:Co-worker Co-worker: ⊣⌐	Click one or other of these buttons to add an extra box to the right or left of the chart box that you click on.
Manager: ⨆	Click on this button and then click on the chart box above which you wish to create a higher level. Note: the box you click on is demoted.
Assistant: ⊏⌐|	Click on this button and then on the box to which you wish to add an assistant box.

Deleting boxes

To delete a structure chart box, select the box and delete it by pressing the *Delete* key. Note that if a box is deleted which has subordinate levels, these are not deleted, they move up one level.

 To cater for more variety in a chart, different group styles may be chosen from the **Styles** menu. An example of a vertical group style can be seen in the chart illustrated in Task 7.

Task 5: Adding a co-worker

Open the document **Chelmer Estates Management Structure** saved in the last task.

1   Double click on the organisation chart to run MS Organisation Chart 2.0.

2   Click on the co-worker to the right button and then click on the rightmost box of the second level to create an extra box at that level.

3   Add the following text to this box

Sandra Jones

Financial Advisor

4   Return to the document and save it.

Task 6: Adding co-managers to a chart

The aim of this task is to create the structure shown below which has a co-manager level.

1   Start a new document and choose **Insert-Object** and select **MS Organization Chart 2.0** and click on **OK** .

2   Delete two of the lower level boxes by selecting them and pressing the *Delete* key. Note two or more boxes may be selected at once by holding down the *Shift* key during the selection process.

3   Click on the one remaining subordinate box and choose **Co-manager** from the **Styles** menu.

4   Click on the **Subordinate** button and click on the top level box, thereby creating two co-managers.

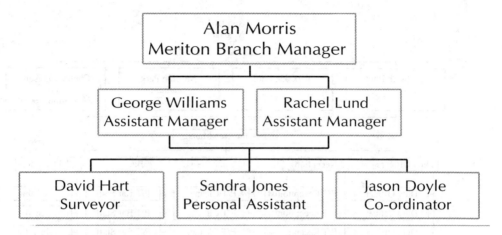

5   Click on the **Subordinate** button and add a subordinate to the co-managers by clicking on one of them. Repeat to add another two subordinates of the co-managers.

6   Add the text, names and positions as illustrated. Embed the chart in the document and save as **Organisation chart examples**.

Task 7: Adding groups of co-workers

In this task a second chart will be added to the document **Organisation chart examples** as illustrated below. To cater for the illustration of a variety of levels this chart illustrates a different type of organisation.

1   Open the document **Organisation chart examples**, make a blank line beneath the last chart and using Insert-Object add a second chart.

2   To select the boxes at level 2 choose Edit-Select levels and choose 2 through 2.

3   Next open the Styles menu and select co-managers. Choose a left co-worker and click on the leftmost co-manager to create four co-managers.

4   Click on the **Subordinate** button and click on one of the co-managers. Click on the **Subordinate** button again and add a subordinate of the last subordinate. Add four additional co-workers.

5   Click on the **Subordinate** button and click on leftmost box at the lowest level. Choose Styles and click on the top middle button (vertical group). Click on Co-worker and add a co-worker to this box. Repeat to add the third co-worker.

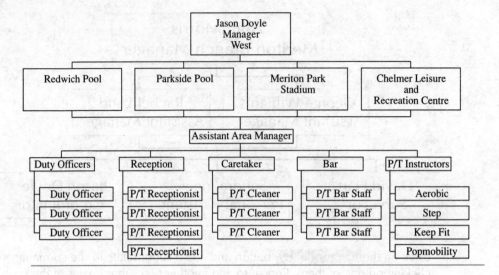

6 Add the other lowest level vertical groups, as illustrated, in the same way as described above. Add the text to the boxes, return to the document and save.

Editing an organisational chart

Text in the boxes in an organisational chart can be edited and its font, alignment and colour can be altered using the Text menu. The colour, line style and shadow effects of the boxes can be changed using the Boxes menu. The background colour of the whole chart can be set using the Chart menu.

Task 8: Editing colours, line styles and shadows

1 Open the document **Chelmer Estates Management Structure**. Select the top level box. Using Text-Font (Insert-Object-MS Organisation Chart 2.0) alter the font of the text. As the whole box is selected all the text in the box will reflect the change you make. Try selecting a portion of the text within the box and altering its font. You will find that only the selected text is changed.

2 Investigate changing the colour of the text using Text-Color.

3 Select all the boxes using Edit-Select Levels All and change the colour of the box background using Boxes-Color. If you wish to experiment then select different levels and apply different colours to the boxes. Remember, however, that for a serious chart too many colours will look gaudy so colours should be chosen with care. If in doubt then choose fewer rather than more colours.

4 Select boxes and levels and investigate the options in the Boxes menu. Again take care when choosing these for a serious chart; err on the side of fewer effects to avoid making your chart look too busy.

5 Finally, through **Chart-Background Color** you may choose the background for the whole chart. When choosing this and other colours in the chart, take into account any other colours you have used your document.

6 Experiment with this chart, return to the document and save. Experiment with changing text, colour and line style in the other two charts created in this unit.

Using Office applications together

What you will learn in this unit

All the Office Applications are powerful and often you can use them to produce
documents for which they were not originally designed, such as slides from Word or
a sales report from Excel. However, the purpose of an Office suite of applications is
to allow you to switch to the appropriate application for the task in hand and to
embed or link data from other applications.

If you installed Microsoft Office, you can use the Office Binder to keep related files
together. For example, if you have a Word document, a Microsoft Excel workbook,
and PowerPoint slides that make up a single report, you can place them in a binder
to work on them together. This is a useful organisational tool.

This unit will demonstrate some of the ways in which Office applications can be
used. By the end of this unit you will be able to:

■ use Word's insert Excel worksheet facility

■ create a PowerPoint presentation from a Word outline

■ use embedding and linking.

Inserting an Excel worksheet

If you wish to add a table of figures to your document and you want to be able to
perform more than simple calculations upon them, you can insert an Excel worksheet. This can be done without having to start Excel separately by using the
Insert Microsoft Excel Worksheet button on the standard toolbar. When you
click on this button a drop down list of worksheet size appears so that you can
choose the size of the worksheet. This is not critical as the size of the worksheet can
be altered later. The worksheet appears as an object in the document as illustrated
below.

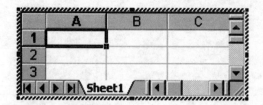

Data and formulae can be added as if you were in Excel and while this object is
active the toolbars give you access to Excel's functions and commands. When you
have completed the worksheet click outside it to insert it into the document. It looks
like a normal Word table, but unlike a table it can only be edited by double-clicking

on it to open the Excel workspace. Features such as font size, borders and shading can be applied to make the table's presentation and layout consistent with the rest of the document.

By sizing the worksheet area, using the sizing handles, you can control what is embedded into the document so that not all the data in the worksheet need appear. You can also add extra sheets, but these data will be hidden unless you display that particular sheet before embedding the worksheet. If you share the document electronically then the underlying data and sheets become accessible when the embedded worksheet is opened.

Task 1: Inserting an Excel spreadsheet

Although Word allows you to do calculations in tables, if you want to perform some repetitive calculations then Excel's fill function is useful and the use of this will be illustrated in this task.

1   Open the document **Sales** created in Unit 15, and select the first nine rows (excluding totals) and copy them.

2   Click on the **Insert Microsoft Excel Worksheet** button and choose a 9 × 4 grid. Paste in the data you have copied to the clipboard. Edit the dates so that Excel recognises them as dates and if necessary use **Format-Cells** to adjust the date formatting. You will probably have to be content with American date formatting so choose a format that gives the month number rather than name.

3   Click in the document to embed the worksheet. The columns may not be wide enough so double click on the embedded worksheet and drag the column headers to widen them. Embed the worksheet to see the result.

4   Double-click on the worksheet and select column D and choose **Insert-Columns**. Add the following data to this column.

Registration date

3-Nov-96

6-Jun-97

4-Feb-97

20-Oct-97

14-Sep-97

13-Aug-97

6-Nov-97

25-Nov-97

5   Widen the worksheet space by dragging on its sizing handle and in cell F2 add the formula =(E2-D2)/7 to calculate the number of weeks the properties have been on the books. Format this cell as an integer.

6   Select column F (F2 to F9) and use Edit-Fill-Down to complete it. Embed the worksheet and save.

Creating a PowerPoint presentation from a Word outline

You can use an existing Word document to create a PowerPoint presentation. To set up the slides in a presentation, PowerPoint uses the heading styles in your Word document. For example, each paragraph formatted with the Heading 1 style becomes the title of a new slide, each Heading 2 becomes the first level of text, and so on. To create a PowerPoint presentation from a Word document:

1   open the document you want to use to create a PowerPoint presentation

2   choose File-Send To and then select Microsoft PowerPoint.

If you're already working in PowerPoint, you can import a Word document into PowerPoint. In PowerPoint, choose File-Open and in the Files of type box, select All Outlines. In the File name box, enter the file name and location of the Word document.

You can also insert slides from a Word outline into an existing presentation. In PowerPoint, display the slide after which you want to insert the new slides. Choose Insert-Slides from Outline, and then select the Word document you want.

Task 2: Creating a slide presentation from a Word outline

For this task you will need both Word and PowerPoint.

1   Open the document **Letting**, choose File-Send To, and then select Microsoft PowerPoint.

2   PowerPoint opens in Outline View showing the headings from this document.

3   Experiment with changing the heading levels in this outline, using the **Promote** and **Demote** buttons. You will have to promote several heading to the top level to give you more slides.

4   You can also add and delete text to complete the slide show. To see how to apply formatting, design and other effects, refer to the PowerPoint basic skills companion book.

5   If you want to save the PowerPoint presentation formatting, save this as a PowerPoint presentation.

Linking and embedding

Information can be shared between Office applications by using linked and embedded objects. Information from other applications that support object linking and embedding can also be shared. If the information you want to use was created in an application that does not support linked and embedded objects, you can still copy and paste information from the file created by that application, to share the information between programs.

The main differences between linked objects and embedded objects are where the data are stored and how they are updated after you place them in the destination file. With a linked object, information is updated only if you modify the source file. Linked data are stored in the source file. The destination file stores only the location of the source file and displays a representation of the linked data. Use linked objects if file size is a consideration. With an embedded object, information in the destination file does not change if you modify the source file. Embedded objects become part of the destination file and, once inserted, are no longer part of the source file. Double-click the embedded object to open it in the source program.

Task 3: Linking Word and Excel

For this task you will need both Word and Excel. In Task 1 we have already seen how to embed a worksheet in Word and if you are entering new data then this is probably the best way to handle it. On the other hand, data may be already available in Excel and you may wish to link them to a document so that they can be kept up-to-date. To illustrate this we will copy and paste the data from task 1 into Excel.

1   Open the document **Sales** last updated in Task 1 and double click on the embedded worksheet. Select the data and copy it. Start Excel and paste the data into a new worksheet. Save it as **Sales**.

2   Now copy the data from the spreadsheet and return to Word and open a new document. Choose **Edit-Paste Special**, choose **Paste Link** and leave the **Formatted text** option highlighted and click on **OK**. A table of data will be pasted into the document.

3   Return to Excel and make some changes to the dates. Display Word again and note that the changes made are reflected in the Word document. It is not necessary to save the Word document or the changes to the Excel worksheet **Sales**.

Task 4: Linking Word and PowerPoint

For this task you will need both Word and PowerPoint.

1   Open the document **Sales**, select and copy the data in the Word table.

2   Start PowerPoint, choosing a new presentation and select a blank slide.

3 Choose **Edit-Paste Special**, choose **Paste Link** and click on **OK** . A table of data will be pasted into the slide. Drag to resize the table.

4 Return to Word and make some changes to the text in the table. Display PowerPoint again and note that the changes made are reflected in the table in the slide. It is not necessary to save the PowerPoint presentation or the changes to **Sales**.

What you will learn in this unit

You are probably familiar with the concept of mail merge and should be able to create a standard letter and set of data and merge them to produce a set of standard letters. The basics of mail merge are covered in the companion book *Word 97 Basic Skills*.

Mail merges can be used for completing other standard documentation as well as letters, for example data concerning records of achievement can be printed out on a certificate. A standard form using a table can be designed so that data elements can be printed in a standard fashion, as in a report that uses data from a database.

These applications tend to be a little more permanent and unlike a 'one-off' mail shot where all the letters are printed in one 'run', it may be desirable to print out a selected set of standard documents at regular intervals, such as monthly or annually.

If you are storing data in a more permanent fashion then you may consider creating a database, or the data may already be available to you in an existing database. It is very easy to use Access and Word together in context of mail merging.

By the end of this unit you will be able to:

■ use selected data sets for mail merge

■ use data stored in an Access database for mail merging.

Basic mail merging

Two documents are required for a mail merge.

■ The *standard document*. This contains the standard text plus areas which are marked as 'replaceable', i.e. personal information can be slotted into them.

■ The *data document*. This is a document containing the personal information which is to be slotted into the standard letter. Each person's information is in a separate paragraph. The source of this data may be an Access database.

Task 1: Mail merging

In this task a standard letter will be created based on the template **Value and Saleability** (created in Unit 1).

1   Use File-New to open a new document based on the template **Value and Saleability**. Don't fill it in but save it as **Saleability Merge**. Edit the third paragraph in the letter to read:

We regard valuation as lying reasonably in the region of and would suggest an initial asking price of subject to contract as a test of market reaction.

2   Save the document and choose Tools-Mail Merge and the Mail Merge dialog
     box appears.

3   Click on the Create button. Choose Form Letters and click on the
     Active Window button. The next step is to specify the data source or to
     create the data source. The active window, Saleability Merge, becomes the basis
     for the form letters.

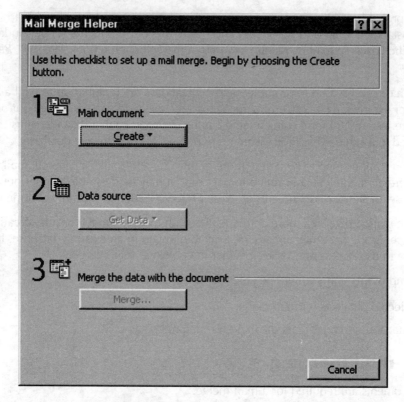

4   Click on the Get Data button. Choose Create Data Source and the Create
     Data Source dialog box is displayed. In this box you define the names of your
     replaceable fields.

5   Click on FirstName (in the Field Name in Header Row box) and click on the
     Remove Field Name button. Repeat for all fields except **Title**, **LastName**,
     Company and **PostalCode**.

6   Type Street into the Field Name box and click on Add Field Name . Repeat for
     Town and again for County, Initials, Property, Ref, Valprice and Startprice. Use the
     'Move' arrow buttons to reorder the field headers so that they are in the order
     Ref, Title, Initials, LastName, Street, Town, County, PostalCode, Property, Valprice
     and Startprice.

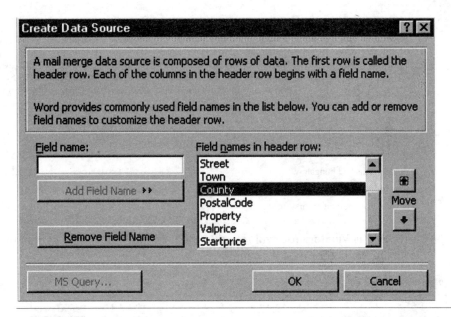

7   Click on **OK**. Save your data source as **Vendor**.

8   Choose **Edit Data Source** and a form for entering data records will be displayed.

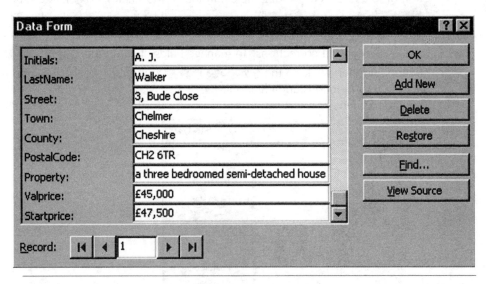

9   Enter the following records.

Use the *Tab* key to move from one box to the next. After each record is entered click on the **Add New** button until the last one is complete and then click on **OK**.

Ref	Title	Initials	LastName	Street	Town	County	PostalCode
136/SJC/01	Mr	A. J.	Walker	3 Bude Close	Chelmer	Cheshire	CH2 6TR
461/JER/02	Miss	D.	Cartwright	2 Woodford Road	Meriton	Cheshire	CH9 3DR
297/SJC/01	Mr	D. J.	Harris	15 Pownall Lane	Chelmer	Cheshire	CH3 3CJ
88/HJ/03	Mr	P. W.	Robinson	4 The Crescent	Branford	Staffordshire	ST10 4RT
205/SJC/01	Mrs	F.	Swift	Flat 1, Gracelands	Chelmer	Cheshire	CH2 5AQ

Property	Valprice	Startprice
a three bedroomed semi-detached house.	£45,000	£47,500
a two bedroomed mid-terraced house.	£33,000	£34,950
a modern detached bungalow.	£80,000	£82,500
a four bedroomed detached house.	£300,000	£310,000
a modern one-bedroomed first floor flat.	£38,000	£40,000

10 Save this as **Vendor**. You will return to the letter document. Notice that there is an extra toolbar for mail merging.

11 If you wish to edit your data file click on the **Mail Merge Helper** button otherwise carry on to the next step. To edit data, either to add or correct information or to add or remove data fields, in the Helper dialog box click on the **Edit** button of the Data Source section. Select the name of the data file (in this case it is **Vendor**). To edit the data records simply move through them and make the required corrections. To manage fields click on the **View Source** button and then click on the **Manage Fields** button. Make the required field additions or deletions and click on Mail Merge Main Document to return to the main document.

12 Position the insertion point after the words Our Ref:. Click on the **Insert Merge Field** button to display a drop-down list of the fields in the data file and click on Ref. Under this insert a date field (tick Update Automatically in the Date and Time dialog box).

13 Below the date add the name and address, click on the **Insert Merge Field** button and highlight **Title**. Build up the address and greeting as shown below (don't forget to type spaces between <<Title>> and <<Initials>> etc.).

<<Title>> <<Initials>> <<LastName>>

<<Street>>

<<Town>>

<<County>>

<<PostalCode>>

Dear <<Title>> <<LastName>>

Re: <<Street>>, <<Town>>

14 Add the replaceable fields to the body of the letter as shown:

We found the property to comprise <<Property>>.

We regard valuation as lying reasonably in the region of <<Valprice>> and would suggest an initial asking price of <<Startprice>>, subject to contract as a test of market reaction.

15 Save these additions to the document **Saleability Merge**.

16 Click on the **View Merged Data** button to see how the merged document will look.

17 You may wish to click on the **tick** button in the merge tool bar to check the data file. The most common error is where the number of fields in a record does not correspond with the number of fields that have been specified. Choose the Simulate the merge and report errors in a new document option.

18 Click on the **Merge to Printer** button in the Mail Merge tool bar to print the merged letters. One letter will be produced for each record of data.

19 If you wish to merge the letters to a file rather than printing them, this can be done by clicking on the **Merge to new Document** button on the mail merge tool bar. Each letter in the new document will be separated from the next by a section break. Don't forget to save this new document if you wish to keep the merge for later printing.

Sorting and selecting records for merging

Word allows you to sort your data records in an order you choose. You can also filter out selected data records so that only these are used in the merge. To do this click on the **Mail Merge** button 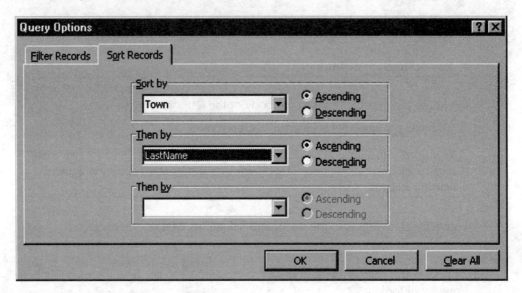 in the tool bar.

This will display the Merge dialog box and if you click on the **Query Options** button you can sort and filter records.

Task 2: Filtering

1   With the document **Saleability Merge** open, click on the **Mail Merge** button and use the **Query Options** to filter out the records of properties in Chelmer. Set the **Filter records** criterion as shown below and click on **OK** .

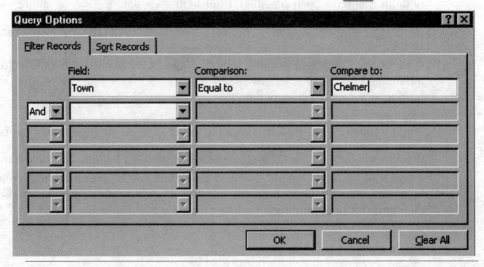

2 Click on the ▐ **View Merged Data** ▌ button to see how the merged document will look. To move through the records use the ▐ **Record navigator** ▌ buttons.

3 Try to merge either to the printer or to a document. Note that the filter will remain in force and is saved with the document, so if a different set of records is required for the next merge then the filter will need to be edited first.

Printing envelopes and labels

As well as producing merged letters, Word provides a facility to print envelopes or labels by merging an address list. These two facilities will be explored in the following tasks.

Task 3: Printing envelopes

1 With the standard letter created in the last task still open, choose Tools-Mail Merge.

2 Click on the ▐ **Create** ▌ button and choose Envelopes. Next choose ▐ **New Main Document** ▌ .

3 Click on the ▐ **Get Data** ▌ button. Next click on Open Data Source, and select the directory (folder) of the file **Vendor**. Highlight **Vendor** and click on ▐ **Open** ▌ after highlighting this file. Next click on Set Up Main Document.

4 On the ▐ **Envelopes Options** ▌ tab, select the envelope size you want, and adjust the address format and position on the envelope. On the ▐ **Printing Options** ▌ tab, make sure that the selected envelope feed options are correct for your printer, and then click ▐ **OK** ▌ .

5 In the Envelope Address dialog box, insert the merge fields for the address information as shown below.

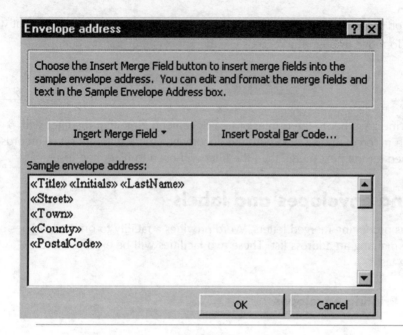

6 Click on **OK** and you will be returned to the Mail Merge Helper dialog box. Click on the **Merge** button.

7 In the Merge To box, chose New Document or Printer. If you choose Printer the envelopes will be printed straight away; choosing New Document will allow for later printing. Click on **Merge** .

 Note that as for document merges, it is possible to print envelopes for selected addressees only by clicking Query Options, and then specifying criteria for selecting the data records. These options are set separately from the main merge.

Task 4: Printing labels

The steps to printing labels are essentially the same as those for printing envelopes. In the second step choose Mailing labels and in step 4, select the type of labels you require.

Mail merging from Access

If you have Access as part of your Office Suite then it makes sense to keep the data records in an Access database. A mail merge can be performed in Access in conjunction with Word. In Word a standard letter can be produced and Access can provide the data (usually names and addresses) to be merged with the standard letter.

Task 5: Mail merging

For this task you will need Access as well as Word. The same data will be used as for the Word mail merge. First a database needs to be created and to save typing the data file **Vendors.doc** will be exported to a new Access database.

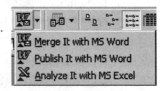

1   Create a new database in Access called **House Sales**. Create a new table **Vendor** as shown below and enter the data from Task 1 into this new table. Use the **Ref** as the Primary key. To set the Primary key, position the cursor in the Ref field row and click on the **Primary key** button in the toolbar.

⊞ Vendor : Table		_ □ ✕
Field Name	**Data Type**	**Description**
🔑 Ref	Text	Size 20
Title	Text	Size 10
Initials	Text	Size 10
Lastname	Text	Size 50
Street	Text	Size 50
Town	Text	Size 30
County	Text	Size 20
Postcode	Text	Size 15
Property	Text	Size 50
Valprice	Currency	
Startprice	Currency	

2   Close the table. In the Database window, highlight the **Vendor** table and open the Office Links drop down list (on the toolbar) and select Merge It with MS Word.

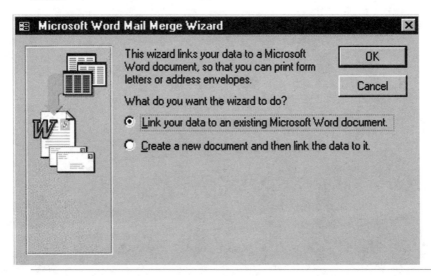

3   Choose the option to **Link your data to an existing Microsoft Word document** and click on OK . Select the document **Saleability Merge** and Word will be loaded in mail merge mode with this document open.

4   It is best to check the merge for errors first: do this by clicking on the View Merged Data button. You can then print the merged document.

 To merge selected records, create a query in Access to retrieve the required records and, with the query highlighted in the database window, use the same procedure as for the table.

Producing HTML documents

What you will learn in this unit

This unit is the first of several that will introduce you to the process of creating documents, known as HyperText Markup Language (HTML) documents, for publication on the World Wide Web. Such documents may be used in both Internet and Intranet (within one organisation) applications.

Producing Web or HTML documents using Word's Web authoring tools is very much like producing a normal document. An HTML document does not support the range of word processing features that normal documents do, as the aim is to keep them simple for transmission over the Internet.

This unit concentrates on basic document production and posting a document on to a World Wide Web (WWW) server. By the end of this unit you should be able to

■ create a basic HTML document

■ convert an existing Word document to an HTML document

■ create a suitable directory structure for storage of HTML documents.

Web authoring tools are available with Word. If they are not available then install them from the Office CD. The Web authoring tools allow you to create HTML documents without having to learn HTML itself. HTML is a set of codes that are embedded in a plain text file, in order to tell an Internet browser how to display them on screen. A browser is a software application that retrieves and displays files on the Internet; familiarity with browser software is assumed in this and the units that follow.

Many HTML codes are concerned with the formatting of text. By selecting styles provided by the Web authoring tools these codes are automatically embedded in the document. In this unit we will concern ourselves with the production of small one page (or one screen) documents. In the next unit the concept of pages and their use in a WWW publishing context will be considered.

The Web Wizard

The quickest way to create a web page is to make use of the Web Wizard. However, in most applications it will be necessary to design unique Web pages, either by designing a page from the beginning or by formatting a Web page that has been created through the use of the Web Wizard. In order to demonstrate more fully the formatting of Web pages, the next few sections create a Web page without the support of the Wizard. We recommend that you return to the use of the Wizard after you have completed the tasks in this and the following units.

To use the Wizard choose File-New, select the Web Pages tab and double click on the Web Page Wizard. This will open a new HTML document and display a list of Web Page Layouts for you to choose from as illustrated below. Once you have chosen the type of layout, you can then choose a style, which will set fonts and background. You can then edit the document by replacing the example text with your own.

Task 1: Creating and saving a new HTML document using the Web Wizard

1 Choose File-New, select the Web Pages tab and double click on the Web Page Wizard.

2 Select Simple Layout and click on Next. Choose a visual style such as Jazzy and click on Finish.

3 Replace the text with the text illustrated and save as **Selling your home**. Note that the links are not active and will need to be defined. Setting up links is described in the following unit.

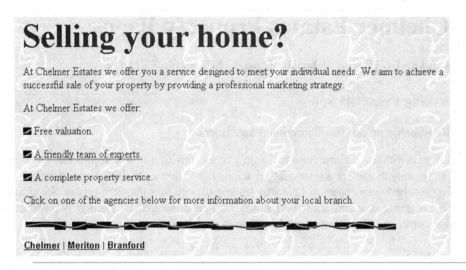

4 Type the name of the document **Selling Your Home** and click on Save .

Creating a new HTML document

To create a new HTML document you choose File-New and choose a Blank Web Page template from the Web pages tab. When you choose Blank Web Page a new document will open that has an HTML formatting toolbar.

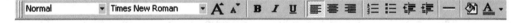

Some buttons are the same as those in the Word document formatting toolbar but others are new such as the Horizontal Line button. There is no longer a Font and Size drop-down list box, only a Style list box. If you open the Style list box you will see many pre-defined styles and we will start our document creation with an investigation of some of these.

Task 2: Creating and saving a new HTML document

This task introduces you to the styles, Normal and Heading. Although Word offers the usual heading styles, Heading 1 etc, many browsers use standard normal and heading styles which are defined as Normal, H1, H2, H3, H4, H5 and H6. In this task the styles H1, H2, H3 and H4 will be used. You can use the styles Heading 1 etc. in the document but the resulting display of these in various browsers may differ from browser to browser.

You may create a new HTML document, as illustrated on the opposite page, as follows.

1 Choose File-New Web Pages and select Blank Web Page and click on OK .

Chelmer Estates Property Pages

8 Maple Mews, Maple Road, Meriton, Staffs

Asking Price £45,950

Reasonably priced two bedroomed apartment

Located within a purpose built two-storey block, this first floor flat provides an ideal opportunity to acquire a reasonably spacious flat within a competitive price range. Approached via a communal hallway leading to only four flats, the private accommodation is arranged around a central hallway with generous lounge, kitchen, two bedrooms and bathroom. **Gas fired central heating is installed**.

Location

From our Meriton office proceed along Chelmer Road turning right into Hornchurch Road. Continue along Hornchurch Road to the traffic lights, turn left into Blacksmith Lane and Maple Road is the third turning on the right. The property can be found on the right hand side.

Viewing by appointment only.

---

2 Open the style box and select H1 (the standard HTML heading 1). Type in **Chelmer Estates Property Pages**.

---

3 On the next line select the style H2 and type in the property address as illustrated. Use style H3 for the asking price and H4 for the next heading. Use the Normal style for the three paragraphs and H4 for the other heading. Make text bold in the same way as for Word documents.

---

4 Choose File Save notice that HTML Document (*.htm) should be in the Save As Type list box. (If necessary open the list box and select the file type .htm).

---

5 Type the name of the document, **8 Maple Mews**, and click on Save .

The codes given for the style name are the codes that are embedded in the document to tell the browser to display the text in a particular style. If you wish to see the codes then you can view the source code using View-HTML Source. (Save the document before you do this and use View-Exit HTML Source to return to the document.) However, if you wish to decipher them then you will need to refer to a book on HTML authoring. It is not necessary to learn these codes or 'tags' as the Web authoring tools can create the effects you desire and more quickly.

Opening an existing HTML document

Closing and opening existing HTML documents is accomplished in exactly the same way as for Word documents. If you are not currently using the Web authoring tools you can open an HTML document using **File-Open** and selecting HTML Document (*.htm) from the **Files of type** list box. Select the file and click on **Open** and the document will open with the HTML formatting toolbar instead of the Word document formatting toolbar.

You may work with Word documents and HTML documents open at the same time and use the **Window** menu to switch between them; the appropriate formatting toolbar will be displayed for the active document.

Previewing a document using your browser

On the standard toolbar there is a **Web Page Preview** button that allows you to view your document with Internet Explorer, the Microsoft browser. If the browser is not running then clicking on this button will start the browser and display your document. If you have not saved your document you will be prompted to do so before the document is displayed by the browser. It is useful to preview your document from time to time as you might try to apply formatting which is ignored by the browser. As the level of sophistication of browsers increases then the formatting that they can display will probably also become more sophisticated. However, it is worth remembering that your target audience may be using a variety of browsers.

Text formatting and rules

As for Word documents, bold, italic and underlining may be applied to HTML documents. To change the font size click on either the **Increase Font Size** or the **Decrease Font Size** button (on the HTML formatting toolbar) to alter the size of selected text. Text alignment, either left or centre can be set using the alignment buttons.

To change the font (typeface), colour and size of any selected text then use the **Format-Font** command to display the **Font** dialog box. Use the drop-down list boxes to select the combination of formatting you desire and click on **OK**.

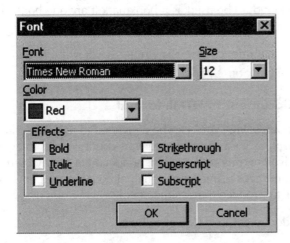

Preformatted text

You may have noticed that your browser ignores extra spaces in the Normal and Heading styles. Many browsers also ignore tabs. Sometimes you may wish to set text out in a particular way so that it aligns neatly. To do this you can use preformatted text. Any text which has the Preformatted style applied to it will be displayed in Courier non-proportionally spaced font exactly as it has been typed. Since Courier is a non-proportionally spaced font, spaces may be used to 'line-up' text (a Web page is not a true word-processed document). The preformatted text looks very much like the Typewriter style but, please note, browsers ignore tabs and spaces in this style.

Horizontal line

This is a neat way of dividing your Web page up. A standard horizontal line ▬ or 'rule' can be added by clicking on the `Horizontal Line` button. Formatting in terms of borders and shading is not available although it is possible to create tables, which will be considered in a later unit.

Task 3: Formatting and Fonts

1 Open the document **8 Maple Mews** created in the last task. Position the insertion point at the end of the first heading and click on the `Horizontal Line` button. This should add a horizontal rule under this heading.

2 Select the **Price** heading and change font to Arial. Click in the main heading and centre it by clicking on the `Center` button on the formatting toolbar. Save and preview in browser.

Giving your document a title

Every HTML document (page) that you create should have a title. If you do not specify one, Word will use the file name. The title is the text that appears on the title bar of the browser window and would be used as a bookmark if anyone book-marked your page when it is published on the Web.

If you wish to alter your document title, choose File-Properties, key the title into the Title box in the dialog box and click on `OK`.

Converting an existing document to HTML format

Any document that you can open using Word can be converted to an HTML document. The Internet Assistant will, as far as possible, convert existing styles in your document to their HTML equivalent. Before converting a document it may be useful to review the styles used in it, perhaps using AutoFormat, although once converted you can easily re-assign styles to produce the desired effect.

You may convert an existing document to HTML as follows.

1 Choose File-Open. Select the drive and directory where the document is stored. Select the file, and click on `Open`.

2   Choose File-Save As HTML.

3   Choose the folder and either accept Word's choice of file name or type the name of your file and then click on **Save** .

(!)   Not all Word elements are preserved when a document is converted to HTML.

Task 4: Converting to HTML

In this task the document **Budgeting Advice** (as used in Unit 4) will be converted into an HTML document.

1   Open the file Budgeting Advice (Unit 4 version) and use File-Save As HTML. The file is now named **Budgeting Advice.htm** and the title is **Budgeting Advice**.

2   Go through the document and apply some heading styles (H1, H2 and H3 should be enough) and add some horizontal rules. Note that if the original document uses borders these will be converted to horizontal rules. Save and preview in browser.

3   Move 'CHELMER ESTATES' to the top of the page and centre align it.

4   Review the document and make any further changes you require, for example colour and font. You should discover that the border has been converted into a horizontal rule. Save and preview it using your browser. Note that if the document is already open in your browser you can use the browser's **Refresh** button to update to your current saved version.

Storing HTML documents

It is unlikely that you will store your entire Web publication in one htm file. In particular, if you wish to use graphics or other multi-media objects then these will be stored as separate files. It is easiest, particularly if you are new to Web publishing, to store all the files together in the same directory. In Unit 23 you will see how to create links between the files. If you keep files together in the same directory, when you move them onto your service provider's Web server, the links between them will work as they did on your local directory.

Publishing a document on the WWW

When you have completed your pages and tested them they will need to be uploaded to your service provider's computer. It is likely that you will be allocated one directory on that computer. You will need software for transferring files and this is available on the Web. The actual software you use may depend on your service provider but it is generally straightforward to use. The details of the operation and use of such software is beyond the scope of this book.

Viewing the HTML source

It is perfectly possible to create acceptable HTML documents using the Web authoring tools, but if you want to embellish the document then you can do so by editing the HTML source directly. In order to do this you will need to know more about markup tags, definitions of which are given in Appendix 4. Any significant discussion of mark-up tags is beyond the scope of this book; refer to your Office manual.

Creating linked HTML pages

What you will learn in this unit

A document, published on paper, is usually read sequentially. Readers may often skip sections, however, or refer back to previous sections in the document that they are reading. Each Web document (page) is a file that is in electronic format, so, to give the viewer the ability to view your publication non-sequentially, you must provide links within and between pages.

If your page is large, you will want to provide the viewer with the ability to 'jump' to different headings within the page. Your viewer will also find it useful if you provide links back to the top of your document, so that they can 'jump' to another heading.

By the end of this unit you should be able to

■ create links within a document

■ create links to local files within your directory

■ create links to other files on the WWW.

Understanding links

A link is composed of two elements.

1   A *destination* which may be a place:

   ■ within the same document

   ■ a local file (commonly image files which are considered in the next unit)

   ■ or a file somewhere else on the WWW.

2   A *tag* giving the name of the place to link to, which when activated invokes a 'jumping' action to that place. This is inserted into your document using the Insert-Hyperlink command. The link will appear as 'hot' text (graphics can also be used) which when clicked on will activate the 'jump'. 'Hot' text is usually a different colour from the normal text to identify it as a link. In addition, the mouse pointer will change shape to a pointing finger when positioned over link text or graphics. If, when a link has been visited, your viewer returns to the previously displayed page, the linking text may be displayed in a different colour indicating that the link has been visited.

Creating links within the same document

First you must provide destinations in your document to which your links provide 'jumps'. This is done by creating an 'anchor' in the text using a bookmark. You may create several bookmarks within the document, usually at the beginning, the end and at each heading. When you add an anchor bookmark to an HTML document an anchor name tag is inserted into the source in the form:

<A NAME = "Contents"> Contents </A>

where <A NAME> is the anchor name tag, **"Contents"** is the bookmark name and the one you will specify in your linking tag, and **Contents** is the text in the document to which the bookmark is attached.

Add a bookmark to your document as follows.

1   Position your insertion point at the beginning of the text (such as a heading) that you want to bookmark. Choose Insert-Bookmark and key in a name for your bookmark. Choose one that you will recognise when you later create links to it from other places in your document.

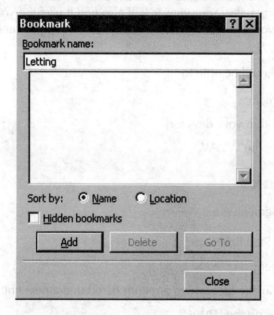

2   Click on   **Add** . Repeat this process to add all the anchor bookmarks required in your document. Save your document and, if you wish, inspect the source to note the use of the tags.

Through the use of the Insert-Bookmark command bookmarks may be deleted or renamed as described in Unit 8. As a document is revised you may wish to move a bookmark by deleting and re-creating it elsewhere. If you delete a bookmark altogether, or rename one, check that you also remove or edit link tags that refer to that bookmark.

The second stage is to add links to the document. When you add a link to an HTML document a **H**ypertext **ref**erence tag is inserted into the source which, for a bookmark, is of the form:

<A HREF="#Letting" >Letting</A>

where **"#Letting"** is the anchor bookmark name and **Letting** is the link text that appears in the document.

Create links to bookmarks as follows.

1 Select the text that is to form the hyperlink. Choose Insert-Hyperlink.

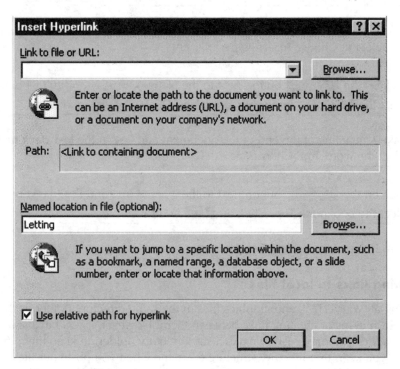

2 Click on the **Browse** button next to the Named location in file text box and select the bookmark you wish the link to refer to (and jump to if activated). Click on **OK** . The link text will appear underlined in a different colour (the default is blue) in your document.

3 Repeat this procedure to add all the links to the document and then save the document.

4 You may test your links by switching to Web Browse View (click on the **Web Page Preview** button) and clicking on the links.

Task 1: Creating links within a document

In this task internal links will be created in the HTML document **Budgeting advice.htm** created in the last unit.

1 Open **Budgeting advice.htm**

2 Position your insertion point at the beginning of IMPORTANT QUESTIONS. Choose Insert-Bookmark, key in the name *Important_questions* for the book

mark. Note that, as you cannot use a space in a bookmark name, an underscore makes a good substitute. Click on **Add** .

3 Position your insertion point at the very beginning of the document. Choose Insert-Bookmark, key in Top for the bookmark, and click on **Add** . Save.

4 Make a new line below the main heading and key in the ***Important Questions*** and select it. Choose Insert-Hyperlink.

5 Click on the **Browse** button next to the Named location in file text box and select the bookmark ***Important_questions***. Click on **OK** and save.

6 Make a new line at the end of the document and key in the text ***Back to Top***. Select the word **Top**. Choose Insert-Hyperlink.

7 Click on the **Browse** button next to the Named location in file text box and select the bookmark **Top**. Click on **OK** and save.

8 In Web Page Preview test out your links.

Creating links to local files

Keeping all your HTML and graphics files in the same directory (folder) is the simplest in terms of creating links between them. However, if you have several graphics files you may wish to make a sub-directory (folder) to keep them in. As long as you keep the directory structure the same when you post your files on the Web you should not have any problems. If you view the HTML source code you will see that links to local files are achieved by tags of the form:

<A HREF="Guide.htm">Guidelines for publishing Web document</A>

for a file in the same directory (folder), and

<A HREF="Web/Guide.htm">Guidelines for publishing Web document</A>

for a file in a sub-directory (folder) called Web. Note that directory (folder) separators are forward slashes.

The procedure for inserting a hyperlink to a local file is practically the same as that for a link within a document.

1 Select the text that is to form the hyperlink. Choose Insert-Hyperlink.

2 Click on the **Browse** button in the Link to file or URL section and select the directory (folder) in which the file is stored and select the file you wish the link to refer to (and open if activated). Click on **Open** . Click on **OK** . This will create a relative link.

3 Repeat this procedure to add to the document all links to local files and then save the document.

4 You may test your links by switching to Web Browse View (click on the [Web Page Preview] button) and clicking on a link which will open the local file. Alternatively you can test them out using your browser.

 You can use this procedure to add links to normal word documents so that you can work with them in the same way as you would read HTML documents.

Task 2: Creating links with local documents

1 Create a home page for Chelmer Estates that looks similar to the example below, using this opportunity to practise the formatting techniques introduced in the last unit. Save as **homepage.htm**.

Chelmer Estates

Welcome to Chelmer Estates, with offices in Chelmer, Meriton, Branford and a new one opening soon in Oxley, we cover Cheshire, Staffordshire and Derbyshire. We are a long established (1965) firm and pride ourselves in our friendly efficient service. Don't delay in finding your new home, register with us now!

Property Pages

Budgeting Advice

A Guide to Selling your Home

A Guide to Letting your Home

Planning a Successful Move

Register on our Mailing list

---

2 Select the **Letting** heading and choose Insert-Hyperlink.

 3 Click on the [Browse] button next to Link to file or URL and select the directory (folder) in which you saved the file **Budgeting advice.htm** (created in the last unit), then click on this file and then click on [Open]. Note that it is best to keep all related files in the same directory (folder). Click on [OK] and the link will be created. Save and test the link.

4 Now create a link in the **Budgeting advice** file which will return the viewer to the home page. Save this file and test this link.

Creating links to files on the WWW

You may wish to include links in your page to other sites on the WWW. To do this you will need to enter the URL (Uniform Resource Locator) in the File or URL text box of the Hyperlink dialog box.

These are files over which you have no control so, before you create hyperlinks, it's a good idea, if possible, to check with the authors of the pages to which you are linking. They might have good reasons for you not to link to their pages: they may, for example, be planning to move or delete the page.

Even if you don't let the author of a page know that you are linking to his or her site, you should check all the links on your pages periodically. The Web is constantly in flux, and readers commonly experience the frustration of following links that lead to dead ends because the files have moved or been deleted. It is good Web publishing practice to try to save your viewers this frustration.

Before you begin this procedure, it is good practice to save the file in which you are creating the hyperlink. As for other links, this is done as follows.

1   Select the text which is to form the hyperlink. Choose Insert-HyperLink.

2   In the Link to file or URL box, type the URL of the file you have chosen as the destination of your hyperlink. This should be absolutely correct, including upper and lower case and punctuation. Alternatively use the Browse button to search for the page you wish to link to. Click on OK.

3   Repeat this procedure to add all links to WWW files to the document and save the document. Test out the links and do not forget to check regularly that they still work.

Task 3: Creating links with WWW documents

Browse the WWW to find several sites that interest you, preferably on the same theme. Switch to Word and create a simple HTML document into which links to these sites can be added. Select the text you wish to make a hyperlink and choose Insert-HyperLink. Using the Browse button of the Link to file or URL box, locate the page that interests you and click on OK. Save this document as **My interests** and test it.

Design elements in HTLM documents

What you will learn in this unit

Despite the fairly basic text handling capabilities associated with HTML documents, they do cater for the use of lists, tables and graphics. Using these features, and particularly with good use of colour, the very attractive documents that are seen on many Web sites can be produced. If you are inexperienced at document design the best way to start is to look at other peoples' documents and model your designs on the ones that you find attractive. Do not be too ambitious initially; start with some relatively simple designs and build on these.

By introducing lists, tables, graphics and multimedia this unit aims to give you a basis from which you can begin to experiment with design features. The Web Wizard allows you to choose and then customise various layouts, but if you want a little more understanding of design features, this unit introduces, in particular, the use of

■ lists

■ tables

■ images, and

■ multi-media.

Lists

There are three types of list that you may want to include in an HTML document. These are: bulleted lists, numbered (or lettered) lists and lists of terms and definitions. It is straightforward to create a bulleted or numbered list, using the buttons on the toolbar as you would for a normal word document and switching off the numbering (or bulleting) when finished. Alternatively, you can key in the text for the list, select it and use the Format-Bullets and Numbering command.

If you want to use Roman numerals or letters for a 'numbered' list you can select these through the **Numbered** tab of the Bullets and Numbering dialog box. Bullets may be changed in similar way, but if you choose a graphic for a bullet then note that the source code for the list is different from that for a standard bulleted list.

The underlying source code for a numbered or standard bulleted list is of the form shown in the following table.

Standard Bulleted List	Numbered List
<UL>	<OL>
<LI>First item	<LI>First item
<LI>Second item	<LI>Second item
<LI>Third item, etc.	<LI>Third item, etc.
</UL>	</OL>

Variations to first line of list (HTML source)

<UL TYPE=SQUARE>	*square bullets*	<OL TYPE=A>	*capital letters*
<UL TYPE=DISC>	*round bullets*	<OL TYPE=a>	*lower case letters*
<UL TYPE=CIRCLE>	*circle bullets*	<OL TYPE=I>	*Roman capitals*
		<OL TYPE=i>	*Roman numerals*

Task 1: Numbered list

The document used in this task would probably not be posted to an Internet site but would more likely be used in an Intranet situation. An Intranet works like the Internet but restricts access to selected users, for example, within an organisation, and allows organisational documents to be accessible using a browser.

1 Start a new blank Web page and key in the heading as illustrated below. Use Heading 2 style for the heading and use a horizontal rule to separate the heading from the list.

Code of Practice

---

1. General
2. Instructions
3. For sale boards
4. Published material
5. Offers
6. Access to Premises
7. Clients' Money
8. Conflict of Interest
9. Financial Services
10. Interpretation and Definitions

---

2 Click on the **Numbering** button in the toolbar and key in the bullet points. Save the document as **Code of Practice**. View using Web Page Preview.

3 You may wish to experiment with different types of numbering by reformatting the list using **Format-Bullets and Numbering**.

4 If you wish, investigate the underlying source code.

Nested lists

Lists can be 'nested', one inside the other, to give several levels of indents (or a multi-level list). When you are nesting lists, you can use bullets for one level and numbers for another. A bulleted outer list and a numbered inner list make an effective combination. Changes in emphasis, using bold, italic and font size, can be used to control the level of prominence of list items. You may create a nested list as follows.

1 Type the entries in your list.

2 Select the list and use **Format-Bullets and Numbering**. It doesn't matter that at this stage all the list items are at the same level.

3 Select the entries you want to nest within the larger list, and then click on the **Increase Indent** button on the toolbar. While these entries are selected you can apply the type of bullet or number you require.

Task 2 A nested list

In this task we shall import the text of the document **Code of Practice** into our HTML document created in the last task. There are various lists and multi-level lists in this document.

1   Open both the HTML and Word versions of **Code of Practice**. Using the Window menu view the HTML version and add a horizontal rule at the end of the numbered list.

2   Switch to the Word document and copy the text and heading of 'General'. Move back to the HTML document and paste. Select the list text just pasted and click on the Numbering button to remove numbering and then click on it to re-create it. Using Format-Bullets and Numbering, apply a lowercase letter numbering. Save the HTML document.

3   To experiment with multi-level lists select the section on **Offers up to and including point d)**. Copy and paste into the HTML version. Select the list text and remove the numbering. Reapply letter numbering as before. Select the part of the text that should be the next level of bulleting, click on the Bullets button and the Increase Indent button.

4   When viewed by the browser, you may find that after the second level of bulleting the lettering returns to 'a'. This can be put right directly in the HTML source but after you have done this do not use Word to edit the file. The cure is to remove the </OL> tag before the <UL> list and the <OL Type="a"> tag after it. It is better to use multi-level lists that have numbers within bullets unless you wish to edit the source code directly.

5   To revisit the work on links in the last unit, bookmark the two headings and create links to these from the numbered list at the top of the page. Save, preview, test and close the file.

Tables

A table is a compact and readable way of displaying items of information. A table can be used to display text, links, graphics or any other items that can be incorporated into a Web page. Tables can be enhanced with borders, colours and graphics to give more visual impact to the page. Create a simple table for text as follows:

1   Choose Table-Insert Table. This is equivalent to inserting <TABLE> and </TABLE> tags in your document.

2   Drag across the grid to select the number of rows and columns you need.

3   Type text in the rows and columns of your table. If you want to change the width of your columns, drag column borders with the mouse.

4 Format your table using commands from the Table menu. There are the following options.

a) **Table Properties**, to determine how other text on the page wraps around your table; distance of surrounding text from the table; background colour of the table; and space between columns.

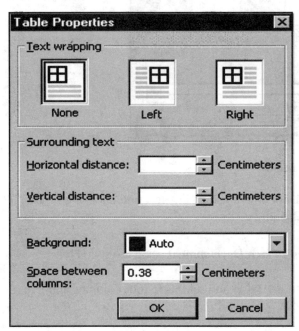

b) **Cell Properties**, to define the alignment of text within the selected cell(s); to precisely specify cell width and height; and to specify the background colour of the cell(s).

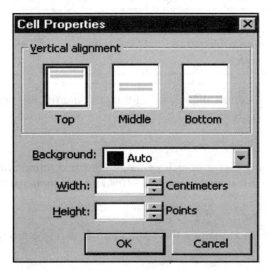

c) **Borders**, to add a border to the table.

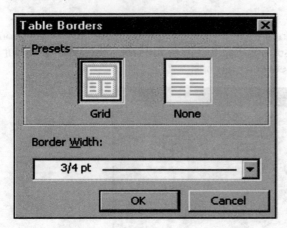

Task 3 Creating a table

1 Open a new HTML document using **File-New** and choosing **Blank Web** page
   from the **Web Pages** tab.

2 Add the title ***Bishop's Place Development*** using the style H1.

3 Add a table using **Insert-Table** and set this to four columns and five rows. Add
   the text shown below.

Plot No	House Type and Accommodation	Completion Date	Sales Price
3	5 bed detached with double garage	February 98	£322,500
4	5 bed detached with double garage	February 98	£327,500
5	5 bed detached with double garage	March 98	£325,000
6	5 bed detached with triple garage with games room over	March 98	£355,950

4 Select the first column and centre align it, select the last column and right align
   it. Click in the first cell and choose **Table-Cell properties** and choose **Middle** for
   the vertical alignment.

5 Select the top row and using **Cell properties** change the background colour of
   these cells. With this row still selected use **Table-Borders** and increase the width
   of the borders.

6 If you wish, experiment with formatting this table in other ways before saving as
   Bishop's Place.

 If you save a Word document containing a table as an HTML document, the table
will be preserved in the HTML document.

Linking and positioning an image

A graphic that will be displayed in your document when it is loaded into a browser can be added to your HTML document using Insert-Picture. This kind of graphic is called an 'inline graphic', or 'image', and uses the <IMG> tag in the source. You should use these types of graphics judiciously, for two reasons.

1   Inline graphics will not automatically be displayed by every browser. Some browsers are unable to display graphics at all, and most browsers allow users to choose not to download graphics in order to increase browsing speed. Therefore, your page should be understandable even if users can't see the graphics. You should always include alternative text (the ALT attribute) to display in place of these graphics.

2   The fewer inline graphics you include, the quicker your file can be downloaded and browsed through. It is good Web publishing practice not to slow down your users with extremely large (or a large number of) inline graphics. You can speed up your file by reducing the number of colours in your graphics, and also by including HEIGHT and WIDTH attributes.

Inline graphics are commonly used as decorative elements to make a Web page more attractive, for example to create 'fancy' bullet characters. Another common use is to provide a graphical 'hot spot' that the user clicks in order to activate a hyperlink.

There are two graphics file formats that are used by browsers: GIF files (their extension is .gif) and JPG files (their extension is .jpg usually pronounced jay-peg). The GIF file format is typically used for inline graphics. If you convert an existing Word document that has an inline graphic in it, to HTML form, the graphic will be converted to a GIF file and will be linked to the document automatically. When you use Insert-Picture, if you choose a graphic that is not in this format then it will be converted and the converted graphic file will be stored in the same directory (folder) as the htm file.

You may insert a graphic into your document as follows.

1   Choose Insert-Picture From File and the Insert-Picture dialog box appears (see opposite page).

2   Using the Look in box select the directory (folder) in which the graphics file is stored. Select the file from the Name box and click on **Insert** . Clipart can be inserted by choosing Insert-Picture Clipart.

You may convert an existing document containing an image to HTML format as follows.

1   Create the document you wish to convert using the Normal template. Add graphics or create your own using Insert-Object Microsoft Word picture. If you want to add WordArt then use Insert-Object Microsoft Word picture and then Insert-Picture WordArt to create the WordArt in the picture work space.

2   Choose File-Save As HTML.

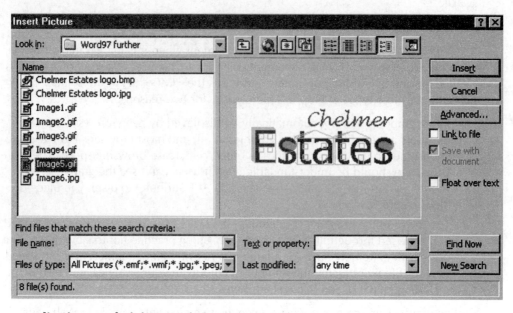

Aligning and sizing an image

An image on its own on a line may be centred or left aligned as for text. If the image and text are used on the same line then, by default, text is aligned with the bottom of the image. If text wrapping is desired then select the image and use Format-Picture. Under the **Position** tab, illustrated below, left or right text wrapping can be selected.

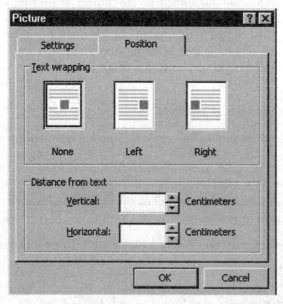

Usually, graphics are displayed at their natural size, but you can alter the size of a graphic by dragging the sizing handles. This will define, in pixels, the HEIGHT and WIDTH attributes in the source code <IMG> tag. These attributes are included in the <IMG> tag as shown in the following example:

<IMG SRC="IMAGE1.GIF" HEIGHT=90 WIDTH=90>

If the viewer of your page has a browser that cannot display your picture then an alternative text caption can be provided via the **Picture** dialog box (Format-Picture). Click on the **Settings** tab and type your caption into the Text: box in the Picture Placeholder section.

Task 4: Adding an image

1 Open the HTML document **Bishop's Place** and add some WordArt as follows.

2 Choose Insert-Object Microsoft Word picture, and use Insert-Picture WordArt to create some WordArt with formatting of your choice for the text 'Bishop's Place' in the picture work space.

3 Reset the boundary of the picture work space and click on Close Picture. Adjust the size of the WordArt to fit across the top of the page and save. This will convert the image into a graphics file that can be viewed by a browser.

Background images

A background to your Web page can be produced from a graphic that is repeated on the screen in a wallpapered or tiled effect. It may be a company logo and is usually created in faint pastel colours so that foreground text and graphics are not masked by it. Word offers a number of different textured backgrounds, which can be added as follows.

1 Choose Format-Background Fill Effects to open the Fill Effects dialog box from which a textured background can be chosen. If you just want a plain colour then select from the background palette after selecting Format-Background.

2 If you want to use your own graphic as textured wallpaper then click on the Other Texture button and select the file you require.

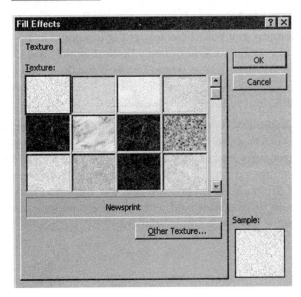

Text and links colours

You can also specify the colour in which text will be displayed, as well as the colour of visited (followed) and unvisited hyperlinks (TEXT, VLINK, and LINK attributes, respectively). To change these colours use Format-Text Colors.

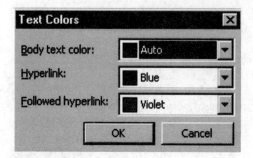

Fun with images for bullets

As you probably noticed when the bulleted list was considered earlier in this unit, Word offers a choice of small graphics for bullets. If one of these is chosen, an image tag <IMG> is added before the text of the point, and the list tags as described earlier are not used. If you have created your own images that you wish to use as bullet points then click on the **More** button under the **Bulleted** tab of the Bullets and Numbering dialog box, to display the File Open dialog box. To create space around graphic bullet points use Format-Picture and set Increase the horizontal distance to text.

Images and links

There is another way to include graphics in your HTML documents: through hyperlinks. Hyperlinked graphics don't show up when your document is downloaded. The user accesses them by activating a hyperlink. This is the preferred method for linking to graphics that are very large or important.

Images themselves can be used to invoke links just as the usual text links. Using this technique your page could contain a menu of fancy buttons, which you could create using WordArt, which when clicked would invoke a link to another page.

Task 5 Links to images

In our Estate Agency application we could make available pictures of properties on the Web pages. By using links to these pictures, viewers can elect whether or not to look at the picture, if the property interests them, and do not have to wait for pictures to download which they do not want to see. We shall investigate this effect by using an impression of the house to be built on Plot 5 at Bishop's Place below. Either scan this image or use the file **House.gif**, which you will be able to obtain on CD-Rom from your lecturer if you are a college student.

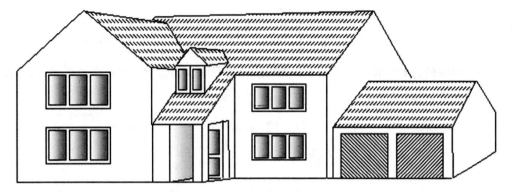

1 Move the file **House.gif** to the same directory (folder) as that in which you have the document **Bishop's Place.**

2 Open the HTML document **Bishop's Place** and select the text *5 bed detached with double garage* in the first row in the table.

3 Choose Insert-Hyperlink and click on the **Browse** button by the Link to file or URL box. In the Files of type box select Internet files and select the directory in which **House.gif** is stored, highlight this file, click on **OK** and click on **OK** again.

4 Test out this link. When clicked it will display the image on its own and the viewer can use the browser's **Back** button to return to the price list page.

Task 6 Images as links

In visiting Web sites, you will probably have noticed that pages often contain images that you can click on to link to another page. In this task we will create some WordArt saying 'Home page' that will be used as a link to the home page.

1 Open the HTML document **Bishop's Place** and move to the end of the document.

2 Choose Insert-Object Microsoft Word Picture and then choose Insert-Picture WordArt and choose a style for your WordArt.

3 Type in the text *Home Page* and choose a font and size for your WordArt. Choose a size of around 14pts as you don't want the link to be too big.

4 Set the picture boundary and close the picture. Save the document to save the WordArt as an image.

5 Select the picture and choose Insert-Hyperlink, browse for the file **homepage.htm**, created in the last unit and select it as the link. Save and test out the link.

Bishop's Place

Development	Bishop's Place, Eyebrook Road, Bowdon
Sales Negotiator	Ann Dilorenzo
Telephone No	0161-926-9392
Sales Office opening Hours	Open 7 days 10 a.m. – 5 p.m.

Plot No	House Type and Accommodation	Completion Date	Sales Price
3	5 bed detached with double garage	February 98	£322,500
4	5 bed detached with double garage	February 98	£327,500
5	5 bed detached with double garage	March 98	£325,000
6	5 bed detached with triple garage with games room over	March 98	£355,950

Sold

SHOW HOME: PLOT 2

RESERVATION DEPOSIT £300   TENURE: FREEHOLD

Completion Dates:	These are for guidance only, and our Sales Negotiator will keep you advised of any variations.
Sales Price:	These particulars are subject to contract and availability at the time of mailing. We would recommend you contact our Sales Office as soon as possible.

Sound and video

Sound

You can have a background sound play automatically when someone opens your Web page.

1   Choose Insert-Background Sound, and click Properties.

2   In the Sound box, enter the address, or URL, of the sound file you want, or click on **Browse** to locate the file.

3   In the Loop box, click the number of times you want the sound to repeat. If you want it to loop continually while the Web page is open, click Infinite.

 To review the sound while you are creating the Web page, choose Insert-Background Sound and select Play. To stop the sound, select Stop.

Remember that visitors to your Web site will only be able to hear background sounds if they must have a sound system installed and their Web browser supports the sound format of the file you inserted. Common sound files formats are WAV, MID, AU, AIF, RMI, SND and MP2 (MPEG audio).

As the background sound plays automatically every time your page is opened or returned to, your visitors could find it annoying. For the same reason you should exercise caution when selecting Infinite for a sound looping option. You might be better adding the background sound to one of your pages that is visited less often. As with large graphics, you could insert a hyperlink so that the user can click on a link to download a sound file.

Video

You can add an inline video to your Web page, which means the video will be downloaded when the user opens the page. You can determine whether the video will play when the page is opened or when the user points to the video with the mouse. Because not all Web browsers support inline video you may want to provide alternative text and images or avoid presenting essential information in videos.

1   Save your document and choose Insert-Video. In the Video box under Source, type the address or URL of the video file you want, or click on the **Browse** button to search for the file.

2   In the Alternate image box, type the address or URL of the graphics file that you want to designate as a substitute when the viewer's browser doesn't support videos or when the viewer turns off the display of videos.

3   In the Alternate text box, type the text that you want to appear in place of the video.

4   In the Start list, click an option to specify how the video will play on a Web page. Open causes the video to play when the user downloads the Web page; Mouse-over causes the video to play when the pointer moves over the video; Both causes the video to play in both scenarios.

5   In the Loop box, enter the number of times you want the video to repeat. If you want to display video controls, such as "Start" and "Stop", while you're authoring Web pages, tick the Display video controls check box.

Note that the video will play after you insert it. If you've selected the Mouse-over option for video playback, the video will also play in your Web page document when your mouse moves over it.

 Video files can be very large and take a long time to download. It is advisable to insert a hyperlink to a video, so that the viewer can click the hyperlink to download the video and play it.

Forms and feedback in HTML documents

What you will learn in this unit

A form incorporated into an HTML document provides a means for viewers to interact with you through your pages. An HTML form is created in much the same way as an on-line form, incorporating GUI features such as checkboxes, radio (option) buttons and drop-down lists that are familiar features of dialog boxes.

Unlike other aspects of HTML, forms involve two-way communication and will only function if your service provider runs software to pick up the responses. You will need to sort out how and where your responses will be stored so that you can retrieve them for analysis.

A form can be created in a separate document or it can be included as part of a larger page. All formatting that can be used in an HTML document can be used in a form, and the tags that collect data and send the form provide the interactivity.

A form is enclosed by the <FORM>...</FORM> tags. Within the form, data is collected by text boxes, tick boxes, option groups and drop-down lists, all of which are implemented by <INPUT...> tags.

The Control Toolbox

The Control Toolbox allows you to add controls to the form in a similar way to that for on-line forms. The buttons allow you to create a form field and define options for it. There are also additional buttons as there are extra features in HTML forms. We will introduce some of these in the tasks in this unit.

To add controls to a form you need to be in Form Design mode. The document will switch into design mode as you add controls from the the toolbox to it, but you can switch between Form Design Mode and the normal editing mode by clicking on the **Design Mode** button.

Sending the form

You can add a button to the form so that your viewers can click on it to send their responses. Clicking on the **Submit** button in the Control Toolbox will create a button which when clicked by the viewer will send the form's contents back to you.

Submission Information

You may need to specify the properties of the **Submit** button and these are briefly summarised below. You should contact your system administrator or service provider for specific information relating to forms.

Action

Specifies the URL of the script on your server to which you want to submit the contents of the form. If you do not specify an Action, the default is the current document.

Encoding

This attribute specifies the format of the form's data. The default value of Encoding is application/x-www-form-urlencoded.

Method

The Method property specifies the way data is submitted. The default Method is Get.

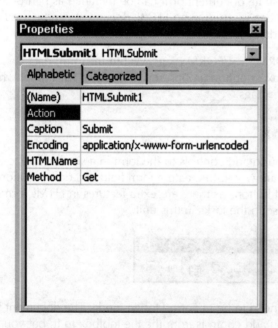

Reset

To clear a form, a reset button that clears the form's contents can be provided so that if the viewer wants to start again they can clear all inputs. Clicking on the **Reset** button of the Control Toolbox will add a reset button to the form.

Task 1: Creating a simple feedback form

This Task creates a simple form requesting a viewer's name, e-mail address and phone number. The form as seen in Form Design Mode is illustrated below.

Feedback Form

We would like to follow up your enquiry, please send us your details

<u>Top of Form 1</u>

Name: ☐

E-mail address: ☐

Tel. No: ☐

| Submit | Reset |

<u>Bottom of Form 1</u>

1 Start a new document, adding a heading (using style H2) entitled **Feedback Form**. Add a horizontal rule and save the document as **Feedback.htm**.

2 Choose File-Properties to give the form the title **Simple Form**. Add the text *We would like to follow up your enquiry, please send us your details*.

3 Type in *Name*: and click on the **Text box Form Field** button. A text box field will be added to the form. Click on the **Properties** button and set HTMLName as Lastname. Note you do not have to set this property but it may make it easier to identify the feedback data. Close the Properties window.

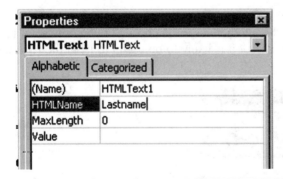

4 Make a new line and key in the text *E-mail address*: click on the **Text box Form Field** button. Display the properties and key in *Email* as the HTMLname of the field.

5 Make the next line one for the viewer to key in their telephone number. Give the HTMLname **Phone** to this field and use the default settings.

6 Next add the **Submit** and **Reset** buttons simply by clicking on the
   Submit and **Reset** buttons in the Control Toolbox.

7 Save and your form is ready for use. If you wish to alter the size of the text box
   controls, return to Form Design Mode, select the text box you wish to alter and
   drag its sizing handle to make it the size you require.

When a viewer completes the form and they click on the **Submit** button, the data
he or she has entered will be passed to you by your Internet service provider. The
data that you receive may be of the form:

Lastname=Other&Email=a.n.other@univ.ac.uk&Phone=01234567890

or it may be processed so that you receive it in a form suitable for importing into a
database or spreadsheet. Check with your system administrator or service provider,
in order to identify the format in which you will receive data from forms.

Checkboxes and radio (option group) buttons

Some responses may be of a simple yes/no nature, for example, 'Do you require a
brochure?' A check box is a useful way of providing yes/no alternatives. You may
wish to specify an option group where several choices are offered but you only
want to allow the viewer to choose one: these are known as radio buttons. A check
box is square and a radio button is round (hence 'radio').

A checkbox is added by clicking on the **Check box** button in the control toolbox.
If the viewer selects the check box, the data that is returned is set to 'on' (true) as
opposed to 'off' (false) for not checked. If no default value for the check box is specified then the check box is assigned the value of *off* or not checked.

With radio buttons, the same NAME should be used for all the radios in the set, as
you only want to allow one of the alternatives to be chosen (if you only want to use
one set you could leave this blank but it is likely to be useful to label the returned
answers).

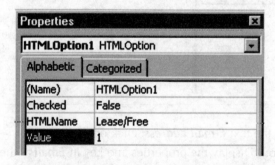

You should also set the **Value** property: if it were omitted *Lease/Free* would contain
the value *on* (true or yes) whatever was selected, which is of little use. It is usual to
number them but other 'values' may be chosen. If the **Checked** property for each
option button in the set is left as False, then all the buttons will be empty when the

form is first opened. If you want to provide a default choice then set the Checked property to 'true' for the option you wish to set as checked by default.

Task 2: Check boxes and option groups

In this task we will create a section of the on-line form created in Task 1 of Unit 18. Later we shall add to this form to create a complete HTML version.

1   Start a new document, add a heading (use style H3) entitled *Type of property you are interested in* and add a horizontal rule. Save the document as *Property enquiry.htm*.

2   Add a table three columns by two rows and complete it as illustrated below, adding the check boxes using the **Check box** button in the Control Toolbox. You may add HTML names, using the same names as the label. If you wish, you may border the table.

Type of property you are interested in:

Detached ☐	Semi-detached ☐	Bungalow ☐
Terrace ☐	Flat/Apartment ☐	

3   Under this an option group can be added to allow the user to select from the options Leasehold/Freehold/Either. To do this add another row to the table (you may differentiate this by suitable use of bordering) and add the **Text** and **Option** buttons as illustrated below. Set the HTMLname for each button to Lease/Free and set the Value to 1, 2, 3 for each button consecutively. Save the form.

Leasehold ○	Freehold ○	Leasehold or Freehold ○

Text areas

The text box control only accepts one line of text and is defined by the HTML source <INPUT..> tag. If you want to allow your viewer to enter several lines, for example to provide you with their comments, use the Textarea control in the Control Toolbox (implemented in HTML source by <TEXTAREA...>... ...</TEXTAREA> tags). The text area can be sized using its sizing handles.

Drop down lists

A drop-down list is a neat way of offering a set of alternatives as we have seen for an on-line form. They are added by clicking on the Dropdown box control in the Control Toolbox (implemented in HTML source using the tags <SELECT...> and <OPTION...>).

Task 3: Adding a text area and drop-down list to the form

1 Continuing with the **Property** enquiry form, add a text area to the bottom of the form as illustrated. Drag the text area box to the size that you require. You could add an extra row to the table and merge the cells to give room for the text area. Use an HTMLname, for example, **addinfo**. Save the form.

If there are any further details you would like to give us to aid our search for suitable properties please use the space below:

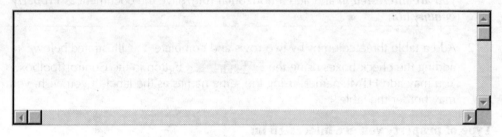

2 A drop-down list is used to select the person's title, i.e. Mr, Mrs etc. Type *Title*: and click on the ▮ **Dropdown box** ▮ button. Click on the ▮ **Properties** ▮ button and in the DisplayValues property type the list of values you want, separating each with a semi-colon, i.e. Mr;Mrs;Miss;Ms;Mr &Mrs;Dr etc. Set the HTMLname to **Title**. An example of how this might look is shown below. Save the form.

Your name:

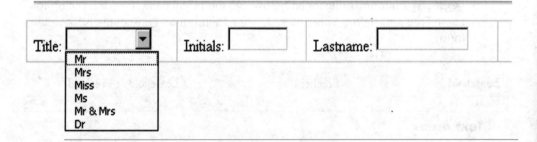

3 Using the form below as a guide, add text boxes for the address and check boxes for the price ranges. Why is it better to use check boxes for these than option buttons?

4 Add a ▮ **Submit** ▮ and a ▮ **Reset** ▮ button and save the form. Unfortunately, instructions for posting the form and for data retrieval cannot be given, and data analysis can only be discussed in general terms below.

If you would like us to add your details to our mailing list so that we can send you up-to-date details of our comprehensive list of properties, please take five minutes to complete and send this form.

Your name:

Title: [Mr ▼]   Initials: [   ]   Last name: [   ]

Your address:

Street: [   ]   Town: [   ]

County: [   ]   Postcode: [   ]

E-mail address: [   ]

Check this box if you are a first time buyer ☐

Type of property you are interested in:

Detached ☐   Semi-detached ☐   Bungalow ☐

Terrace ☐   Flat/Apartment ☐

Leasehold ○   Freehold ○   Leasehold or Freehold ○

Please indicate your preferred price range

£30,000-£50,000 ☐   £50,000-£70,000 ☐   £70,000-£100,000 ☐

£100,000-£150,000 ☐   £150,000-£250,000 ☐   £250,000 and above ☐

If there are any further details you would like to give us to aid our search for suitable properties please use the space below:

[   ]

Thank you for your co-operation, please send us your details by clicking on this button [Submit]

To clear all entries in the form click on [Reset]

Analysing feedback

Data may be returned to you in a variety of ways depending on your Internet service provider. They may be in the form of simple text strings as illustrated earlier or possibly in a form that can be imported into a database. Once data are imported into a database, they can be queried, counted, sorted and grouped in answer to the questions posed in the form. You will probably find using the HTMLnames property useful as these names correspond to field names in your database of answers. Also, using numerical values in option groups could be useful for finding the average response, especially if you are asking the strongly agree/agree/neither agree or disagree/disagree/strongly disagree type of questions.

Toolbar buttons and customising Word

Toolbar buttons - standard

New document; Open document; Save document

Print; Print Preview; Spelling & Grammar

Cut; Copy; Paste; Paint Formats

Undo; Redo

Insert Hyperlink; Web Toolbar

Tables and Borders; Insert rows; Insert Excel Worksheet; Columns; Drawing

Show/Hide white space characters; Zoom Control; Help

Formatting

Style drop down list

Font drop down list; Size drop down list

Bold, Italics, Underlining

Alignment – left, centre, right, justified

Numbered list; Bulleted list; Decrease Indent; Increase Indent

Border drop down list; Highlight drop down list; Font Color drop down list

Tables and Borders

Button name	Function
Draw Table	Allows you to draw table outline
Eraser	Removes lines in table
Line Style	Selects style of line from the drop down list and draw on the table to apply it
Line Weight	Selects line weight (thickness) from the drop down list and draw on the table to apply it
Border Color	Selects colour from the drop down list and draw on the table to apply it
Borders drop down list	Selects which sides of a cell should be bordered
Shading drop down list	Selects colour of shading for a cell or selection
Merge Cells	Makes two or more cells into one
Split Cells	Makes one cell into two or more
Align Top	Aligns text at top of cell
Centre Vertically	Aligns text in the middle of a cell
Align Bottom	Aligns text at the bottom of a cell
Distribute Rows Evenly	Selected rows are given an equal share of available height
Distribute Columns Evenly	Selected columns are given an equal share of available width
Table AutoFormat	Provides autoformatting for the table
Change Text Direction	Alters text from horizontal to vertical and back
Sort Ascending	Sorts rows into ascending order according to column selected
Sort Descending	Sorts rows into descending order according to column selected
AutoSum	Totals figures in a row or column

WordArt

Button name	Function
Insert WordArt	Adds more WordArt
Edit Text	Edits the text in the selected WordArt
Gallery	Displays the selection of WordArt styles
Format WordArt	Displays Format dialog box
WordArt Shape	Chooses a WordArt shape
Free Rotate	Rotates WordArt
WordArt Same Letter Heights	Adjusts WordArt letter heights
WordArt Vertical text	Swops from horizontal to vertical text (and vice versa)
WordArt Alignment	Adjusts alignment
WordArt Character Spacing	Adjusts letter spacing

Picture

Button name	Function
Insert Picture	Opens the Picture workspace
Image Control	Allows you to choose colour, greyscale or black and white
More Contrast	Increases contrast of image
Less Contrast	Reduces contrast of image
More Brightness	Increases brightness of image
Less Brightness	Reduces brightness of image
Crop	Reduces image by discarding part of it
Line Style	Choice of line styles for border
Text Wrapping	Choice of text wrapping
Format Picture	Displays Format dialog box

| Set Transparent Color | Sets one colour as transparent, i.e. clear, so that you can see what is behind the image |
| Reset picture | Returns the picture to its original formatting |

Drawing

Draw ▾	**Draw Menu**	Displays menu of drawing options
	Group, Ungroup, Regroup	Works with a selected set of objects by grouping or ungrouping them
Order		
	Bring to Front, Send to Back, Bring Forward, Send Backward	Controls layered position of selected
	Bring in Front of Text, Send Behind Text	Brings the selected drawing object in front or behind the text
	Grid	Allows options for grid to be set for aligning drawing objects
Nudge		
	Up, Down, Left, Right	Nudges selected object up, down, left, or right
Align or distribute		
	Align Left, Centre, Right	Aligns selected objects to the left, centrally around a vertical axis, or to the right.
	Align Top, Middle, Bottom	Aligns selected objects to the top, centrally around a horizontal axis, or to the bottom
	Distribute Horizontally, Vertically	Spaces selected object evenly

232

Rotate or flip

	Free Rotate	Rotates the selected drawing object freely to any angle
	Rotate Left, Right	Rotates the selected drawing object 90 degrees to the left or right
	Flip Horizontal, Vertical	Flips the selected drawing object from left to right or top to bottom
	Edit Points	Displays the vertices on Freeform objects so they may be reshaped
	Select Objects	Displays an arrow pointer used for selecting several objects
	Line, Arrow, Rectangle, Oval	Lets you draw the chosen shape in your document
	Text Box	Lets you draw a text box in your document
	Insert WordArt	Starts WordArt
	Fill, Line, Font Color	Displays a drop-down choice of fill colours for the selected object, line or font
	Line, Dash or Arrow Style	Specifies the line, dash or arrow style for the selected line
	Shadow	Allows the selection of various shadow effects
	3-D	Allows the selection of various three dimentional effects

Forms

Button name	Function
Text Form Field	Creates a text box
Check Box Form Field	Creates a check box
Drop down Form Field	Creates a drop down list box
Form Field Options	Displays the options dialog box
Draw Table	Allows you to draw table outline
Insert Rows	Adds rows to a table
Insert Frame	Adds a frame
Form Field Shading	Switches form field shading on or off
Protect Form	Locks or unlocks the form

HTML formatting

H1 ▼	Style drop down list
Times New Roman ▼	Font drop down list
A⁺ A⁻	Increase Font Size; Decrease Font Size
B *I* <u>U</u>	Bold, Italics, Underlining
≡ ≡ ≡	Alignment – Left, Centre, Right
⅓☰ ☰ ⯈ ⯇	Numbered list; Bulleted list; Decrease Indent; Increase Indent
—	Horizontal rule
🎨 A ▼	Background; Font Color drop down list

Customising Word

Word can be customised to suit the particular user or the circumstances in which it is being used. In this Quick Reference the options available from the Tools menu will be investigated. The options available from Tools-Options are grouped into categories, which are

- view
- track changes
- save
- print

- general
- user information
- spelling and grammar

- edit
- compatibility
- file locations

Not all these will be discussed, only those options which it is considered the reader may wish to change. To change any of the other options, consult the Help information and the manual to be sure that you know the effect of any change you make.

View

In this category the options available affect the window display, text and non-printing characters. You may set the width of the style area (an area displayed to the left of the document), in Normal View only, which indicates the style applied to each paragraph.

Window

By clicking in the appropriate check boxes, you may select whether or not to display the scroll bars and the status bar. Options are slightly different depending on which view you are currently in. If, in Normal View, the Style Area width is increased from its default value of zero, the document is displayed with a left margin showing the style name applied to the corresponding text.

Heading 2	**View**
Normal	In this category the c
	characters. You may
	left of the document
Heading 3	**Windows Display**

Show and Non-Printing Characters

It is best to leave these options as their default values. There may be occasions when hidden characters such as paragraph marks are required to be seen. However, this is unlikely as it is easy to switch between displaying paragraph marks or not.

Save

Here it is possible to choose between fast saving or creating a backup of your document. It is better to choose to create a backup copy. You should get into the habit of saving your work every few minutes or so. Word provides an AutoRecovery feature and it will regularly save the document, you can adjust the time interval between saves. Sensitive documents may be password protected but be cautious using this.

General

Here you can alter the measurement units that Word uses. You may choose between centimetres, inches, points, or picas. You can specify the number of recently opened files that will be displayed on the **File** menu.

Spelling and Grammar

Word can be customised so that it checks spelling and grammar as you type, or not by ticking the options. Options may be set to allow the spell checker to ignore words that are in upper case and/or words that contain numbers. Through the **Custom Dictionaries** button it is possible to set up your own dictionary. The **Always Suggest** box may be used to speed up checking if this is off. Also you may select to check spelling from the main dictionary alone.

Edit

The one setting you may wish to alter is that of **Typing Replaces Selection**, particularly if you are new to Word. New users of Word can make selections by mistake and if this is followed by, say, pressing *Enter* then the selection disappears. It has been replaced by a paragraph mark. **Edit-Undo** will remedy this but a new user might not recognise what has happened soon enough. If this option is switched off, by clicking in the check box to remove the tick, then this problem is avoided.

Other settings in this category, which you may wish to alter, are the operation of the drag and drop feature or the selection of text in units of whole words.

Print

There is one option in this section you may wish to use, which is **Reverse Print Order**. This will cause a document to be printed from the last page to the first.

Customising toolbars

If you find you use a command often, you might want to set up the toolbars so they have precisely the buttons you want to use, for example adding the **Insert Chart** button to the standard toolbar.

To add a button to a toolbar:

1 Choose **View-Toolbars-Customize**

2 Click on the
   Commands tab,
   and select a cate-
   gory that includes
   the button you
   want to add. The
   buttons, with their
   descriptions,
   appear on the right
   in a scrollable list
   box. The **Chart**
   button is found in
   the Insert category.

3 When you find the
   button you want to
   add, drag it and
   drop it on the
   toolbar where you
   want it. You can create your own toolbar by dropping the button anywhere
   except on an existing toolbar. You can drag and drop as many buttons as you
   want.

4 When you finish adding buttons to toolbars, click on the **Close** button.

Keyboard equivalents

Apply formatting using shortcut keys

Format characters using shortcut keys

To	Press
Change the font	CTRL+SHIFT+F
Change the font size	CTRL+SHIFT+P
Increase the font size	CTRL+SHIFT+>
Decrease the font size	CTRL+SHIFT+<
Increase the font size by 1 point	CTRL+]
Decrease the font size by 1 point	CTRL+[

To	Press
Change the formatting of characters (Format-Font)	CTRL+D
Change the case of letters	SHIFT+F3
Format letters as all capitals	CTRL+SHIFT+A
Apply or remove bold formatting	CTRL+B
Apply or remove an underline	CTRL+U
Underline single words	CTRL+SHIFT+W
Double-underline text	CTRL+SHIFT+D
Apply hidden text formatting	CTRL+SHIFT+H
Apply italic formatting	CTRL+I
Format letters as small capitals	CTRL+SHIFT+K
Apply subscripts (automatic spacing)	CTRL+= (equals sign)
Apply superscripts (automatic spacing)	CTRL+SHIFT+ = (equals sign)
Remove manual character formatting	CTRL+SPACEBAR
Change the selection to Symbol font	CTRL+SHIFT+Q

To	*Press*
Display nonprinting characters	*CTRL+SHIFT+** (asterisk)
Review text formatting	*SHIFT+F1* (then click in the text to be reviewed)
Copy formats	*CTRL+SHIFT+C*
Paste formats	*CTRL+SHIFT+V*

Format paragraphs using shortcut keys

When setting line spacing, to	*Press*
Single-space lines	*CTRL+1*
Double-space lines	*CTRL+2*
Set 1.5-line spacing	*CTRL+5*
Add or remove one line of space preceding a paragraph	*CTRL+0* (zero)

When setting paragraph alignments and indents, to	*Press*
Centre a paragraph	*CTRL+E*
Justify a paragraph	*CTRL+J*
Left align a paragraph	*CTRL+L*
Right align a paragraph	*CTRL+R*
Indent a paragraph from the left	*CTRL+M*
Remove a paragraph indent from the left	*CTRL+SHIFT+M*
Create a hanging indent	*CTRL+T*
Reduce a hanging indent	*CTRL+SHIFT+T*
Remove paragraph formatting	*CTRL+Q*

When applying styles, to	*. Press*
Apply a style	*CTRL+SHIFT+S*
Start AutoFormat	*CTRL+K*
Apply the Normal style	*CTRL+SHIFT+N*
Apply the Heading 1 style	*ALT+CTRL +1*
Apply the Heading 2 style	*ALT+CTRL +2*
Apply the Heading 3 style	*ALT+CTRL +3*
Apply the List style	*CTRL+SHIFT+L*

Function key shortcuts

	Function key	SHIFT	CTRL	CTRL+SHIFT	ALT	ALT+SHIFT
F1	Get Online Help or the Office Assistant	Context sensitive Help or Reveal Formatting			Go to next field	Go to previous field
F2	Move text or graphics	Copy text	Print Preview command (File menu)			Save command (File menu)
F3	Insert an AutoText entry	Change the case of letters	Cut to the Spike	Insert the contents of the Spike	Create an AutoText entry	
F4	Repeat the last action	Repeat a Find or Go To action	Close the window		Quit Word	Quit Word
F5	Carry out the Go To command (Edit menu)	Move to a previous revision	Restore the document window size	Edit a bookmark	Restore the program window size	
F6	Go to next pane	Go to the previous pane	Go to the next window	Go to the previous window		
F7	Carry out the Spelling command (Tools Menu)	Carry out the Thesaurus command (Tools menu)	Carry out the Move command (Control menu)	Update linked information Word source document	Find next misspelling (Automatic Spell Checking enabled)	
F8	Extend a selection	Shrink a selection	Carry out the Size command (Document Control	Extend a selection (or block)	Run a macro	
F9	Update selected fields	Switch between a field code and its result	Insert an empty field	Unlink a field	Switch between all field codes results	Run GOTO BUTTON or MACRO BUTTON the field that displays the field results

F10	Activate the menu bar	Display a shortcut menu	Maximise the document window	Activate the ruler	Maximise the program window
F11	Go to the next field	Go to the previous field	Lock a field	Unlock a field	Display Visual Basic code
F12	Carry out the Save As Command (File menu)	Carry out the Save Command (File menu)	Carry out the Open command (File menu)	Carry out the Print command (File menu)	

File Management

Features in the File-Open dialog box

The last six buttons illustrated below will be explained (you should be familiar with the Look in box; the Up One Level button and the Search Web are only of use if you are connected to the Web).

The Look in Favorites button will display a list of subdirectories (folders) which you have added to your favourites list using the Add to Favorites button. To do this, display the directory (folder), highlight it and click on the Add to Favorites button. To remove a folder from your favorite list, display the list, highlight the folder and press Delete (this does not delete the actual folder only its entry in the favorite list).

The last five buttons control how the file list is displayed: List , Details , Properties , Preview .

- List just displays a list of file names.

- Details gives file name, size, type and when last modified.

- Properties displays the associated properties of the highlighted file, such as author, creation date, title, number of revisions, etc.

- Preview displays a preview of the highlighted document.

- Commands and Settings displays advanced features that are not covered in this book. Refer to the Office Assistant for more details.

Finding files

In the lower section of the File-Open dialog box you can specify criteria to select files from the current directory (folder). Specify one criterion or more as described below and click on the Find Now button. The New Search button will clear the criteria so that you can specify new ones.

In the File Name box you can use the 'wildcards' * for any characters and ? for any one character to select files, for instance s* will find all files beginning with the letter s, and Sales Report ? will find files such as Sales Report 1, Sales Report 2 etc.

Files of types allow you to specify the type of file, for example text files instead of Word files.

The text or property box allows you to specify a word or phrase contained in the document and only files containing that word or phrase will be displayed.

The last modified drop down list box allows you to limit the displayed files to certain time periods, for instance 'this week' as illustrated below.

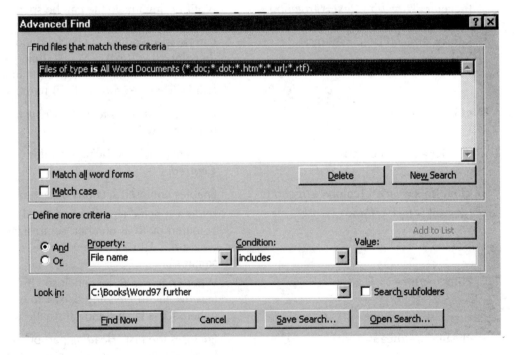

Advanced Find file

If the file you are searching for is not in the current subdirectory folder you can click on the **Advanced** button to display the Advanced Find dialog box. Through this dialog box you could search the whole of drive C and include all subfolders but you would want to narrow this down to, say, a file name.

You can specify which file property you want to search on and which criteria you want for the search. Searches can be saved so that you can re-use them.

HTML tags

Below is an alphabetical list of some frequently used HTML tags with a brief definition. If you intend to edit HTML sources then you should refer to a book on using HTML.

Tag	Meaning
\<a href="*URL***">***link text***\</a>**	Creates an **Anchor** for a **hypertext reference**, so that clicking on the *link text* retrieves the specified *URL*.
\<a name="*label***">***target text***\</a>**	Creates a target for an internal *hypertext reference*, where the href="#*label*" instead of external href="URL", as previous.
\<body [background="*image filename***"] [bgcolor="#***rrggbb***"] [text="#***rrggbb***"] [link="#***rrggbb***"] [vlink="#***rrggbb***"] [alink="#***rrggbb***"]> ... \</body>**	Encloses the **Body** part of a document. A **.gif** or **.jpg** image file can be specified for a 'tiled' **background**; colours can be specified for the background (**bgcolor**), text (**text**), link text (**link**), visited links (**vlink**), and activating links (**alink**). These *rrggbb* are RGB numbers.
**\ **	At the end of some text, the *Break* tag forces a new line.
\<center> .. .. \</center>	Elements enclosed by tags display **Centred**.
\<font [face="*face***"] [color="#***rrggbb***"] [size=***n***] > text \</font>**	Enables enclosed sections of text to be set to a specific typeface, e.g. Arial; coloured by RGB number; set to sizes where *n* is 1 to 7 (1 being the smallest).
\<h*n***>...\</h***n***>**	Where *n* is 1 to 6, text enclosed by tags display in *Heading* sizes 1 to 6 (where h1 is largest and h6 smallest).
\<head> ... \</head>	Encloses the first, **Heading** part of an HTML document. Usually set automatically by editor.
\<hr>	Inserts a Horizontal Ruler line.
\<html> ... \</html>	These tags enclose the entire HTML document.

<img src=""*image filename*" **[align=***position*] **[alt="***description text*"] **[border=***n*] **[width=***n*] **[height=***n*]>**	Loads an ***inline Image*** of the source filename. The align *position* options top, bottom, middle, left and right define image positions and text flow round them. The alt text displays in text-only browsers. For border, the *n* sets a width. For height and width, *n* sets the size in pixels.
<li>	***List item*** – see the **<ol>** and **<ul>** tags below.
<ol [type="number type"**>** **<li>** first List Item **<li>** second List Item **</ol>**	List Items between *Ordered List* tags display are prefixed by sequential numbers. Type sets the number or letter style to be used.
<p>	***Paragraph*** tag, causes a line-break and blank line.
<title> ... </title>	Text appears in browser's ***Title*** bar at top of screen.
<ul> **<li>** a List Item **<li>** another List Item **<li>** yet another List Item **</ul>**	List Items between *Unordered List* tags display are prefixed with bullets.
<table [border=*n*] **[cell spacing=***n*] **[cell padding=***n*] > ... </table>**	Encloses the table part of the document. The thickness of the outer border, the gap between borders and the distance between text and inner border, are set by specifying *n*.
<tr> ... </tr>	Encloses a table row, which usually encloses several table items
<td [align=*hposition*] **[valign=***vposition*] **[width=***n*] > ... </td>**	Encloses a table item. The align *hposition* options left, center, or right define horizontal alignment. The valign *vposition* options top, middle, or bottom define vertical alignment. The width of the cell can be specified by setting *n*.

Index